At the Centre of Government

AT THE CENTRE

OF

GOVERNMENT

The Prime Minister

and the

Limits on Political Power

IAN BRODIE

McGill-Queen's University Press

Montreal & Kingston | London | Chicago

ISBN 978-0-7735-5290-6 (cloth)
ISBN 978-0-7735-5377-4 (EPDF)
ISBN 978-0-7735-5378-1 (EPUB)

Legal deposit second quarter 2018
Bibliothèque nationale du Québec

Printed in Canada on acid-free paper that is 100% ancient forest free
(100% post-consumer recycled), processed chlorine free

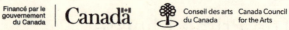

We acknowledge the support of the Canada Council for the Arts,
which last year invested $153 million to bring the arts to Canadians
throughout the country. Nous remercions le Conseil des arts du
Canada de son soutien. L'an dernier, le Conseil a investi 153 millions
de dollars pour mettre de l'art dans la vie des Canadiennes et des
Canadiens de tout le pays.

Library and Archives Canada Cataloguing in Publication

Brodie, Ian Ross, 1967–, author
At the centre of government : the Prime Minister and
the limits on political power / Ian Brodie.

Includes bibliographical references and index.
Issued in print and electronic formats.
ISBN 978-0-7735-5290-6 (hardcover).
ISBN 978-0-7735-5377-4 (EPDF).
ISBN 978-0-7735-5378-1 (EPUB)

1. Canada – Politics and government. 2. Legislative power – Canada.
3. Executive power – Canada. 4. Canada. Parliament – Powers and
duties. 5. Separation of powers – Canada. 6. Federal government –
Canada. 7. Constitutional law – Canada. 8. Prime ministers – Canada.
9. Canada. Office of the Prime Minister. I. Title.

JL75.B72 2018   320.971   C2018-900620-X
                                        C2018-900621-8

This book was designed and typeset by studio oneonone
in Minion 10.5/13.

Contents

Acknowledgments | vii

Preface: Getting to Government: An Autobiographical Note | ix

1 Governing from the Centre: How We Came to See the PM as a Dictator | 3

2 The Origins of Cabinet Government | 13

3 Delegation and Its Limits: The Core Powers of a Prime Minister | 26

4 Making a Cabinet | 53

5 The Executive Branch and Parliament | 75

6 Managing a Government Agenda | 109

7 Prime Ministers and Political Parties | 130

8 Democratizing or Bureaucratizing the Constitution? | 156

Afterword: Leaving Government: Another Autobiographical Note | 180

Notes | 187

Works Cited | 191

Index | 199

Acknowledgments

From 1988, when I gave up my engineering studies and transferred to McGill's undergraduate program in political science, until 2003, when I took a leave of absence from the faculty of the University of Western Ontario, I was a student of democratic government. Then, from spring 2003, when I went to work for Stephen Harper in the Opposition Leader's Office on Parliament Hill, until I left his Prime Minister's Office in June 2008, I was a practitioner of democratic government. Like an astronaut who spends years training on the ground for a space mission that might last only a few days, I spent fifteen years studying democratic government to prepare for my six years in democratic government. My academic training was excellent preparation for the "real world" of Canadian politics.

I have long been blessed with superb teachers. At McGill, I learned from J.R. Mallory and Chris Manfredi, and well as Mike Lusztig and later Pat James. At the University of Calgary, I found a real home filled with outstanding teachers like Tom Flanagan, Roger Gibbins, Les Pal, Barry Cooper, David Taras, Stan Drabek, David Bercuson, Neil Nevitte, Keith Archer, and, of course, Rainer Knopff and Ted Morton. Ted, in particular, was a wonderful supervisor and went on to show how a political career can be enriched by a lifetime of scholarship. Teaching at Western, I was blessed with colleagues like the late Bob Young, Peter Neary, Ian Holloway, Grant Huscroft, Don Abelson, and Miriam Lapp. I thank them all.

In practical politics, I also had some superb teachers. My parents understood the connection between the kind of community we lived in and the need for good people in elected office. At a very young age I campaigned for Alan Redway, John Bosley and the late Bob Elgie. Later in life I have been door to door with many other candidates, in particular Rob Anders, my former student. In London, the irrepressible George Burns, Chris Essex, Len Letissier, Salim Mansur, Al Gretzky, and Marian Meinen all taught me lasting lessons.

In 2003, Tom Flanagan agreed to hire me in order to get my wife, Vida, onto Harper's staff. Everyone involved knows she was a more valuable member of Harper's Team than I ever was. But Flanagan gave us both the opportunity to work on the Hill, and we are grateful for that.

In Ottawa, I found so many teachers that I will overlook some if I try to list them all. Thank you all, especially those who worked for me. I will only single out the two who saw the best and worst of me, on the best and worst days in government: thank you to Lanny Cardow and Jeff Bertrand.

A very special thank you goes to Stephen Harper, who made the entire enterprise possible. He saw potential in me for both opposition and government. Because of his confidence, I had a unique opportunity to learn and to serve. Working for Stephen Harper was an unparalleled honour, and I am grateful for the endless political lessons I learned from him. Also, a very special thanks to Vida, Chloe, and Lachan, who gave the most important support throughout.

My last thank you goes to two great Scotsmen, now both gone. First, to the late Neil McLean: a great teacher does not let the curriculum get in the way of teaching. Neil was a great teacher, a footballer, a gunner, a patriot, and a tory. His advice to me was "Be your own kind of tory"; I have tried to follow that advice ever since. And secondly, to my dear friend, the late Senator Doug Finley. At a low moment in Harper's political career, Doug, Patrick Muttart, and I gathered around a table in the Wellington Building and resolved that we were not yet finished. In our all-too-brief time together, Doug never failed to remind us of the moral stakes of what we were up to.

Preface

Getting to Government: An Autobiographical Note

Students and academic colleagues sometimes ask me how I got from a junior academic post to the PMO chief of staff? There is no "typical" background for a PMO chief of staff. Some chiefs have been political aides and organizers for years. Some have been government officials drawn into political service. The scope of the job varies with the personality and needs of the prime minister. Some chiefs have been thinkers and some have been doers. Others have been political fixers. Some have policy expertise. Others do not. Some run the day-to-day operations of the PMO. Others have more strategic responsibilities. So, it can be hard to explain how I ended up at the centre of government.

I first met Stephen Harper when I was a student at the University of Calgary. I had arrived in Calgary to be a master's student in political science on 3 August 1990, the day after Saddam Hussein's forces invaded Kuwait. In those days, the University of Calgary was making a name for itself as an up and coming centre for the social sciences. Roger Gibbins, then the head of Department of Political Science, was at the height of his intellectual power, setting out new academic and political ideas about Canadian federalism. In 1991, he spent a summer in Ottawa advising the Mulroney government about its efforts to move on from the failure of the Meech Lake Accord. Ted Morton and Rainer Knopff had just finished *Charter Politics* (Knopff and Morton 1992) and were working on a concept they referred to as the "Court Party" (Morton and Knopff 2000). David Bercuson, the historian, and Barry Cooper had just finished writing *Deconfederation* (1991), their explanation of why Quebec should leave Confederation. Neil Nevitte had brought the World Values Survey to Canada and was pumping out research about longer-term value change in Canada. Les Pal had finished *Interests of State* (1993), his volume on how the Trudeau government had used its funding and bureaucratic power to shift Canadian political culture. Tom Flanagan was energetically tackling many subjects in the discipline. David Taras was researching the Canadian news media. Keith Archer was researching the inner workings of political parties. Guy Laforest and Janet Ajzenstat had left the department by 1990 but returned often. They and so many others had turned the department into a dynamic place to study politics in Canada.

While the Department of Political Science was devoted to its academic mission, its close connection to the political tumult of Alberta gave it an energy and vibrancy that was intoxicating to young graduate students. Peter Lougheed co-taught the department's seminar on Canadian federalism with Gibbins. Preston Manning was a frequent visitor to the department. He arranged monthly discussions on various issues in Canadian politics and offered free sandwiches to anyone who wanted to join. For a graduate student, free food and the opportunity to hear senior scholars and a thoughtful politician talk about politics was irresistible. I was a young transplant from Ontario, with five years at McGill under my belt. The free-flow of ideas and the willingness of so many learned people to tackle sacred cows of central Canada's political culture was riveting. The wild west mentality of early 1990s Calgary was just the tonic for the veneration of hierarchy and order I had learned back east. My years at McGill coincided with self-destructive and pointless politics in Quebec. The courts struck down Quebec's Bill 101 provisions on public signs while I was living in Montreal and the federalist Bourassa government used the notwithstanding clause to enact a revised version of the signs law in Bill 178. The episode provoked a poisonous public debate. The Mulroney government was trying to heal wounds with the Meech Lake Accord. I supported the Meech Lake Accord and then, realizing the terrible path it laid out for Canadian politics, abandoned both the Accord and the PC Party. I was ready to challenge the established thinking on Canadian federalism and, especially, the Charter of Rights. The dominant views of Pierre Trudeau's Charter of Rights and Brian Mulroney's attack on the Charter's "notwithstanding clause" underlined the need for new thinking. I had attended a standing room only seminar on the Quebec sign case at McGill's law school and seen Pierre Trudeau sitting with Quebec Chief Justice Jules Deschenes in the front row of the Moot Court Room debating the Charter and Bill 101 with former PQ Premier Pierre-Marc Johnson, then a faculty member at McGill. The raw politics of the moment cured me of any illusions about Charter and Canadian federalism. In 1990, there was no better place for political iconoclasm than the University of Calgary. I had been introduced to skeptical ideas about the Charter by McGill's Chris Manfredi. That led me to Ted and Rainer's work on the Charter of Rights and the courts. Hanging around the University of Calgary's Department of Political Science brought me in touch with Manning, Jason Kenney, some of the writers at Alberta Report, Ezra Levant, Danielle Smith, Rob Anders, and countless other activists.

And it brought me to meet Stephen Harper at one of Manning's monthly seminars. The topic for discussion that day was the Indian Act, and Harper impressed me with his optimism about the potential of First Nations reserves as economic and social units if they could be freed from the legislative restrictions of the Indian Act. Flanagan had not yet written his award-winning attack on the Act, *First Nations, Second Thoughts* (2000), and I had never given much thought to the state of Canada's reserves, but the conversation that day was unlike any I had ever had at McGill. In 1993, Harper was elected to the House of Commons for Calgary West but did not serve out his term. He resigned his seat to become President of the National Citizens' Coalition. Shortly after he joined the NCC, he came to speak in a Canadian politics class I was teaching. His visit was the first chance I had the opportunity to talk with him personally. At that time he was a close friend of Tom Flanagan's, and I was able to keep in touch with him through Tom. When I graduated with a PhD in 1997 and left Calgary for the University of Western Ontario, Ted hosted a combined farewell and thirtieth birthday party for me at his house. Harper, Jason Kenney, Rob Anders, and many other local activists rubbed shoulders with friends from the department, including its newest recruit, Lisa Young. Lisa, a scholar who has probably never voted for a conservative party, always reminds me that her introduction to Calgary society was a deep dive into the future Conservative caucus.

In London, I was drawn more deeply into Reform Party politics. A young student named Ray Novak guessed my political views and invited me to a local meeting for the London North-Centre riding association. I ended up meeting George Burns, the riding president, Chris Essex, a UWO math professor who had run for a Reform nomination in 1997, and Ken Kalopsis, soon to become President of the Reform Party Executive Council. Manning used the 1998 Reform Convention in London to launch the United Alternative, an effort to entice federal PC supporters into joining a Manning-sponsored vehicle to unite federal conservatives and defeat the Liberals in 2000. Ken was a strong supporter of the effort. I was skeptical at first. Then, as the United Alternative got caught up in a PC Party effort to unseat Joe Clark as leader, I opposed it. George became a public leader of the Stop UA movement, and I leant a hand to his effort. The pro-unity logic was compelling for most Reform members and the UA became the Canadian Alliance. But through the debate about the UA I realized that Reformers were getting hungry for more success in Ottawa and having doubts about Manning's leadership.

Once the Canadian Alliance leadership campaign began, I called Harper and urged him to run. I told him I thought the field was open and that grassroots members were looking for a conservative alternative to Manning. He did not see much opportunity in the Canadian Alliance and ended up backing Tom Long. I backed Stockwell Day, who proved my instincts correct. Day ran a successful insurgent's campaign against Manning. A leadership campaign is a battle of membership sales and member mobilization. Day's compelling personal story, his upbeat personality, his overt faith, and his sunny arguments for conservative ideas contrasted sharply with Manning's front-runner campaign of high-level endorsements and widely advertised "moderation" designed to appeal to urban professionals in Ontario.

Day lost the 2000 election, but under his leadership the Canadian Alliance built an organization and a profile in Ontario's hinterland. Manning's supporters refused to recognize the legitimacy of Day's leadership and were, justly, critical of missteps made in the 2000 campaign. Day tried to appear sensible and sensitive to the criticisms, but his opponents were only interested in deposing him, not improving the party. I defended Day in London in a public debate with Lynette Corbett, then a law student and Manning stalwart who would eventually join us in Ottawa as a political staffer. I was not part of an organized "save Day" campaign. There was no such thing. Eventually George and I met with a delegation of Day's staff – one was Dave Penner, later the director of appointments in the Prime Minister's Office – that was trying to form such a group. Later, I was asked if I would move to Ottawa to become director of research and policy in Day's Parliament Hill office. But as the internal discord became worse, Ted Morton went to Ottawa as Day's research and policy director instead. Ted had become an elected stand-by senator at that point, and his profile and wisdom stabilized the organization. Eventually, a group of dissident Canadian Alliance MPs left the caucus, first to form the "Democratic Reform Caucus" and then to join a coalition of opposition parties with Clark's PCs. Most days I try to forget this period of Canadian politics. I unearth it for the benefit of readers who were fortunate not to experience any of it first-hand. Everyone involved in the chaos was learning that parties need focus, professionalism, and strong leadership.

Day could not maintain his hold on the Alliance leadership and resigned the post to seek a new mandate from party members. I still hoped Harper would run, and when I heard there might be a Draft Harper campaign, I called him right away. By this point, the Canadian Alliance was on the verge of self-destruction. I told him that he had to run since he was the only credible candidate who could hold the party together. Tom Flanagan eventually became his campaign manager and Ray Novak his executive assistant. I arranged a small organizational meeting for him in London and then a huge rally with 800 supporters. He went on to win the leadership handily, and I lost touch with the organization for a while. Harper was busy reuniting the Canadian Alliance caucus and bringing the Democratic Representative Caucus group back into the fold. His tenacity in putting the Alliance back together proved to be only the first demonstration of his skills at uniting people.

Then, in early 2003, Flanagan called me at home and asked what plans I had for my upcoming sabbatical. Flanagan had become Harper's chief of staff by that point. I told him I was planning to take a year to write a book about the Department of Justice. He needed an event organizer for Harper's office, and the only one he knew was my wife, Vida. He asked if he could hire Vida for a year while I was on sabbatical. I passed him to Vida. She insisted Tom had to hire both of us on the parliamentary staff. Vida would be the event planner, and Flanagan promised, "We'll find something for you to do, Ian. Speeches or policy or something like that."

As I started getting ready to move to Ottawa, I had already been involved in the Canadian Alliance campaign for the by-election in the Perth–Middlesex riding. John Richardson, a Liberal, has been elected in 2000 but resigned abruptly in autumn 2002. It turned out he had been seriously ill for some time. The riding perfectly illustrated the futility of the PC Party–Canadian Alliance division of efforts. Richardson had won the 2000 election with just over 40 percent of the vote. The PC and Alliance candidates, combined, took more than half the votes. Garnet Bloomfield, a former Liberal MP, had run twice for Reform and then the Canadian Alliance, both times against Gary Schellenberger, the PC candidate. Both times, Schellenberger had finished second and Bloomfield third. My friend Marian Meinen thought it was time for new blood, and she successfully challenged Bloomfield for the Alliance nomination. The Liberal nomination became a battlefield in the ongoing conflict between the Chrétien and Martin factions of that party. The results of the initial nomination meeting were overturned and on a second meeting a different candidate won the Liberal nomination. The internal Liberal mess raised expectations that both Schellenberger and Meinen had a chance to win the seat. As it became clearer that the riding would become a bellwether in the national competition between the PC Party and Canadian Alliance, the Alliance poured resources into Perth Middlesex.

In early 2003, at about the time Flanagan was recruiting Vida to Ottawa, he and Harper sent a new campaign manager to Perth–Middlesex. The Meinen campaign's ground game was bad. She did not live in the riding, and the leadership of the Alliance riding association were increasingly unhappy that Harper had brought the Democratic Reform Caucus "rebels" back into the fold. Ottawa had sent a series of people to help the campaign, all of whom seemed to make things worse. Eventually, Harper hired a former Ontario political organizer then living in New Brunswick to run the Perth–Middlesex. Doug Finley drove straight from New Brunswick to Stratford to take over. He asked me to come see him at a B&B in Stratford, and when I arrived I found him in such ill health that I wondered if he would survive the day. He had contracted a cold before leaving for Stratford, and the long trek had made it worse. I gave him my assessment of the situation without being entirely certain he had absorbed any of what I had had to say. He thanked me, told me he was bringing in some other people to help, and asked me to come back the next day. When I returned, he had recovered his health and had nearly a dozen people from the nearby riding of Haldimand–Norfolk working in the campaign office. I eventually met Diane Finley, Doug's beloved wife and a future minister. Perth–Middlesex was the most fun riding-level campaign I had ever worked on. I was sad to leave Perth–Middlesex and Marian when it came time to join Vida in Ottawa.

We went on to lose the by-election. Gary Schellenberger and the PCs won. Someday, a historian will write a proper account of the Perth–Middlesex campaign. It was the turning point in Canada's early twenty-first-century political history. Losing Perth–Middlesex – Marian finished third – convinced Harper of many things. First, that the Canadian Alliance could not succeed without joining forces with the PC Party. Peter MacKay won the PC leadership in June 2003, and with the obstructionist Joe Clark gone negotiations to create the Conservative Party moved quickly. Secondly, it convinced him that a strong, professional ground organization was essential. Divisions among party activists could not get in the way of professionalizing the ground campaign. Thirdly, it convinced him to clean house in the Canadian Alliance campaign organization. He brought Doug to Ottawa, first as a "trainer," then as field manager for the second Harper leadership race, and finally as national campaign director. I chaired the small group that secured the support of Canadian Alliance members for the new Conservative Party. When PC members did the same, a new leadership campaign was on. Flanagan asked me to run Harper's tour team for the 2004 leadership campaign. Over the previous six months I had shown some management talent by getting Harper's tour and communications teams working together. Jim Armour, Harper's communications director, and I worked on several drafts of the speech Harper used to launch his second leadership race. During the day, I worked for the party's acting leader in the House, Dr Grant Hill, and at night I volunteered with the Harper campaign. As tour director, I once again worked closely with Doug. On voting day, Doug, Vida, and almost everyone else decamped to Toronto, where the results would be announced. I was in charge of the group left behind at Harper HQ in Ottawa, monitoring problems being reported by our scrutineers in the field – scrutineers are always the most important people on voting day – and making preparations for Harper's return to Ottawa.

Harper and the Toronto group took the train back to Ottawa the next day. On the ride, Tom sat with Vida for a few minutes to discuss how the campaign had gone and the next steps in our political work. "What does Ian want to do?" he asked. Vida and I had talked about our next steps as the leadership came to a close. She would stay on as Harper's event coordinator while we tried to start a family. I had long wanted to be executive director of the Canadian Alliance, the full-time staff member in charge of non-parliamentary party affairs, and hoped to become executive director of the new Conservative Party. Cyril McFate, a former air force officer, Reform candidate, and party organizer, had been holding the fort as interim executive director during the leadership race. Doug was going to become national campaign director and director of political operations for the party. He and I had worked well together for a year at that point. So, Vida told Tom to move me off the Hill to be executive director. When the train arrived at Ottawa Station to the cheers of a small welcoming party, Flanagan and Harper asked me to take charge at Conservative HQ.[1]

Setting up the new party in the wake of the leadership was the experience of a lifetime. If I had retired from politics having only done that I would have counted myself fortunate. It gave me the chance to work with the greatest political fundraiser in Canadian history, and probably the greatest political fundraiser in North America, Irving Gerstein. Irving had been raising money for the PC Party for decades and his constant, youthful enthusiasm for staying up to date makes him eager to embrace innovation after innovation. He started out raising money in the days of unregulated party finance, when national election campaigns were still funded with a handful of large corporate donations from Toronto and Montreal. After Joe Clark won the PC leadership in 1976, Irving became PC Canada Fund Chair and pioneered the use of direct mail fundraising for the party. By 2003, direct mail had become a science and applying the discipline of the PC Canada Fund to the grassroots enthusiasm of the Canadian Alliance membership list turned out to be a stellar success. Fundraising using professional telephone banks was also coming to Canada, and I enjoyed watching Irving's unflappability at managing the cultural change involved. Irving is still in the business, working to perfect the art and science of online fundraising. On Irving's recommendation, Harper asked Nicole Courtois-Eaton to oversee the organization of the first Conservative Convention, held in Montreal in 2005. Irving and Nicole eventually ended up in the Senate. Vida joined us in the convention effort. I was lucky to have a former UWO student, Rebecca Thompson, riding herd on the policy process leading to the convention. She went on to be a PMO staffer, a Sun TV host, and a senior aide at Queen's Park. I picked up an intern from Trinity Western University – Donna Robertson – on the recommendation of Paul Wilson, later a PMO policy director and now a Carleton professor. I dropped Donna into the job of pulling together the constitutional amendment resolutions for the convention. She later became a PMO staffer as well. I worked closely with Conservative Party CFO Susan Kehoe and eventually recruited David From to professionalize the party's IT and information management operation, particularly CIMS, the party's constituent information management system. Doug consolidated an outstanding group of political organizers, including future campaign manager Jenni Byrne. We were firing on all cylinders. The 2004 election was upon us as soon as the leadership wrapped up, and we held the Martin team, once thought to be invincible, to a minority.

Between the 2004 campaign and the fall of the Martin government in November 2005, the Harper team went through some periods of introspection. Tom Flanagan and Ken Boessenkool, two of Harper's closest advisors, left to pursue other endeavors. They had both invested heavily in getting Harper to the edge of victory, but after the 2004 effort they lost interest in pursuing Harper's future. Tom and Doug, thankfully, managed to recruit Patrick Muttart to join the team, and we found ways to bring more of the PC Party's best minds to the group as well. When Phil Murphy left the team as Harper's chief of staff, Doug and Irving convinced Harper to hire me as his successor. He put me in charge of the Opposition Leader's Office on Parliament Hill and, at the same time, of redrafting Harper's platform for the coming campaign. In 2004, we had run on a hastily assembled platform that featured an inordinately complex tax plan devised by Ken Boessenkool (Conservative Party of Canada 2004). That plan, which involved changes to the brackets at which various tax rates kicked in and a generous tax deduction for children, was probably very generous to middle income families but no one could explain it in the midst of the campaign and it was forgotten almost as soon as it was announced.

My mandate from Harper was to draft a shorter, sharper, and more memorable platform. The problem with promising to cut taxes is to convince voters that you will deliver on the promise. By autumn 2005, Canadians had been hearing about tax cuts for a decade. Few Canadians believed they had seen any changes in their own taxes. Many governments, including conservative governments, had *talked* about reducing taxes but too often all they really did was introduce tax breaks for particular industries or certain kinds of investments. Those governments had poisoned the well on tax cuts. We had to find something clearer and more recognizable. Mark Cameron, Bruce Carson, Patrick, and I worked on the issue through autumn 2005. We looked at a lot of options, and eventually recommended a two-point cut to the Goods and Services Tax (GST). I was not certain what Harper would say when we presented the recommendation. He had wanted a short, sharp, memorable plan, and cutting the GST would be a high profile, cut-through-the-clutter promise. We had to be certain we could deliver it, though, because if we promised it and did not end up getting to 5 percent the voters would never trust anything else we said. When Harper agreed to campaign on cutting the GST by two points, I knew we were serious about winning.

The 2005–06 federal election campaign was an invigorating experience. Doug stayed in the war room to direct the campaign from there. I travelled with Harper to ensure the tour group and the war room were always on the same page. At the same time, I worked with Harper's transition team, headed by the legendary Derek Burney. Until very late in the campaign, I could not tell Derek who was slated to be PMO Chief of Staff because I did not know myself and I sensed Derek had not had any indication from Harper about his choice. In the last full week of the campaign, I left the tour group for a few hours to fly to Ottawa and pick up the binder of transition recommendations that Derek's group had drafted. I handed it to Harper when I returned to the tour group, late on Wednesday, 18 January. The next morning, we discussed its contents on the campaign airplane. After dictating a few changes that Harper wanted communicated to Derek's group, he turned to me and asked, "So, are you ready to be PMO chief of staff?" Without nearly enough thought, I answered "Yup." And with that, we were done. This academic was about to become PMO chief of staff.

At the Centre of Government

1

Governing from the Centre: How We Came to See the PM as a Dictator

Canada's prime minister is a dictator. The Sun King of Canadian government. More powerful than the chief executive of any other democratic country. Cabinet is dead – reduced to a mere focus group for the prime minister. Parliament is dead and not to be taken seriously. Canada's form of government no longer has checks and balances. There is nothing to block a prime minister from imposing his will on government. He governs with the help a few hand-picked advisors or "courtiers," like Zeus aloft in the clouds sending lightning bolts from on high into government departments. The vast machinery of government looks nice on paper but mainly exists to feed information upward to the first minister and then implement whatever decisions come back from the top. This is the picture Canadians have had of their government for about a generation now. It's the picture of government I had when I moved into my office as chief of staff to the prime minister. I had, after all, spent my adult life studying Canadian government as a full time political scientist. The academic studies of Canadian government almost all echo this line. Like my fellow citizens, I also got impressions of government from the news media and in particular from political journalists. They report on Ottawa with much the same mindset. A Canadian prime minister is all-powerful.

Is this right? Are prime ministers really dictators? Are there really no limits on how far prime ministers can impose their will on the Government of Canada?

When political scientists ponder these questions, they ask whether we have a *constitutional* system of government? A constitution, in the terminology of the discipline, does more than merely put together a particular government in a particular way. A *successful* constitution puts together a government in a way that limits the powers of government and limits the powers of individual officeholders within that government. A constitution first enables the government to control the governed. It then obliges government to control itself, in James Madison's deft phrase (*Federalist* no. 51 in Hamilton 2001). Sometimes we say a constitution protects rights and liberties, as we have since the 1982 constitutional reform made the Charter of Rights and Freedoms part of our constitutional law. Sometimes we use less legalistic language and say a constitution establishes a system of checks and balances. Sometimes we say we are guided by more specific ideas like the rule of law. But these ways of talking about a constitution all have the same question at their root. Is political power in a given country somehow restricted or limited? Can prime ministers really get away with imposing their view on everyone else? Is its form of government *constitutional*? When we say that the prime minister is a dictator, that is a very serious claim. We are really saying that the government can no longer control itself. A dictatorship is not a constitutional form of government. If the prime minister is a dictator, that is the same as saying Canada no longer has a *constitutional* form of government. It means that our constitution has become a dead letter.

University professors, journalists, and Canadian citizens often insist that the prime ministership is, in some sense, a dictatorship. Maybe that's good for the country. After all, shouldn't academics, journalists, and citizens worry about the quality of our democracy? Shouldn't we all be sensitive to threats to that democracy and be quick to raise the alarm if we see one? Shouldn't citizens be skeptical about government and government power? Of course, the answer to all these questions is a resounding *Yes!* We should be constantly on guard for threats to our form of government. But we should also be aware that, when our worries about the quality of our democracy become a frame for seeing the world around us, we are at risk of losing perspective. Once the idea is set in our minds that the prime minister is a dictator, confirmation bias sets in. Even trained political scientists – maybe *especially* trained political scientists – may miss contrary trends. Blinkers are a good way to ensure that horses are not spooked by what is going on around them. When an idea like "the prime minister is a dictator" becomes a blinker, we can miss important developments and misjudge the importance of others. This book, which draws on both political science and personal experience, is an effort to encourage you to pull off the blinkers and look again at our form of government. My time in politics filled me with awe and wonder at the form of government we have inherited from our ancestors and the pages that follow are my effort at sharing what I found.

Governing from the Centre

Where did we come up with the idea that a Canadian prime minister is too powerful? Where did we come up with the idea that he is a dictator?

Like so many ideas on the common culture, this one began in academia. Canadian academics have worried about the "presidentialization" of the prime ministership for a long time, but the first rigorous arguments that power is unduly centralized in the executive branch are from Donald Savoie. Until 1999, Savoie was not a public figure. He was widely respected in academic and government circles for his expertise in public administration. For years, he wrote about the dilemmas of regional development, a long-standing bugbear of Canadian public policy, and the evolving challenges of bureaucracy. Perhaps his most influential work was *The Politics of Public Spending in Canada* (1990). Almost thirty years after its publication, the book is still a compelling look at how the federal government decides to spend money. In it, Savoie shows the challenge of restraining the federal budget when the federal government has so many "spenders" – government departments and ministers always pushing for more money – and only a few "guardians" – departments and ministers charged with resisting the spenders. Savoie coins the "musical ride rule" to describe how government agency heads, when asked for ways to reduce their budgets, offer up high-profile and politically popular operations, like the RCMP's Musical Ride and the Canadian Force's Snowbird aerial acrobatics team, to take the first cut. Every political staffer who reads *The Politics of Public Spending* laughs at the familiarity of the game.

Savoie's 2000 book, *Governing from the Centre*, catapulted him into a level of media and public attention that public administration specialists never get. He started the research for the book by having breakfast with a Chrétien Cabinet minister who told him "You academics don't get it, do you? Cabinet is nothing more than a focus group for the prime minister" (Savoie 2008). That comment led Savoie to focus his study on the role of the prime minister, the Prime Minister's Office, the Privy Council Office, and the Department of Finance – the branches of government usually referred to as the "central agencies" – in shaping "policies, programs and decisions" (213). He concluded that "prime ministers, beginning with [Pierre] Trudeau, had gradually but systematically strengthened their position at the expense of everyone else, from Parliament to the cabinet and the senior public service" (ibid.). *Governing from the Centre* traces how and why power has been centralized within government in Canada, away from departments and ministers toward the prime minister, a few bureaucrats, aides and ministers deputized by the prime minister, and the central agencies of government that empower the prime minister, namely the prime minister's department, the Privy Council Office (PCO) and his political office, the Prime Minister's Office (PMO). In Savoie's view, the trend to centralization begins with Pierre Trudeau's effort to formalize the Cabinet decision-making process and rationalize support for decisions by expanding PCO, PMO, and the Treasury Board Secretariat. It continues through the governments of Brian Mulroney and Jean Chrétien, with ministers becoming less and less equal at the Cabinet table and successive prime ministers using their levers of power to impose their priorities and policies on everyone else. A prime minister with a majority government "can drive virtually whatever initiative or measure they might favour. Cabinet and Parliament are there, but with a majority of seats a prime minister can manipulate them when it comes to issues that matter a great deal to him" (Savoie 2000, 106). Ergo, Cabinet has become nothing more than a focus group for prime ministers. When a prime minister feels a minister or department has erred or fallen afoul of prime ministerial priorities, the centre governs from on high, hurling lightning bolts into the machinery of government to set things right, overriding ministerial and public service authorities as needed. Whereas once, textbooks could describe a prime minister as *primus inter pares*, first among equals, Savoie claims there is no more "inter" or "pares," just the "primus."

As Savoie himself wrote later, the book was released just as Ottawa was seized with a public inquiry into allegations that Prime Minister Chrétien's political aides were ultimately responsible for the pepper-spraying of protesters at the 1997 APEC Summit in Vancouver. Media attention to his book and its provocative argument took off quickly. Savoie recounts how *The Globe and Mail* gave the book front page coverage and the Canadian edition of *Time* asked him to write a piece based on the book. Book reviews and Savoie's own interviews blanketed the country for weeks. The book became a bestseller, with many printings of the softcover edition.

Only a year later, Jeffrey Simpson, at the time the national affairs columnist for *The Globe and Mail*, produced a more popular version of the argument in his book, *The Friendly Dictatorship*. Where Savoie's sketch of the concentration of power reached back to Pierre Trudeau's government, Simpson's concerns were immediate and starkly tied to the Chrétien government. Jean Chrétien's third straight election win, with his third straight majority government, in 2000 made Simpson wonder if Canada had become a de facto one-party state: "An effective parliamentary system presumes at least one party is ready and capable of replacing the existing government by winning an election" (2001, x). While Simpson did not want to make predictions about the future, he did not think that either the Canadian Alliance or the federal PC Party had "absorbed the lessons of Canadian political history," that the only way to defeat the Liberals was to move to the centre of the political spectrum. He found himself unenthusiastic about the Liberal re-election platform and the prospects of their third term. Now, a one-party state need not necessarily be a dictatorship if the governing party has its own internal checks and balances. The long period of LDP rule in Japan has been marked by factional jockeying inside the governing party and, at times, frequent turnover of leaders. But

Simpson saw almost no prospect of the Canadian Liberal Party displacing Chrétien as its leader: "The perils of intra-party review" – of the like that had toppled Joe Clark as PC Party leader in 1983 – "can plague opposition party leaders ... But a prime minister faces no such peril" (7). The security of Chrétien's leadership had turned Cabinet into policymaking cipher: Cabinet "chews over general policy directions ... As a mini-sounding board that meets the day before caucus the cabinet can provide the prime minister with a preview of what he can expect from the backbenches. Again, the dynamics of prime ministerial government apply: information and impressions are funnelled upwards to the prime minister; decisions come back to down to ministers and caucus" (33–4).

Simpson, more than Savoie, focused on Chrétien's leadership, but like Savoie he saw longer term, structural trends tending to centralize power in the hands of the prime minister. A prime minister, once in power, "has a myriad of tools at his disposal for squelching dissent in the cabinet, in caucus, and among the rank and file ... Once elected, the prime minister shapes his government as he sees fit without the slightest formal check on his prerogative" (14). Canadian prime ministers are simply more powerful than the chief executive of any other democratic country. The prime minister of France serves at the pleasure of the president of the republic. The US president is hemmed in by congressional checks and balances. The prime minister of Australia often lacks a majority in that country's senate. And the British prime minister is restrained by the semi-federal system brought about by devolution to Scotland and Wales. Moreover, the sheer size of the British House of Commons means there are always backbench MPs in safe constituencies willing to overthrow even the likes of the Iron Lady, Margaret Thatcher. Who, Simpson wondered, could imagine such a thing happening to a Canadian prime minister? After all, Brian Mulroney had held his caucus together despite his government plumbing the very depths of public support in the early 1990s.

The Other Side

Any provocative academic book, especially one that gets public recognition, attracts challenges and criticisms from other academics. *Governing from the Centre* was no exception. The equally respected public administration scholar Herman Bakvis raised early questions about Savoie's argument. He questioned whether Chrétien had centralized political power in his own hands. Bakvis argued that Chrétien was actually driven by his experience as a minister in Pierre Trudeau's government to empower ministers to act on their own accord (2001). Chrétien often resented the meddling of central agencies in his work as a minister and prided himself on not checking in with Trudeau regularly to ask for his approval. Bakvis notes that the relatively light Cabinet agenda of the Chrétien years might reflect this decision to empower ministers. With so much government business handled by minister, there was little for Cabinet to do collectively except act as a sounding board for the prime minister.

Graham White mounted even more thorough questions about the Savoie argument (2005, 2012): "Cabinet was never intended to be democratic" (2005, 12). In a piece entitled "First Minister as Autocrat?" (2005, chapter 3), he runs through contributing factors. Both PMO and PCO have grown since the 1960s, and the clerk of the Privy Council is not simply the Cabinet secretary but also the prime minister's deputy minister. PCO and the clerk serve the prime minister's agenda more directly than most other departments do. Central agencies like PCO now intrude in the operations of operating departments more regularly than was once the case, and deputy ministers nearly all have experience in a central agency before being promoted to the top jobs. Canada's PMO is relatively large and exclusively partisan. Moreover, between 1939 and 2003, no Canadian prime minister was ousted by his party, unlike the prime ministers of Australia, New Zealand, Ireland, and the UK. Canadian prime ministers are more likely to have extended terms in the office. While any prime minister is busy and can only concentrate on a few issues of special concern, a prime minister can and does impose his will on the rest of the Cabinet. The key question, for White, is how often does this really happen? Certainly, a prime minister is the boss of the government, and wins a 40–1 vote in Cabinet if they cast that single vote. But how representative is Savoie's account of the centralization of power, White wonders? Savoie relies on anonymous comments to buttress his argument. The public portrait of a prime minister can be profoundly out of step with his private conduct in Cabinet. A prime minister's main power may come from being interested in a broader range of Cabinet agenda items than others, and the power to defer or accelerate Cabinet agenda items as needed.

The major practical retort to Savoie's book comes from Eddie Goldenberg, a long-time political aide to Jean Chrétien and his last PMO chief of staff. In his 2006 memoir, *The Way It Works*, Goldenberg tackles what he calls a "great deal of myth" about PMO and "the centre" that arose during the Chrétien years. He tackles Savoie and Simpson head on for creating an impression of "an inordinate, inappropriate and almost undemocratic concentration of power at 'the centre' and, more particularly, in the PMO" (Goldenberg 2006, 20). But, he argues, the "role of the office of the head of government is far too complex to be captured by pithy sound bites" (ibid.). Goldenberg's analysis is a first-person one and deeply informed by his long career in government.

Chrétien, he explains, wanted his PMO to be a strategic player but not a micromanager of government. The role of the PMO began to evolve in the 1960s as the role of the federal government expanded. The growing complexity of government created a need for coordination across departments and between ministers, and the growth of television as a medium for political communication focused and centralized attention on prime ministers at the expense of local MPs and regional ministers (73–4). The PMO, Goldenberg argues, has an oversight role that is essential but which no other government institution is able to do. It should not be, he argues, a parallel cabinet or public service. It is, however, designed to serve the prime minister of the day without becoming detached from or independent of the prime minister. Coordination "isn't something sinister," Goldenberg writes (75). The centre has to ensure the government gets its arguments out to the public. It has to provide the prime minister with blunt advice that ministers and other parliamentarians have trouble providing. It has to herd by keeping track of where ministers are travelling. It has to make appointments to public offices, although this is almost a no-win job. It has to act as a gatekeeper so the prime minister is not overloaded. And everyone at the centre must be wary about what they say, in case a casual comment is seen by a minister or public servant as a command from the boss.

The most compelling part of Goldenberg's argument, though, is his pithy and funny stories about Chrétien's efforts to get his Cabinet to set the government's priorities collectively: "During the Chrétien years there were a number of different – and unsuccessful – attempts made to involve the whole Cabinet in priority setting" (97); when it came to the budget, they "tried a number of different approaches to involving the whole Cabinet in priority setting, and have discovered that Cabinet is too large and diverse as a group to be able to take into account the whole mix of considerations that go into the allocation of spending priorities." There is also a syndrome he calls PIMBY (please in my back Yard), in which every minister wants money spent in their ministry or province. "The result of PIMBY and all of the competing interests in any Cabinet is that only the prime minister, usually in conjunction with the minister of finance, can make the final decisions on the determination of spending priorities" (98). Sometimes, he recounts, Cabinet meetings are weighty and serious, producing "profoundly important and rational decisions" (99). But most Cabinet meetings deal with relatively routine issues "of importance to some ministers, but not necessarily to the whole country" (100). During Chrétien's first term in office, in the course of a long set of interviews with ministers about the government's priorities, Goldenberg and Chrétien's policy director, Chaviva Hosek, found that most minister are so busy with their own department responsibilities (not to mention political issues in the riding) that they give little serious thought to the government's larger agenda (104). Goldenberg and Hosek's consultations produced two kinds of priority lists: either things the government should do in a minister's own department or home region, or vague ideas of what the government might do overall. Goldenberg reminds us that there are some decisions that only a prime minister can make.

Both sides of argument might be true. Possibly, since the late 1960s, power has been centralized within the executive branch on some matters. Goldenberg emphasizes the need to coordinate government and for the prime minister to set priorities and an overall direction as the scope of government grows. Yet, the very growth of government that increases the need for clear priorities and direction also gives ministers powers and freedom to act within those parameters. The balance of power within Cabinet and the broader executive branch almost certainly shifts over time. In any case, soon after Savoie and Simpson put their fears of prime ministerial power on the record, Chrétien was toppled from office by his own caucus. Paul Martin was either fired or quit as finance minister in June 2002 and began an open campaign for the Liberal leadership. That autumn, Chrétien was forced to announce he would step down as Liberal leader in 2004, and his party called a leadership convention for the end of 2003. Martin's success in dividing the government caucus against Chrétien should have led both academics and journalists to reconsider the Savoie and Simpson theories. But the dominant thinking about Canadian constitutionalism did not get revised much.

The Harper Era

Instead, Savoie and Simpson's worries about the centralization of power under Pierre Trudeau, Brian Mulroney, and Jean Chrétien laid the foundation for the dominant view of Stephen Harper's government. Harper's tenure is almost universally recognized as a time of unprecedented centralization of power in the prime minister's hands. First, the effort to impose professionalism and predictability in government communications was said to make PMO communications officers – all five or six of them – centralizers of power. Over time, increasingly shrill titles authored by journalists, former public servants, and even a few former MPs screamed about Harper's governing style from bookstore shelves: *Sheeple: Caucus Confidential in Stephen Harper's Ottawa* (Turner 2009), *Harperland: The Politics of Control* (Martin 2010), *Rogue in Power: Why Stephen Harper Is Remaking Canada by Stealth* (Nadeau 2011), *The War on Science: Muzzled Scientists and Wilful Blindness in Stephen Harper's*

Canada (Turner 2013), *Harperism: How Stephen Harper and His Think Tank Colleagues Have Transformed Canada* (Gutstein 2014), *Irresponsible Government* (Rathgeber 2014), *Kill the Messengers: Stephen Harper's Assault on Your Right to Know* (Bourrie 2015), *The Arrogant Autocrat: Stephen Harper's Takeover of Canada* (Hurtig 2015), *Dismantling Canada* (Jeffrey 2015), *Unaccountable: Truth and Lies on Parliament Hill* (Page 2015), and *Party of One* (Harris 2014).

I am hopelessly conflicted when it comes to the Harper government. I had a senior role in the government during its early years; after I left, many friends and relatives stayed to work for the government. While I was chief of staff, I was a courtier and probably did my share of governing by lightning bolts. But soon after I left Harper's office I moved abroad and by the time the 2011 election was over I had only a few friends left in government. By 2012, my main personal attachment to the Harper government was my brother, Neil, who manfully carried on in the service of Tony Clement until the government was defeated in 2015. I returned to the academic world in 2013 and gained further distance. Despite my history and my friendships and my brother, I hope that nine years of reflection has given me a bit of distance and not dulled my first-hand insights. The reader will be the final judge.

There is much to be said for the view that the prime minister is a dictator. The next chapter turns to the historical record about the origins of Cabinet or responsible government to see how much the centralization of power in the executive and the prime minister represents a departure from the original idea of Cabinet government. Chapter 3 draws on my first-hand experience to set out where the prime minister is inevitably drawn into government decisions. These are the areas where power is most naturally centralized in Ottawa. Then, in chapter 4 I turn to the decisions that must be made in constructing and maintaining a Cabinet. Is it true that a prime minister has a free hand in putting together and working with a Cabinet as Savoie and Simpson would have us believe? In chapter 5, I argue that Parliament is very much alive as a decision-making institution, and I demonstrate how the battle between government and opposition to allocate Parliament's time shows it is not subordinate to Cabinet and the prime minister. Chapter 6 looks at the two roles of a cabinet minister and the challenge of ensuring the government's agenda is not simply the sum of several ministerial agendas. From the PMO point of view, the government agenda can be divided into a strategic component on the one hand and issues management on the other. In chapter 7, the text turns to the prime minister's role as a party leader. The prime minister's power over party caucus and party organization is much misunderstood, and that misunderstanding was reflected in the Reform Bill proposed by Michael Chong. Partisanship has a useful purpose, and a Senate without partisans is a dangerous innovation. Finally, chapter 8 returns to the state of constitutionalism in Canada. It defends our system of government against criticisms made by the late Peter Aucoin and revisits the Harper government's decision to prorogue Parliament in 2008. It also defends constitutionalism against the arguments for technocratic government made by scholars of public administration. Canada's constitutional order *is* weak in checking the government's spending plans, and I offer some suggestions on how that can be strengthened.

2

The Origins of Cabinet Government

The argument made by Savoie and the others – that power has been centralized in the federal government – is a simple one, but that simplicity comes at a cost. Let us say that power has been centralized in the prime minister's hands since 1968, or since 1993, or since 2006. What do we make of that? Does the trend mark a departure for Canada? Does it undermine our system of government? To answer these questions, we have to go back farther in the historical record than Pierre Trudeau's reorganization of the Cabinet committee system and the reform of PCO. We need a better historical context, and we have to ask different questions. How did we end up with this form of government? Where did Cabinet, or responsible, government come from? What was the alternative? And what arguments were made in favour of responsible government? We can only say whether recent trends have subverted responsible government once we have that historical context in mind. Without it, we cannot pass judgement on the bigger question about the quality of Canadian democracy. Was Cabinet government ever supposed to be a *constitutional* form of government?

To answer these questions, let us turn our minds back to the point in our history when it was not clear what form of government Canada would have, to the first half of the nineteenth century. Responsible, Cabinet government was a conscious choice for Canada, the result of a debate. To get the historical context we need, we have to turn our minds back to the time when responsible government was up for discussion. The proponents of responsible government favoured it over other forms of government. They thought responsible government would have advantages for Canada. By understanding their arguments, we can see what they thought of its scope and limits and see the other forms of government that were rejected. We can ask ourselves: did responsible government's proponents foresee that it could or would be subverted and become "undemocratic"? What steps or safeguards did they try to build into the form of government they created? Was there a "democratic deficit" at the core of Cabinet government from the beginning?

In this discussion, I will use the terms "Cabinet government" and "responsible government" interchangeably. The terms are usually used to emphasize one aspect of our form of government over the other – "Cabinet government" to emphasize the centrality of Cabinet and the executive branch, and "responsible government" to emphasize how a prime minister and Cabinet are identified and then how they relate to the House of Commons. The British North American colonies had something that looked like a Cabinet before the establishment of responsible government, and for some purposes it is helpful to distinguish the two terms (Bowden 2016). But for the present purpose there is no need to draw such a distinction.

Uncovering the Origins of Responsible Government

Uncovering the origins of responsible government is tricky. There are so many historic moments that divert us. The first diversion is Confederation itself. The plan of 1867 to confederate the first seven provinces was an ambitious idea, so ambitious that we often date Canada's political history from that decade-long effort from 1864 to 1873.[1] Subsequent generations have hardly amended the constitutional handwork of the Confederation generation, so we are right to pause every 1 July to admire their wisdom and foresight. Among their wise decisions taken at the Confederation conferences was the one to continue responsible, Cabinet government at both the Dominion and provincial levels. The delegates opted, as the BNA Act puts it, for a constitution "similar in principle to that of the United Kingdom." The most substantial debate about responsible government during that decade was over British Columbia, where local leaders were not certain that conditions were ripe for that form of government just yet (Ajzenstat et al. 1999, 23–55). So if, by 1867, responsible government was widely seen as the proper form of government for Confederation we need to delve further to find the original debate about it.

Responsible government was introduced in British North America in 1840s. The Act of Union, 1840, paved the way for responsible government, and some date the beginning of responsible government from 1841 (Champion 2011). Governments did not change in the British North American colonies using the principle of the confidence convention until 1848, after a letter from Colonial Secretary Earl Grey to the governors instructed them to follow that principle in 1847. The mechanism for the latter change was simple, orderly, and informal. No legislation was passed. No amendments to the British legislation establishing the colonies was required. Grey's letter created no great tumult. In 1848, new governments were formed, first in Nova Scotia, then in the United Province of Canada and New Brunswick. Similar transitions took place later in the other colonies. As colonial governors found governments with the confidence of the local legislatures, responsible government became an established fact. The orderliness of British North America, so calm compared to the upheavals in Europe in 1848, followed a quarter-century long debate about the best form of government for the colonies. Lord Durham's *Report* had made a case for responsible government, and so the 1837 rebellions in Upper and Lower Canada are part of the debate about responsible government. The rebellions demonstrated the shortcomings of the colonial form of government and divided the rebel reformers from the colonial authorities. When reading the history of the rebellions, we should be careful, as Janet Ajzenstat has argued, not to ignore or downplay the fundamental divisions among the reformers themselves (Ajzenstat 1995, 210), or, worse, pretend that the natural march of history toward democracy required the adoption of responsible government. Instead, we should follow Ajzenstat's lead and put our focus on the long debates about the form of government best suited to the colonies. Those debates were important ones, conducted by leaders who understood it had broader implications reaching far beyond the colonies.

The Responsible Government Debate

In the Canadas, the debate over the best form of government for the colonies took place against the backdrop of the Constitutional Act, 1791. That British statute responded to the influx of English-speaking settlers from the United States and elsewhere by dividing the old Province of Quebec in two. Upper and Lower Canada were each granted an elected legislative assembly and its consent was needed to levy taxes and spend the proceeds. Each colony was also given an upper house, a legislative council that was appointed by its colonial governor. To see to the colony's day-to-day needs, an executive council appointed by the governor. While the governor appears to have the upper hand in this arrangement, the military commanders and noblemen dispatched from London came and went. Some were capable and some were not. While it is tempting to see the political conflicts of the period as pitting sensible local leaders against London's blundering or arrogant governors, the reality was more complex. Over time, a small clique of local notables formed in each colony and these cliques, the Chateau Clique in Lower Canada and the Family Compact in Upper Canada, allied themselves to the governors, pursuing their own agendas and interests through the executive and legislative councils. The legislative assemblies then came to be dominated by leaders who claimed mandates from "the people" to decry the corruption of the cliques. A similar dynamic played out in Nova Scotia under the representative form of government established in 1758.

In Lower Canada, the conflict was compounded by English-French divisions. As the largely English-speaking, commercial, and urban Chateau Clique solidified its political position and filled out the appointed councils, politically ambitious French-Canadian reformers consolidated their control of the assembly. Louis-Joseph Papineau became speaker of the Legislative Assembly in 1815 and began drafting plans for a more purely democratic form of government in the colony. Papineau and some reformers in Upper Canada argued that the imposition of British institutions in 1791 had subjected colonists to the "rule of intolerant and unjust elites" (209). Papineau portrayed himself not just as a democrat – the voice of the people – but given the dynamics in Lower Canada as the voice of a particular nationality, permanently shut out of political power (211). In her analysis of his program, Ajzenstat reminds us that Papineau did not claim to speak for the people in the sense of a "shifting and continually changing aggregation of groups and interests" of the sort we think of today when we think of a political majority, but rather a permanent and homogeneous body of citizens. He viewed his own party, the Patriotes, as the party of that permanent body of citizens and foresaw no need to consider the alternation of political parties in power as an element of democracy for the colony. The Patriote program of constitutional reform would have had the elected assembly taking on the executive power and erased the separation of legislative and executive powers. The assembly would devise its own budget policy and initiate its own legislative program (216–18).

British efforts to resolve the political dysfunction created by the 1791 Act by sending out governors with better skills in the arts of political accommodation missed the mark, and when Lower Canada fell into a series of economic, agricultural, and public health crises, the impasse sharpened. In 1837, the Legislative Assembly in Lower Canada refused to grant supply to the colonial administration. The long-standing inability of Lower Canada's form of government to gain the consent of the population was a profound failure. Just as Shays' Rebellion, an armed uprising in Massachusetts, exposed the weakness of the Articles of Confederation, the 1837 rebellions in exposed the weakness of the 1791 and 1758 arrangements in British North America. By this time, "it was apparent to all that the colonies could not continue under the practices that had grown up in the decade succeeding 1791. It was a period of founding, or re-founding" (225).

In the 1820s, the early arguments for responsible government can be seen in the writings of Étienne Parent in Lower Canada and Joseph Howe in Nova

Scotia. These two newspaper editors separately pressed the case for political reform at a time when newspaper editorials could result in criminal charges. Parent and Howe both supported party government, with the prospect that no party would become a permanent government. They opposed both the absolutism of the "colonial oligarchs" and understood that the pure democracy advocated by some of their fellow reformers could readily degenerate into democratic absolutism as well (212). Ajzenstat's adroit account of their arguments, and her rendering of Lord Durham's subsequent recommendation of responsible government, help us understand the debate over Canada's form of government, the arguments for responsible government, and the types of alternatives that were considered at the time.

Parent was born to a farming family and advanced through Lower Canada's system of religious schools to become a leading intellectual force of French Canada. Writing in the pages of *Le Canadien* and other outlets, he opposed the permanent alliance of Chateau Clique with the governors of the time and eventually also the democratic absolutism promoted by Papineau and the Patriotes. He served as librarian and then clerk of Lower Canada's assembly and in June 1833 wrote despondently about the inability of the assembly to legislate wisely:

> One has generally so little time to give to public affairs that the sessions [of the assembly] pass in demanding one piece of information after another document after document, testimony after testimony, and years pass before a committee is able to unravel the chaos that is before it. The session ends, everyone returns to his particular affairs, and one returns at the next session as innocent as one was at the beginning of the last. And if in response to popular demand, one passes a law, it is nothing but an outline that has to be retouched at each subsequent session." (217)

Left to their own wits, the deputies drafted incomplete bills that led to half-baked legislation. Each session of the assembly had to devote time and energy to fixing laws that had been approved by the representatives of the people but that then needed to be revised. Sober second thought was often overtaken by legislative debates. If legislation were prepared instead by ministers, a proper legislative program could be presented to the assembly and the legislature would be able to hold someone accountable to explain it. Long before the assembly blocked supply in 1837, Parent saw that the political battles over supply betrayed a fundamental weakness of the colony's form of government. Lower Canada's budget was a mess of local appropriations, each added to the agenda to secure the approval of a local representative. Responsible government, he argued, would bring the money bill rule. The executive would have the sole power to propose taxes and spending to the legislative assembly. By giving the executive the power to draft a budget, Parent saw that the legislature would be free to criticize it and improve government. Parent thought British-style responsible government would be as good for Lower Canada as it had been for Westminster and as it could be for anyone else (224).

Unlike Parent, Joseph Howe was from a loyalist family. But like Parent he attacked Nova Scotia's local clique for its dominance of the colony's government. No matter who won an election, he could see that the same small clique remained in power (219). He was also not satisfied with the democratic absolutism of the radical democrats. His 1839 letters to Colonial Secretary Lord Russell petitioned for responsible government in Nova Scotia, and his arguments echo those of Parent. Where Parent saw the advantages of centralizing fiscal power in the hands of a responsible executive, Howe argued for centralizing the patronage power in the hands of a responsible executive. Howe understood that any form of government needed a cadre of appointed officials, and he assumed that political leaders would appoint and dismiss that cadre. But he argued that this patronage power should be exercised by leaders who had the confidence of the elected house and could account for their exercise of that power to the house. In Howe's view, a responsible Cabinet would have control over what we would call public sector staffing today.

British political figures, especially Westminster's Radicals, followed the Canadian debate about the best form of government for the colony with interest. As Ajzenstat has documented, the Philosophical Radicals, followers of Jeremy Bentham and James Mill's proposals for political reform, had established a caucus in the British House of Commons to pursue these ideas. Bentham had earlier condemned all political parties for sharing interests "opposite to that of the whole uncorrupt portion of the people," and his Radical followers were radical democrats. They aspired to establish a single party of "the people" in Britain, that is "a party to represent the majority and to govern in their name" (Ajzenstat 1988, 56). The Philosophical Radicals saw no value in an independent upper house, either in Westminster or in the colonies, and less value in a strong executive, which should be "no more than a tool of the popular house" (56). The Radicals saw the Patriote cause as a case for pursuing their reform agenda, and they seized upon the 1837 rebellions to advance their views at Westminster. The uprising in Lower Canada, for the Radicals, was a battle between a party of the majority – the Patriotes – and a small colonial elite. The solution they advocated was a radically democratic regime, one where the elected assembly would hold sway and the executive would hold a subordinate position. This "new democratic order" for the new world, as Ajzenstat describes it (55), would see a purely democratic constitution for the colonies, and establish a form of government that Britain would eventually adopt itself.

Melbourne's decision to send out Lord Durham as governor general of the Canadas with an additional commission to investigate the causes of the rebellions responded both to the constitutional crisis in the colonies and to the political situation in Westminster. Durham's *Report*, then, ended up speaking to two audiences: a colonial audience struggling with the 1758 and 1791 constitutions and a Westminster audience with its own agenda for pure democracy. Durham, as Ajzenstat documents, was well acquainted with Westminster's Philosophical Radicals: "Much of the argument in [his] Report is addressed to the Radicals and is meant to refute their claims" (56). Durham's *Report* may not capture the whole debate about what form of government best suits British North America, but in Ajzenstat's hands, the Report comes alive in its full political context. She deftly connects Durham's case for responsible government to the British and modern tradition of political science and constitutional thought. She takes seriously the debate about Canada's form of government.

Responsible government, seen in one light, looks like the type of raw democratic form of government sought by the Radicals and the Patriotes. The colonial executive would be responsible and accountable to the popularly elected assembly. Forcing governors to follow the advice of Cabinets with the confidence of legislative assemblies democratizes the colony. Responsible government also "rendered the colonies more independent" from London, and "spelled the end of the 'family compacts,' the political cliques in each province" that held sway over public decisions by virtue of their alliances with the colonial governors. It would be "easy to conclude," Ajzenstat notes, "that Durham saw 'responsible government' as having a democratic thrust," but "Durham usually writes as if 'responsible government' were a way of restraining democratic demands" (52). He describes it as a measure that will strengthen the political executive so as to enable it to "limit" or "balance" the popular house. It is true that he regarded "responsible government" as valuable because it would be the means, on occasion, by which leaders betraying popular interests could be removed from office. But he seems to have supposed that it would usually work to maintain the executive in office so that it in fact became less responsive to immediate popular demands (ibid.).

For the British Radicals, talk of "balance" was a smokescreen that allowed elites to dominate government and pursue interests that were opposed to those of the people. But, as Ajzenstat argues, Durham was a good democrat, and good government, in the Whig tradition, needs balance (53). In Britain, the constitution was usually described as a "mixed regime," namely a balance among the three estates or social classes – the monarch, the aristocracy, and the commoners. As Ajzenstat reminds us, the standard view of the mixed regime is that it reached its peak in the aristocratic age of British politics and then gave way to the fusion of executive and legislative powers when the independent power of the aristocracy faded (217). But Durham had a modern view of the mixed regime. He agreed with the Radicals "that ministers of the Crown and members of the upper house often – perhaps usually – tried to use their positions to further the narrow interests of party, family, and class" (66). Although he referred to the three estates of the mixed regime, "he has a twofold division in mind" (66). He saw distinctions of wealth and ambition as natural. Distinctions of wealth and ambition, he thought, would emerge among all social classes. A form of government could not be designed to exclude the greedy and ambitious. Instead, a good form of government needed to accommodate and tame the natural skills of the few. Therefore, "if Durham had no trouble prescribing the mixed regime for colonies without a landed class or great differences between rich and poor, it was because he believed that one could always count on a natural crop of ambitious and able trouble makers" (67). The modern mixed regime, Ajzenstat argues, includes a separation of powers, of Cabinet from legislature, that "gives [the] political opposition its foothold in the institutions of government" (Ajzenstat 1987, 119).

Between the establishment of responsible government in British North American colonies and the Confederation of those colonies in 1867, Britain's political parties were shifting and the Westminster House of Commons regularly defeated governments. For a time, observers like Bagehot could describe the Commons as an ongoing "elective" chamber, choosing and dismissing ministries often. This period of "flexible parliamentarianism," to use the phrase of Tom Hockin (1979) turned out to be temporary. In the years following Confederation, the executive regained its powers to dominate Parliament on both sides of the Atlantic. Today, in Hockin's assessment, the "constitutional essence" of responsible government includes the government commanding a majority in the House; the government attempting to answer questions and criticisms in the House; allowing the Opposition to scrutinize government action and to debate the major issues of the day; and elections held at least every five years (1979, 14).

The form of government established in 1791, then, with an elected assembly and an appointed executive failed to provide for popular control of the administration of government and encouraged populist appeals by elected leaders while suppressing legitimate divisions among parties. More direct forms of government proposed by the Radicals would similarly have stripped checks and balances out of the regime. Durham's proposal, implemented during the 1840s, was for responsible party government, a coherent and limited form of government well known in the UK and the colonies.

Assessing Responsible Government

What light does the debate about responsible government, more than 150 years ago, shed on today's argument about the centralization of power in the executive? First, the original proponents of responsible government understood that it would centralize both political power and political accountability. "If we take seriously Durham's own claim to be proposing a measure known in England from 1688, we must suppose he had in mind the strong, relatively independent political executive" (60). As Ajzenstat notes, the tools used by prime ministers and Cabinets to their support in the House have changed since the 1830s. British ministers of that day relied on "bribes of 'place' and pension" to MPs. Contemporary governments rely on "partisan spirit and the promise of advancement" to stay in office. But the replacement of one set of tools with another does not make much of a difference in political practice. Durham, Parent, and Howe all understood that the legislature would hold the power to dismiss a government, but governments were dismissed rarely even in the 1830s. "Only for a comparatively short period in the mid- and late-nineteenth century were the popular houses, in Britain and in the colonies, really able to humble the executive branch and bring ministers to account by making and unmaking governments. Parliamentary systems after that reverted to the strong executive that Durham regarded as the norm" (118fn13).

Brent Rathgeber's recent argument (2014) that responsible government divides the House of Commons into a ministry on the one side and private members on the other is overstated. It is true that private members on the government side have a role in holding the executive to account. Chapter 8 sets out some ways to strengthen that role. Private members on the government side are, however, elected on the basis of the party's platform and national campaign. Voters cast their ballots on the understanding that their local MP is part of a party and a team. Government backbenchers and opposition MPs have different roles to play in our form of government. They share some interests in how Parliament runs, but there are important differences as well.

Moreover, Parent and Durham realized that the money bill rule would further strengthen the executive. Cabinet would not just propose taxing and spending proposals but also "initiate the major legislative programs, and the assembly be confident to review of government budgets and spending" (59). Responsible government would bring order to the "scramble for local appropriations" that had afflicted the legislative assemblies of Upper and Lower Canada (68). Lower Canada had, for example, no education policy but instead had handouts to "this school or that" as the political occasion demanded. Since elected representatives could not rise to higher office, "currying favour with the localities at the expense of the common good was the most profitable course" for them to pursue. With responsible government and the money bill rule, the prospect of advancement would teach "all to think in 'larger' terms and secure the support for the executive that would enable it to proceed in vigorous style." Howe and Durham also understood that the patronage power – the power to hire and fire officials – would reinforce the strength of the executive. Unlike a US President, a first minister would be able to select and dismiss ministers without needing the "advice and consent" of the legislature. Ministers would be able to select and dismiss departmental staff without seeking the approval of the legislature.

Responsible government was also to balance this powerful executive with a liberated opposition. Since the government had the key levers of power in its hands, its opponents in the assembly would be free to oppose. This liberation of the loyal opposition is as much a part of responsible government as the creation of a powerful executive. The opposition would be free from the need to formulate a governing agenda and could therefore avoid all the compromises and accommodations required in government. It could oppose the government with clean hands. An opposition facing a majority government could denounce every government initiative with zeal, secure in its privileges and status. A hungry, ambitious opposition would learn to direct its zeal in a way that improved its chance of taking power. The division of the legislature into government and opposition and the prospect that they may eventually change places are what distinguish responsible government from the purer forms of democracy that appealed to the Philosophical Radicals and the Patriotes.

Comparing these arguments for responsible government to the debates over the US Constitution at the Philadelphia Convention is perilous. After all, Parent, Howe, and Durham were not creating a new form of government. By 1837, responsible government was not a novelty and none of its supporters suggested it was. On the contrary, Durham rejected the Philosophical Radical novel proposals for pure democracy even though they were "so much in tune with the spirit of the age" (57). He chose instead to "advance old arguments for the old constitution" (ibid.). Durham had "argued for mixed government throughout his career in England, and he apparently saw no reason why the colonies of British North America should have anything less than this best constitution" (53). But to Ajzenstat "it is clear that 'balance' as espoused by the British thinkers has the same roots as the American doctrine of the separation of powers – the system of 'checks and balances'" (71). Durham did not use the phrases "separation of powers" or "checks and balances," but "other whigs of the period did not hesitate to describe the British constitution in that language" (ibid.). And those common roots let us draw some rough lessons by comparing the US Constitution and responsible government.

The US form of government was clearly intended to be a *constitutional* one. It pairs a separation of powers with a deliberate set of checks and balances. Since 1789, the relative powers of the branches have ebbed and flowed, and American scholars have worried about the emergence of an "imperial presidency" or an "imperial Congress." Few Canadian observers of US government would say power has become overly concentrated in the executive branch. The United States has a "constitutional" form of government in the sense that its governing institutions are capable of limiting their own reach. As Madison puts it in *Federalist* no. 51 (Hamilton 2001), the separation of powers depends on "giving to those who administer each department [i.e., branch of government] the necessary constitutional means and personal motives to resist encroachment of the others." In the US, this means the president wields a veto, the Senate must "advise and consent" to executive appointments and treaties, and the House of Representatives must initiate appropriations legislation. Responsible government acts differently, but from the same basis, when it divides the legislature into a government side and an opposition side. Each side of the legislature is protected and each side has a job to do. The government initiates legislation and budget plans. The opposition scrutinizes and opposes. The division of the legislature provides the "constitutional means and personal motives" for the opposition parties to resist the government of the day. And it provides the personal motives for them to do so wisely if they aspire to form a government at some point. Madison famously insists in *Federalist* no. 51 that "Ambition must be made to counteract ambition." On this count, the Canadian form of government offers the opportunity for a robust separation of powers. Ambitious opposition politicians will make use of that opportunity when they tire of opposing and become hungry for the powers and perquisites of government.

What impact is the separation of powers supposed to have? The late Martin Diamond reminds us that the separation of powers has two purposes. The American separation of powers is not intended to improve government (or "public policy," to use a more contemporary term) but to improve democracy (1992): The separation of powers, and the checks and balances that follow from it, improve democracy first by preventing a group of ambitious leaders united by passions or interests adverse to the rights of citizens or the public good from overreaching even if they have a democratic mandate in hand. Diamond also argues that the separation of powers improves democracy by heading off another democratic disease, "namely, a tendency to ineptitude, inconstancy, incompetence" (66). The US regime, "is intended to help democracy achieve not only free but also effective government; it has not to maximize either freedom or strength, but work to optimize them" (67). Parent, Howe, Durham, and their allies would have made exactly the same arguments about responsible government. Just as Shays' Rebellion exposed the inadequacy of the Articles of Confederation and drove the Philadelphia Convention to draft a better constitution for the United States, so the 1837 rebellions exposed the inadequacy of the 1791 and 1758 constitutions of British North America. The American founders thought that competent government was indispensable to liberty. Parent, Howe, and Durham would have agreed.

Today, we have difficulty relating to the constitutional arguments of the early nineteenth century. Sometimes, Liberals tell us that the constitutional protection of rights and liberties began in 1982, with the adoption of the Charter of Rights and Freedoms, and too often some Conservatives respond to that argument by pointing to the 1960 Bill of Rights introduced by John Diefenbaker. Liberals respond that the Bill of Rights was lacking because Canada's courts did so little to "enforce" it. This has inured us to the idea that parliamentary government takes away rights and freedoms while judges, interpreting a charter or bill of rights, grant them. While no one can deny the fundamental injustice of some Canadian policies predating the Charter and the Bill of Rights, it is a mark of gross historical illiteracy to pretend that rights and freedoms were not protected in Canada before 1982 or 1960. The entire argument of Parent, Howe, and later the leading figures of the Confederation Conferences was that parliamentary, responsible, Cabinet government itself provided adequate, if fallible, protection of rights and freedoms.

The Broader Impact of Responsible Government

In 1837, Durham argued that the political crisis in Lower Canada was the result of two nations warring in the bosom of a single state. Papineau would not have disagreed, confident in the future political power of the more numerous French-Canadian nation. As Diamond argues, the ancient version of the mixed regime depended on having a divided society and an undivided government. Society was divided into classes and each class had a branch of the regime. Any one branch of the regime could exercise all the powers of government if it could enlist another branch of the regime as an ally. The modern mixed regime, Diamond writes, depends on an undivided society, one without politically significant classes, and a divided government with separated powers. The success of responsible government since 1848 suggests that, whatever divisions Durham saw in Lower Canada in 1837, the two populations were not divided in politically significant ways. They were capable of governing themselves together. As Ajzenstat puts it, Durham intended responsible government to put "French and English on an equal footing" (1988: 10). If Papineau or the Radicals had prevailed in the debate over Canada's form of government, Canada might not have ended up avoiding the challenges of two nations at war in the bosom of a single state.

Joseph Howe realizes that responsible government would shape the political calculations of ambitious politicians and encourage even the most unscrupulous to moderate their strategies and tactics. A British-style constitution, in Ajzenstat's summary of Howe, "encourages demagogues to act like the great statesmen of British history because it rewards their [political] ambition under institutions that curtail" political ambition (223). Those leaders who aim to be first ministers find that to "gratify their ambitions" they must keep the support of "a party that [also] has the support of the country" (ibid.). The challenge of maintaining their party's support even as they win over enough voters to form government attracts energy that would otherwise pursue other objectives, some of them less compatible with free and effective government. And the challenge does not end with winning an election. Once in power, such leaders are subject to the free and zealous scrutiny of the opposition parties and the voters. Responsible government tames rebels with the "salutary clash of elites under a good constitution" (223). By dividing the elected legislature in two, responsible government ensures no leader, even one that speaks for a clear popular majority, can claim to speak for all the people and deny the rights and status of their opponents.

3

Delegation and Its Limits:
The Core Powers of a Prime Minister

A Canadian prime minister is powerful. Years ago, a prime minister was described as *primus inter pares*, or the first among several equal ministers. Today, Savoie argues that there is no longer a *primus* and a *pares*, just a *primus* in Cabinet. But was there ever an era when the prime minister sitting in a Cabinet meeting was truly *inter pares*, among equals? Was the prime minister's position ever akin to that the *Princeps Senatus*, the senior member of the Roman Senate who was always allowed the first word in its debates? Was the prime minister ever *just* the chair of the group? The prime minister's position is inherently powerful. But in what ways is it powerful? And how do those powers come about? Understanding the levers of powers that the prime minister controls helps us also understand the constraints on the prime minister's powers. These are lessons I learned from the transition to power in 2006.

... Ministers Have Some Uses ...

On 24 January 2006, the day after he won the federal election, Stephen Harper boarded his campaign airplane for the last time to fly back to Ottawa from Calgary. After fifty-six days of campaigning, 5,374,000 Canadians had cast a vote for the Conservatives. That was enough for 124 seats in the House of Commons, a slim minority. The mood of the four-hour flight was upbeat. Stephen Harper and I shared a copy of the *Calgary Herald* to see which candidates were joining him in the House and which were not. The change of time zone plus the flight time meant we touched down as the sun was setting over the capital. For the first time, he was greeted at the Canada Reception Centre, the government's small VIP terminal at the Ottawa International Airport. A small but boisterous crowd of campaign workers were gathered to show support. I joined him for the drive straight to the Opposition Leader's beautiful office suite in room 409-S of Parliament's majestic main building, Centre Block, so recognizable in photographs of the Peace Tower. Derek Burney, the head of the Harper transition team, and a senior official of the Privy Council Office were waiting to discuss the transition of power.

As we settled in, the senior official began the conversation with pleasantries about the election campaign and Harper's performance during the election. The best way to break the ice with a politician is to talk politics and most senior officials see enough politicians come and go to know the trick. When the meeting turned to the business of the transition, the official started with a surprising question. "Mr Harper, do you intend to appoint ministers? Is it your intention to have a cabinet?" There was a moment of silence. Harper was taken aback, and so was I. Of course, he intended to appoint ministers. The official continued, deadpan. "PCO's advice is to appoint ministers. You will find ministers have some uses." Pause. "But they are not strictly necessary. The public service is quite capable of briefing you on every issue before the government and to implement your every decision."

At first, I thought the official was testing the limits of Harper's rumoured dictatorial tendencies. But I then realized that the official, like the best teachers, was starting at first principles: Harper had to decide how to organize his government. An effective structure allows a prime minister to pick the files he wants to manage or supervise and delegate the rest. The official continued: "We can organize the Government of Canada so that if you never want to hear about certain issues, you never will." Our Westminster traditions give us many tools to let prime ministers delegate issues to other ministers so they can decide, within boundaries. But there are, I learned, four areas of government policy – four levers of power – where a prime minister can never fully delegate responsibility to others. These four levers of power set the boundaries within which other ministers work.

It is essential to delegate responsibility for almost everything else to ministers because using those four levers of government wisely will take up the bulk of a prime minister's waking hours. Most decisions of the Government of Canada are made well below the level of prime minister. The weekly catalogue of formal decisions of the Government of Canada, the *Canada Gazette*, reports on thousands of decrees, orders, proclamations, and other instruments of decisions each year. The prime minister is not aware of most of them, and a good clerk of the Privy Council and PMO chief of staff have to help ensure that is the case or they, too, will be overwhelmed. Ministers, in almost all cases, have wide discretion to use their ministerial powers as they see fit without checking with the prime minister, PCO, or PMO. But regardless of how a prime minister delegates decisions to others, there are four areas where the prime minister always must be involved. These are decisions about fiscal policy, Canada's foreign relations, the federal government's relations with the provinces, and the management of the government's business before Parliament. It is often wise for a prime minister to leave other ministers to be the government's public face in these areas. Consulting and explaining decisions in these areas of government to the public can be time-consuming. The details of policy in these four areas are tedious and may be best left to others. But no prime minister can afford to delegate these matters entirely. In these four policy areas, the prime minister's involvement is not a variable that reflects the incumbent or some set of courtiers' views about the merits of centralization. They are inherent in our form of government.

Fiscal Policy

First, a prime minister must make the major fiscal decisions of the Government of Canada. The government's budget is *the* essential confidence matter in our parliamentary system, and in a minority government decisions about raising, spending, and borrowing money are matters of parliamentary life and death. Putting a budget, a ways and means motion, or an appropriation bill before the House means gambling on the government's very existence. Only a foolish prime minister would leave the most consequential fiscal policy decisions entirely to someone else. Even in a majority government, the budget involves decisions that cut across every government department. How much money will the government need? How will it be raised? How will it be divided between competing needs? And how will the government try to mobilize its ministers, its parliamentarians, and the broader public to support its fiscal decisions? These are among the most important decisions a government makes, and a prime minister should expect to be involved in all of them.

The prime minister has a finance minister to help him with fiscal policy, and in a time of budget cuts the President of the Treasury Board is also an essential advisor. There must be a relationship between the finance minister and the prime minister if the government is to function. In my time, this involved regular fiscal policy briefings from Finance Minister Jim Flaherty and his officials. When I was in PMO, these meetings were led by Flaherty and his officials. They had the initiative in setting the agenda for these briefings. Later, these briefings were led by PMO staff. Jean Chrétien and Paul Martin sometimes made budget decisions together without meeting face to face (Goldenberg 2006). This cannot have been easy for their political aides or their public service officials. Most of these decisions turned out well, a testament to the professionalism of the public servants and political aides involved and their willingness to do what was needed to overcome the dysfunction at the top.

Flaherty's first budget was structured around the Conservative's 2006 election platform. There were few other budget decisions to make. After that, fiscal decisions involved more give and take between the principals. After Flaherty's untimely passing, Harper explained their relationship in his eulogy:

> The relationship between a Prime Minister and his Finance Minister is always a special one. But this, I can tell you, was more special than most ... [O]n the specifics of the many and complex priorities before us, we often had, at least initially, different views ... As we talked through budget planning meetings, our divergences always narrowed and usually vanished. When they didn't, occasionally I imposed a final decision. Occasionally, I decided he was probably right. And occasionally, I decided he was wrong but let him have his way, just because I got so tired of arguing with him. (Harper 2014)

The first hard decision came in autumn 2006, when the Harper government reversed course on the taxation of income trusts. Early in October, Flaherty and a senior Finance official advised Harper that his government would have to break his high-profile election promise to maintain the existing rules around the taxation of income trusts. Thousands of Canadians held trust units as part of their retirement savings – including, I realized, my father. Hundreds of Canadian firms used income trusts to raise capital. Although I was not a tax policy expert, I knew that reversing ourselves on the issue would spark a massive controversy. The Liberals had considered a move against income trusts a year earlier. A leak about that ignited a furor and sparked a criminal investigation. Changing course on income trusts would require legislation, and possibly a defeat on a confidence matter leading to an early election. Flaherty trusted the advice of his official and pressed his case forcefully. Our election platform committed us to preserving income trusts under the heading of "Security for Seniors." We specifically committed to stopping "the Liberal attack on retirement savings" by not imposing any new taxes on income trusts (Conservative Party of Canada 2006, 32). Given the criminal investigation, we could not risk news of our plan leaking. That limited our ability to consult. Harper told Flaherty and his official to come back with some offsetting tax measures for retirees that would offset any new tax burden on them. About a week later, they returned with a package that satisfied

Harper: a $1,000 per year increase in the age credit for seniors and income splitting for retirement income (Finance Canada 2006). Harper agreed to proceed, and we set the date of 31 October for an announcement.

The offsetting tax changes satisfied most retirees, and a year later Flaherty announced a five-year plan to reduce the corporate tax rate from 22 percent to 15 percent (Finance Canada 2007a). Reducing that rate helped take some of the sting out of the income trust decision. It kept Canada competitive in the search for investments. Harper took severe criticism in caucus and in public for the decision. He would later say that the income trust decision was the hardest decision he had to make in his first year in office. I think we won the public argument that the facts had changed since the election campaign and we had to change policy as a result. The political price we ended up paying was small. But to this day I wonder if we rushed the decision on income trusts. The decision was taken on the advice of Flaherty and the public service, but I wonder if we could have devised a gentler transition to the new regime, one that would not have so suddenly closed off sources of capital for Canadian firms and would not have hurt the retirement savings of Canadians. The right decision was the right one in the longer term. But was the quick implementation fair?

From time to time, Flaherty and others sounded out Harper about reducing the top bracket for personal income taxes. This is traditionally the sort of advice a government gets from business-oriented economists. Harper was never interested in that kind of reform. He later insisted on reducing the GST from 6 percent to 5 percent in autumn 2007, when the early signals of distress were pulsing through credit markets, and thankfully pressed ahead with it. Keeping the GST promise convinced millions of Canadians that Ottawa was listening to their concerns. That popular credibility turned out to be essential during the global financial crisis, when so many other governments lost credibility with their publics. If Congressional Republicans and President Obama had managed to do something similar together, American voters might not have rebelled in such large numbers in the 2016 presidential election. As it turned out, the GST dropped to 5 percent just as the government was trying to design a macro-economic stimulus package to boost spending during the global financial crisis. The timing was fortuitous. All the key tax decisions of the Harper government were made with the same type of give and take between Harper and Flaherty. The five-year plan to reduce corporate tax rates got hashed out in a meeting with Prime Minister Harper, who agreed that announcing corporate tax rates well in advance was important. Without his personal commitment to the plan, he might not have defended it so strongly against the Liberal promise to increase corporate taxes in the 2011 election campaign. Since both he and Flaherty supported with the decision, it stuck.

Despite the importance of the give and take between the two principals in devising fiscal policy, the finance minister has some advantages in the exercise. Outside of major financial crises, the finance minister only has two large deliverables in a year – a federal budget and an economic and fiscal update. Between these two events, the minister is free to meet with Cabinet and caucus colleagues to hear their views on the government's fiscal policy. A finance minister also meets the opposition parties' finance critics to sound out what it will take to earn their wholehearted support. Those discussions are particularly important in a minority government, when every budget must have at least one "give" to each of the opposition parties. While I was his chief of staff, Harper also met separately with the opposition party leaders in the weeks leading up to each budget to listen to what they wanted to see in the document. He figured that the other party leaders would support or defeat the budget for political reasons. But he wanted each leader to be able to point to something in the budget if he decided to support it and included one of the "asks" from each opposition party in each budget. On budget day, I telephoned the offices of the other party leaders to make sure they knew where they would find their "give" in the document. The finance minister meets regularly with provincial finance ministers and, increasingly, with finance ministers from other countries in the G7, the G20, and the regular meetings of IMF and World Bank governors. The IMF, the World Bank, the OECD, and other international financial institutions supply a constant stream of analysis to Ottawa. The finance minister is always welcome in the executive suites of Canada's leading financial institutions, resource companies and industrial firms. The Finance Department is small but well-staffed with experienced and expert officials. The minister can also draw on independent advice and analysis from the C.D. Howe Institute and the Bank of Canada. Finance ministers now names an advisory panel on economic and fiscal policy to meet with them regularly. Few people turn down an offer to serve on such a panel. When selecting a finance minister, the prime minister must pick someone astute enough to be able to get advice and assessments from these sources and meld them with enough political judgement to prepare a draft budget and refine the key questions for the prime minister's ultimate decision. If smaller budget decisions can be managed by the finance minister alone, meetings between the two principals can focus on the most important decisions.

The process for making fiscal policy decisions tends to be highly centralized and secretive. Many of the meetings I attended on fiscal policy had only five attendees – Flaherty and one Finance Department official, Harper, the clerk of the Privy Council, and me. Later in the Harper government these meetings became more formal and larger. The consultations leading up to a budget are as open and accessible or closed as a finance minister and a prime minister want them to be. Finance ministers usually ask the House of Commons Finance Committee to conduct public consultations on the budget starting in August or September of the previous year. The chair of the Finance Committee is therefore a key role. The chair has to manage the demands of MPs from all parties and of all the groups who want to testify. The minister may frame questions or issues for the committee to consider, but the committee is always free to range beyond the minister's interests. It usually publishes a formal call for submissions. Anyone with an interest in budget issues can submit a brief. The committee then calls upon a few groups or experts to appear at hearings in August or autumn. Those hearings are overwhelmingly dominated by interest groups who are petitioning for federal spending. Private consultations with Finance Department officials and political staff usually take place in parallel with the committee's hearings. The committee's report is usually issued before Christmas with dissenting reports from the opposition parties. Unfortunately, because of the academic blinders about Cabinet and Parliament there is little research on how much these reports influence federal budgets (Ulrich 2002). There is only one study of the Finance Committee's work, and that looked at its influence on the design of the GST (Malloy 1996).

Could decision-making around the budget be opened up further? Maybe. With a little political creativity, a finance minister and prime minister could order up all sorts of public consultations. Eddie Goldenberg relates a funny account of Chrétien's efforts to involve all of Cabinet in making budget decisions in 1999. Some ministers, he writes, urged funding for the last item on the agenda of the most recent Cabinet meeting because it was the one item they remembered. Others figured important priorities would be funded anyway and so urged funding for pet projects. Many others voted for their own department's priorities. The results of the process were "so scattered and inconclusive that they allowed the minister of finance and the prime minister to rationalize whatever priorities they chose for the budget as expression the will of Cabinet" (Goldenberg 2006, 109). In the end, the big fiscal decisions rest with the finance minister and the prime minister. Since the big fiscal decisions cut across all of the government's operations, they are naturally centralizing.

One corollary of this centralization is that the prime minister and the finance minister are the only two decision-makers who are able to insert "earmarks" – specific line items of funding for specific recipients – into the budget. Congressional earmarks have become controversial in the United States. There is a long tradition of appropriations committee members in both the House and the Senate inserting all kinds of specific spending directions into spending bills on Capitol Hill. The rules of the House of Representatives recognize and regulate the earmarking process. Congressional Republicans committed to ending earmarks after they won back control of the House in 2010. But in Canada, where only two people can insert them, earmarks are rarely noted by reporters or opposition critics. Jim Flaherty often inserted earmarks for charities that support children with developmental disabilities into his budgets, with Harper's concurrence. The Flaherty family has first-hand experience with developmental disabilities. His 2007 budget also announced a fund to create "Centres of Excellence in Commercialization and Research" at Canadian universities and research hospitals. The budget specified that these centres would be selected based on peer review and private sector advice. But the document went on to say that "as a first step" the government would provide immediate funds to seven centres specified in the budget itself (Finance Canada 2007b, 200). There was no explanation of how those seven centres had been selected. One of the centres was based at the University of Western Ontario, so I was absent from the portion of the meeting that decided the matter. I assume Flaherty recommended the earmark for these centres.

Eddie Goldenberg relates a conversation he once had with Mitchell Sharp regarding his time as Lester Pearson's finance minister from 1965 to 1968: at the time, "the prime minister and his office did not get involved in budgets" (2006, 131). Since the budgets of the day focused on taxes, tariffs, and setting the overall level of public spending for the year, they could be prepared in secret, "with only rudimentary consultation with other departments of government, including even the prime minister" (132). Goldenberg suggests that budget making has changed since 1968 because budgets now express the government's spending priorities and also use the tax system as an instrument of social policy. But I suspect that the high level of trust between Pearson and the veteran Sharp might have made those years of budget making an exception to the need for a prime minister to be closely involved in the key fiscal policy decisions.

The fiscal work of the finance minister is supported by officials in the Department of Finance and by his political aides. Every official in the Finance Department knows that the confidence of the House of Commons in the government of the day is directly tied to its fiscal policy, and that fiscal policy must be driven by the government's overall priorities. I have never heard a current or former official of the department express any concern that the prime minister would be closely involved in making the government's fiscal policy. They gave their best fiscal advice, in private, and accepted whatever decisions Harper and Flaherty made.

Fiscal policy affects almost everything that government does. There is only so much money to go around and, because decisions about money cuts across so much of government, they inevitably involve both the prime minister and the finance minister, and inevitably involve them saying "No" more often than "Yes." The centralization of fiscal policy and the nature of the decisions involved can easily lead to off-the-record complaints from ministers and officials about the decline of Cabinet to visiting public administration scholars.

Foreign Relations

When the Harper government took office, Paul Martin has already agreed to attend a summit of the three North American leaders at the end of March 2006 in Cancun. Our internal polls showed we ran a political risk if we were seen as being too close to President Bush. Holding the prime minister's first meeting with President Bush in the context of the so-called "Three Amigos" summit suited Harper. The summit opened with a tour of Chichen Itza, the pyramids several hours outside Cancun. That arrangement allowed President Bush to give Harper a lift to the site on Marine One and to have an hour-long private conversation on board. I was the other Canadian official on the flight, and this was my introduction to high level meetings between prime ministers and presidents.

At the time, Canada and the US were in the middle of a trade dispute over softwood lumber. Canada would have to decide whether to appeal one of the arbitration panel rulings on the dispute that April. If that appeal went ahead, I knew that our relations with the Bush Administration would be more difficult. The dispute was Harper's first matter of business on board the helicopter. When Harper pointed out Canada had to decide on the appeal within a few weeks, Bush agreed to make a concerted effort at a settlement. By 2006, Bush needed to have a good relationship with Canada. But American officials do not see individual trade disputes as the centrepiece of their relations with Canada, and softwood was not the top issue on the president's mind. His first priority was to find out Harper's views on developments in Haiti. The prospect of Jean-Bertrand Aristide returning to the country was a much bigger worry for his administration than softwood lumber imports.

Prime Minister Harper eventually did travel to the White House for an Oval Office meeting on 6 July 2006. Coincidentally, this was both President Bush's sixtieth birthday and the day before the Calgary Stampede parade. Robert Fife somehow found out that Harper had brought a Calgary Stampede belt buckle as a gift and asked President Bush whether he liked it at the news conference in the White House. Gifts had not yet been exchanged, but when we retired for lunch the White House staff had put the belt buckle right in the middle of the president's place sitting. Warned by Fife's question, Bush made a big fuss about the buckle. "Cheney's going to be jealous," he said as he put it on. The president was charming, engaged, and informed in all the meetings I witnessed. Harper wanted to see if Bush would press Congress to reconsider its decision to force Canadians to have a passport to enter the US. The "Western Hemisphere Travel Initiative" was going to create headaches on both sides of the border. However, Bush was coming to the end of his time in office and focused on the ongoing wars in Iraq and Afghanistan. That limited the progress we could make with his team. He always acknowledged the Canadian effort in Afghanistan and the casualties we had taken in the mission. He wanted to improve our ability to trade and knew the new passport requirement would cause problems. But by mid-2006, settling the softwood dispute was the limit of his ability to deliver on bilateral issues. The day before the meeting in the Oval Office, North Korea had tested a long-range missile, one that public reports estimated could have reached Alaska. The missile fell short, but on the margins of the Oval Office meeting, Stephen Hadley, President Bush's National Security Advisor, asked me what the US should do in the future if such a missile were heading to Vancouver. I told him I hoped the US would help an ally, but the formal arrangement remains outstanding more than ten years later. Hadley's comment showed where bilateral issues with Canada sat in the list of White House priorities.

Just as a prime minister cannot delegate all of the responsibility for fiscal policy to the finance minister, so a prime minister can never fully delegate the responsibility for Canada's foreign relations to other ministers. When presidents of the United States calls to discuss Canada's position on an issue, they do not call the foreign minister, the trade minister, the defence minister, or the international development minister. They call the prime minister. The leaders of other major countries do the same. And so, although foreign relations are not a confidence matter for the government, and although most issues in foreign relations rarely attract public notice, the prime minister is a key actor in Canada's foreign relations. A country that left its international relations in the hands of its foreign, trade, defence, and international development ministers would play virtually no international role at all. At the end of his first year in office, Harper told CTV News how surprised he was at the volume of international work on his plate as prime minister.

The prime minister's foreign relations role has become more important in the era of international telephone service and easier international travel. Summit meetings now take up a great deal of a prime minister's time. Meetings between Roosevelt and Churchill during World War II were infrequent because of the logistics efforts involved in moving them around the world. These days, leaders fly more easily around the world, leading to a proliferation of regular and ad hoc summits. Until 2008, there were only a few top tier summits – ones attended by a US president – and a Canadian prime minister was obliged to attend them all. The annual G7/G8 summit is usually held in early summer and the annual APEC summit in autumn. NATO summits are usually held every two years and the Summit of the Americas every three. The Three Amigos summit is now nearly an annual affair. A Canadian prime minister is also expected to attend two second-tier summits: The Commonwealth and Francophonie summits, held in alternating years. Commonwealth summits were and remain useful since they allow a Canadian prime minister to meet the Queen, a valued advisor. The Francophonie summits are musts because Quebec's premier attends. A year with five summits – a G7/G8, an APEC, a Commonwealth or Francophonie, a North America, and one other – commits Canada's prime minister to about two dozen days of international travel in a year – nearly 7 percent of the prime minister's calendar.

Since the 2008 financial crisis, more summits are crowding the agenda. The annual G20 summit is now a top-tier event. President Obama invited leaders to ad hoc nuclear security summits, making them top-tier events, and some climate change summits also qualify for the top tier. If a prime minister also decides to address the opening of the UN General Assembly in September, that means committing about a month out of every year to summit travel. Some observers think the Canadian prime minister should also attend the East Asia Summit. At some point, world leaders are going to have to reconsider the time commitment involved in all these meetings. Summits have an important role to play. They are, after all, how national leaders meet. But in addition to the time devoted to the meetings themselves, getting to and from summits is an onerous burden. Canada hosted the G8 and the G20 back-to-back in Ontario, but that arrangement was controversial for members of the G20 who were not members of the G8. No one wants to make what is now the G7 look like the executive committee of the G20. As a condition of hosting both summits, Canada probably had to commit to having them at different locations, and that probably explains the huge amount of money set aside to mount the two events. In 2012, Barack Obama tried to host the G8 and NATO summits back-to-back in Chicago. While security concerns forced him to move the G8 to Camp David, some leaders saved travel time by having both meetings in the US one after the other. Perhaps G20 summits could be held in conjunction with the opening of the UN General Assembly; the summit chairmanship could still rotate even if the G20 were always held in the US. Perhaps Commonwealth and Francophonie leaders could agree to meet every third year, like the Summit of the Americas.

Canadian prime ministers typically travel to international summits on the large VIP aircraft of the Royal Canadian Airforce. This aircraft is a converted Airbus 310 originally delivered to Ward Air, then operated by Canadian Airlines, and then sold to the Crown as part of an effort to keep Canadian in business. It has a range of about 10,000 kilometres. It can reach from Ottawa to parts of Europe and all of the United States, a range that suited the needs of Canadian foreign policy at the time it aircraft was purchased. But that range falls short of newer needs. Prime ministers now regularly visit more distant destinations in Europe, Asia, the western hemisphere, and Africa. A routine trip to Asian capitals becomes an onerous undertaking when refueling stops are needed, and that limits Canada's international influence. Prime Minister Harper's trip to the 2007 APEC Summit in Sydney, Australia, required refueling stops at Comox, Pearl Harbour, and New Caledonia. Each stop adds about three hours to the travel time to get to a destination. As the RCAF Airbus fleet comes to the end of its life, its VIP aircraft should be replaced with genuinely long-range jets that match Canada's new foreign policy needs. A trip to Asia, Africa, or South America should be possible without refueling stops.

The prime minister's primary source for assistance in devising fiscal policy is the finance minister and the Finance Department. But there is no similar lead minister for foreign relations in Cabinet. Diplomatic relations are usually handled by a country's foreign minister. Canada's minister of foreign affairs is responsible for the overall "management and direction" of the Department of Foreign Affairs, Trade and Development (now Global Affairs Canada). But the ministers for international trade and international development are meant to "assist" the foreign minister in their policy areas and are the foreign minister's equals at Cabinet. The minister of national defence plays an important role in Canada's foreign relations, and not just when the use of force is required. The Canadian Forces maintains a network of military attachés abroad and trains military forces around the world (Jeffrey 2013). The minister of finance serves as Canada's governor of the World Bank and the International Monetary Fund and oversees some of Canada's most important international relationships. Other ministers have specialized international roles as well. No government would conclude an agreement on international trade issues without involving the minister of agriculture given the critical importance of trade policy to almost every aspect of Canadian agriculture. International health issues inevitably draw on the minister of health, Canada's delegate to the World Health Organization's governing body. Almost every environmental issue now has an international dimension. This puts an onerous burden on the officials in PCO's Foreign and Defence Policy Division and PMO to ensure the prime minister and Cabinet ministers act in a coordinated fashion on international matters. Decisions about foreign relations therefore cut across government policy files in much the same way decisions about fiscal policy do. The prime minister's increased role in foreign relations means we have to keep rethinking the role of the foreign service. This does not necessarily mean dismissing the foreign service as "the institutional response to a surfeit of well-bred, indolent men needing something to do," but it does mean confronting the diminished role of diplomats who are "often sidelined and left to churn out reports that circulate in a bureaucratic vortex" (Bercovici 2016).

This new reality means we also have to rethink how we evaluate Canada's involvement in foreign affairs. Roland Paris, who served as a foreign policy advisor to Prime Minister Justin Trudeau, argues that the Harper government abandoned Canada's postwar record of "liberal internationalism"; Canada once used its "multilateral entrepreneurialism" to "gain a voice in international forums," especially the UN, and then used this influence to advance issues of importance to Canada (Paris 2014, 277). Paris was particularly irked that Harper only made speeches at the UN General Assembly every few years. Underlying Paris's argument is the older view that foreign relations is properly the business of foreign ministers, diplomats, and "their" international organizations. But in the wake of the 2008 global financial crisis Harper oversaw a broad effort to remake the institutions of global financial coordination. Finance Department officials co-chaired the key policy group that supported the G20 in its first few years as a leader-level summit. The Harper government pressed for the reform of the Financial Stability Forum into the Financial Stability Board and for reforms to the IMF. He also pushed for the mutual assessment process of G20 countries. His government helped to lead the first simultaneous recapitalization of the IMF and all the regional development banks. Harper's commitment to double Canada's callable capital at the InterAmerican Development Bank during the 2009 Summit of the Americas reinforced that institution's role and helped to stabilize the finances of Latin America and the Caribbean during the crisis. All the while, the Harper government negotiated a comprehensive trade and economic deal with the European Union and the TransPacific Partnership. Harper was an active player in the biggest restructuring of the global financial architecture since Bretton Woods. That was not traditional postwar diplomatic work, but it fit the needs of the time and reinforced economic multilateralism. Harper was just as committed to multilateralism as any other prime minister has been. Harper's multilateralism was suitable for the times.

In March 2003, Prime Minister Chrétien decided not to involve Canada in the Iraq War. Goldenberg's account does not mention Chrétien getting any advice from diplomats or ministers before making that decision (Goldenberg 2006, 1–5). Foreign Minister Bill Graham and Defence Minister John McCallum were simply invited to help Chrétien plan his lines for the first Question Period after it was announced (6). Diplomats would have tuned into Question Period to get those lines. No one questions a prime minister's right and duty to make decisions regarding war and peace. When the leader of another G7 or G20 nation wants to know where Canada stands on an international issue, no one suggests that the prime minister of Canada defer the call to the foreign or defence minister.

I do not know how Harper would have gotten along with President Trump. Trudeau and his team appear to have made the same mistake we made in 2007 and 2008 by focusing their efforts on preparing to deal with a Hillary Clinton White House. The 2016 US election results surprised everyone and Trudeau has, at the time of writing, managed well by treating President Trump respectfully in public and building private relationships with his daughter, Ivanka, and her husband, Jared Kushner. He has deployed his best ministers to build on the deep relations the Canadian government always maintains with many US Cabinet secretaries and their agencies. This counts as a success by any measure and credit is due to Trudeau and his team for getting off to a good start with the new US administration. If I were still working in PMO, I would worry about establishing relationships with the White House beyond the Trump family. I would want to establish connections to the more nationalistic figures of the administration. As chief of staff to Prime Minister Harper, I dealt with a mature and professional White House team working under a systematic and seasoned president on a clear set of priorities. President Trump is far less predictable, and his White House staff structure is unsettled. That would leave me unsettled.

Dealing with the Provinces

When Stephen Harper decided to travel to the annual meeting of the PC Party of Newfoundland and Labrador in October 2006, I sensed I should travel with him. I did not usually travel with the prime minister on his domestic trips, but a conflict with the province's mercurial premier, Danny

Williams, was already brewing. At the time, the Newfoundland economy was doing well. Its offshore oil resources were valuable and the St John economy was humming. Williams had launched a high profile set of attacks on Paul Martin while he was prime minister, establishing his reputation as a fierce fighter. Harper had made some commitments to Williams regarding the equalization formula during the election campaign, commitments Williams did not think our reform to equalization would respect. Harper's appearance at the PC Party's annual meeting would include a face to face meeting with Williams on his turf and with a large, friendly audience of his provincial supporters on hand. The situation could easily get out of hand, with consequences for the province, for the country, and for our three MPs from Newfoundland. I did not want the prime minister in a tough situation without senior staff support.

In opposition, we had all seen Paul Martin call the premiers to a meeting at his official residence to negotiate an agreement to "save Medicare for a generation." From my outside perspective, watching on television, the entire venture seemed foolish and ill-considered. Holding out the promise of fixing Canada's provincial healthcare systems in a single stroke meant setting yourself up for disappointment. Federal transfers to the provinces can come with incentives and disincentives – carrots and sticks – for various kinds of health programming, and federally funded organizations, when carefully designed to include the provinces, can improve aspects of healthcare.[1] But "saving Medicare for a generation" was the kind of overly ambitious objective that my entire training as a political scientist rejected. Betting that a prime minister could deliver on that kind of promise in a single negotiation with the premiers meant risking the political fate of the government on a process that had a rich history of recent high-profile failures. After Harper took office, I eventually met one of the senior officials in the room for that meeting, and told him how horrified I was at the entire idea of negotiating a blockbuster deal on health transfers with the premiers. He laughed and told me if I had only been in the room I would have been even more horrified. I told the official that, in my view, Harper would never, ever put himself in a similar situation.

Just as a prime minister has many ministers to assist with the international aspect of the job, so a prime minister has many ministers to assist with federal-provincial affairs. Harper had originally appointed Michael Chong to be minister of federal-provincial relations and dispatched Chong to canvass the level of provincial interest in possible reforms to the Senate. This was an issue dear to Harper's heart and to mine. Other major federal-provincial issues were handled by other ministers. Transport Minister Lawrence Cannon put together a new federal-provincial infrastructure program. Environment

Minister Rona Ambrose had to coordinate new environmental initiatives with the provinces. Flaherty and his officials had input into reform of the equalization formula, although from the outset it was clear Harper would drive that reform personally. When issues arose that involved individual provinces, Harper relied heavily on ministers and parliamentarians from those provinces to guide his political strategies. This division of ministerial labour puts an onerous burden on officials in the Federal-Provincial Relations Office and the Prime Minister's Office to ensure the prime minister and Cabinet are coordinated in their approach to federal-provincial matters.

Chong resigned as federal-provincial relations minister a few months later over his principled rejection of Harper's decision to move that the House recognize that the Québécois form a nation within a united Canada. Although I disagreed with Chong's view and tried to persuade him to support Harper's approach, I respected his decision at the time and still do. Later, reports later suggested Harper had overstepped when he made his decision without consulting Chong (see, for example, Malcolmson 2016, 117). When the Bloc Québécois leader, Gilles Duceppe, threatened to bring a resolution about the Québécois to the House earlier that spring, Harper had made clear statements in public and in private that he would respond to any such parliamentary manoeuvre. Harper was constantly in touch with Lawrence Cannon and the rest of the Quebec caucus on the issue. Just as Chrétien's decision regarding Canadian participation in the Iraq War presumably did not surprise any of his ministers, so Harper's decision about the Québécois motion should not have come as a surprise to any of his. Just as Chrétien asked his ministers to help draft lines about his decision for Question Period, so Harper asked his ministers to help explain the Québécois motion.

Harper had a long-standing interest in the details of equalization. The Constitution Act, 1982, commits the federal government to ensuring that the provinces have enough money to provide reasonably comparable levels of public services to their residents and reasonably comparable levels of taxation. Harper was particularly concerned about the way the federal equalization policy treats provincial revenues from natural resources. Our election campaign platform included a commitment to reform this part of the policy, an appeal, if you will, to the vanishingly small constituency of public finance economists in Canada. Some of our other platform commitments were often described as "narrowcasting" – policy proposals intended to appeal to small slivers of the electorate. But the transit pass tax credit and trade tools tax deduction ended up benefitting the hundreds of thousands of Canadians who take public transit and use trade tools every day. Promising equalization reform is genuine narrowcasting.

The 2006 budget reiterated our commitment to reform the equalization formula, and issued a discussion paper on the issue. Over the course of many months in 2006 and early 2007, the briefing notes from PCO about equalization began to mount. When I left PMO in summer 2008, these briefing notes took up an entire drawer in one filing cabinet in my office. Harper spent dozens of hours in meetings devoted to the details of these voluminous briefing notes, generating even more pages of analysis and recommendations. The federal government keeps information about federal-provincial negotiations as secret as it keeps war plans, but the equalization policy community is small, and Newfoundland's officials must have figured out that Harper was not going to reform the equalization formula in the way that maximally benefitted that province. So, the invitation for Harper to speak at the annual meeting of the Newfoundland and Labrador PC Association was not casually offered and not casually accepted. Harper invited Loyola Hearn, the fisheries minister and our regional minister for the province, to fly to Gander with us.

I was curious to see Gander Airport. Gander was once a grand centre for air traffic, a refueling stop for transatlantic jets en route to more central locations in North America. As the technology of commercial passenger jets developed, however, the need for refueling stops at Gander fell. The airport is now constantly in a state of financial crisis and at risk of closing. I had assigned a senior PMO staffer the job of finding enough federal funding to keep Gander open, since the airport was essential to the economic viability of the town, and the people of Gander had famously impressed the rest of the world on 11 September 2001, when they housed and fed thousands of passengers whose flights had been forced to land there after the terrorist attacks earlier that day. Later, when I worked in Washington, DC, for four years, I was always impressed at how many of my friends and neighbours remembered the hospitality Canadians showed to stranded passengers on that day. One small bit of good news on that terrible day made a great impression. Flying into Gander on a small jet like an RCAF Challenger is a remarkable experience. The airport is a gargantuan carpet of concrete bereft of activity but hearkening back to its heyday as a vital hub of intercontinental travel.

Upon landing at the airport, we headed immediately to the Hotel Gander, the location for the PC Party's meeting, a convenient four minutes from the airport. When we arrived, the rest of the Newfoundland and Labrador caucus – Norman Doyle and Fabian Manning – and the President of the Conservative Party's National Council, Don Plett, later a senator, were already on the ground. Premier Williams was hosting a lunch for the delegates to the meeting, and this is where Harper was to speak. The premier's introduction of Harper was effusive and positive. He spoke of the importance of unity within conservative ranks. Harper delivered his remarks and was cheered like no lunch of high spirited Newfoundland partisans had ever cheered a visiting dignitary before. Newfoundland Tories can put on a great show.

Then, to the private meeting. Premier Williams invited Harper upstairs for the business of the trip. Someone had rearranged a guest room for the meeting by pushing the beds against the wall and creating a small sitting area with a few small chairs. Harper and I sat on one side of the room while the premier and his chief of staff sat on the other. Ray Novak, Harper's executive assistant at the time, was outside the door with a couple of RCMP officers. There were no pleasantries extended on either side. The premier laid into Harper directly on the issue of equalization. When Harper began to explain his plans for the reform of equalization, Williams's talk descended into foul language. There was not going to be a conversation or any give and take. Harper hadn't made any decisions on the formula yet, and, in any case, a provincial government has many complex relations with the federal government. A setback in one area of the relationship can be used to lever concessions in another area. Williams's furious attack struck me as incredibly foolish but typical of his past behaviour. Harper excused us, and I told Ray to get the motorcade moving for our return to the airport.

Novak and Harper moved to a safe location in the hotel, and the RCMP pulled the motorcade up to the circular driveway in front of the hotel. I got into one of the cars with Dimitri Soudas, then Harper's deputy press secretary, so we could make a quick departure. I anticipated that Harper and Novak would be out of the hotel soon. But, as we waited, I looked up and realized that Premier Williams was scrumming on the hotel driveway in front of us. Our motorcade was hemmed it – we could not leave without hitting Williams. An unenviable security situation and a terrible political situation. As the premier's press scrum continued, I could see Williams getting more and more animated. The scrum went on longer and longer. After what seemed like an hour but was closer to ten minutes, I thought the premier had made his point and told Soudas to go out and tell Williams's communications director to wrap it up. Soudas was never one for delicacy in a tough situation. When his first effort to persuade the group to wrap up their scrum failed, he began shouting at the premier's communications director about her relationship with her boss. This did the trick. The scrum wrapped up, the rest of our party joined the motorcade, and we made our way to the airport. A few years later, when Premier Williams retired, he nominated his communications director as vice-chair of the Canada-Newfoundland and Labrador Offshore Petroleum Board, a well-paying position. The nomination attracted an uproar of attention, and she soon withdrew her name from consideration.

After the new equalization formula was announced in the 2007 spring budget, Newfoundland, Saskatchewan, and Nova Scotia were all disappointed with the decision. Harper wanted to accommodate the concerns of those three provinces. While the state of relations with Williams made accommodation with the Newfoundland government pretty unlikely, I was confident we could find agreement with the other two. Williams tried to forge a common front with Saskatchewan premier Lorne Calvert and Nova Scotia premier Rodney MacDonald. Harper invited the other two to meet him.

Premier Calvert travelled to Ottawa in May 2007, two months after the budget announcement. Harper invited the premier to meet with him in his office on Parliament Hill. The premier was accompanied by a single staffer. I sat in on the meeting with a senior official. The meeting was short and memorably different from our earlier sit down with Premier Williams. Calvert opened the meeting by asking Harper if he was prepared to be flexible and reopen the equalization formula. The prime minister replied that he had made a decision, announced it, and would not reopen the formula. It treated Saskatchewan fairly and protected the province in case its economy faltered, something he hoped would not happen again. But, he asked, were there any other areas where the federal government and the province could cooperate? Harper was opening the door to a side-deal. I knew that if Calvert played his cards well, Harper would be hard-pressed not to do something that could help him politically. That effort would not be popular with our Saskatchewan MPs who were hoping to see Brad Wall's Saskatchewan Party elected that autumn. Instead of taking up the Harper's offer, Calvert said a few words about his disappointment and then left the room. We never had an opportunity to see if a compromise was possible. Calvert lost the subsequent provincial election.

Harper later met Premier MacDonald. The Nova Scotia premier had supported Harper for the party leadership, and the two men had a relationship going back a few years. Moreover, MacDonald was in constant contact with Peter MacKay, our minister from Nova Scotia. Harper relied heavily on MacKay's political judgement, in particular about Nova Scotia issues, and as political pressure over the equalization reforms mounted MacKay's personal support of Harper's position kept the Atlantic caucus together. When Harper asked MacDonald if there were any outstanding federal-provincial issues that he could try to resolve following the equalization announcement, the premier was ready to respond. He asked Harper to set up an independent panel to calculate what Nova Scotia was owed under the Crown Share Adjustment Payment, a provision of the original Atlantic Accord agreement that the federal government had long claimed was worth very little. This was an ideal "ask" for Nova Scotia. It let us settle an outstanding dispute that did not involve any other provinces. If the panel recommended the CSAP was worth something, Nova Scotia would reap a benefit it would not have to share with any other province. A year later, the panel recommended the federal government pay more than $230 million in back payments to Nova Scotia and commit to hundreds of millions more in the future. For Premier MacDonald, a quarter of a billion-dollar windfall a year away from an election was a major fiscal boost.

Harper rarely met with the provincial premiers as a group, preferring to meet with premiers individually. Aside from the high-profile flops with Williams and Calvert, the meetings I attended were productive, informative, and friendly. One-on-one, premiers can give a prime minister great insight into their view of the world from outside the federal bubble. A private meeting with Premier Robert Ghiz of PEI showed how awarding federal infrastructure funds to provinces on a per capita basis is not terribly useful to a smaller province. The Build Canada Fund infrastructure program ended up with an annual floor of funding to ensure PEI received a useful amount of funding. A private meeting with Gordon Campbell, then the premier of BC, raised the question of why the federal government kept three port authorities competing against each other in the Vancouver area. Port Metro Vancouver was soon formed as a single authority. Every province has its own challenges and in smaller meetings these challenges come to the forefront. The purpose of federalism is to allow each provincial government to deal with provincial issues and priorities in its own way. When the premiers get together in a group, this aspect of federalism moves into the background. They feel the need to present a common front to the prime minister. They become, in effect, an interest group rather than a collection of provincial leaders.

Harper's record in overseeing federal-provincial relations was productive. Well-managed provincial governments that wanted a mutually productive relationship with the Harper government got one. Harper empowered his transport ministers, particularly Lawrence Cannon, to establish a large federal-provincial infrastructure program, known first as the Build Canada Fund and later as the Infrastructure Stimulus Fund. Matching the needs of the provinces with the policy priorities of the funds and the political views of dozens of local Conservative MPs was not easy. The fact that the program came together so smoothly is a credit to the ministers involved, and that success set the stage for the Trudeau government to expand federal infrastructure financing further. The successful negotiation of the Canada-EU trade agreement with the provinces all involved was likewise a success attributable to Harper's strong relationship with Quebec premier Jean Charest and several of the other premiers. Harper and many of his ministers agreed that ensuring a common economic market within Canada was a core federal responsibility. Progress toward a common securities regulator was not a success. Other initiatives, like the unilateral effort at the Canada Jobs Grant, await a comprehensive evaluation. Nonetheless, the Harper approach yielded results.

Parliamentary Affairs

As we will see in chapter 5, the government's scarcest resource is time in Parliament. The House of Commons and Senate only devote a few dozen hours to government business each week, and they only sit for about twenty-six weeks each year. Securing Parliament's approval for policy changes involving legislation is a major challenge for any government. Every day that Parliament sits, the government has to have a list of "must have" bills it needs to get passed. Its House Leader then has to be able to negotiate with the opposition parties to get some of those bills expedited with only a short debate and to manage the business of the House to get the rest passed after a longer debate. If fiscal policy involves allocating scarce money, parliamentary affairs involves allocating the even scarcer resource of Parliament's time. In a minority government, the fate of the ministry depends on the astute management of parliamentary affairs. But even in a majority government, the ministry's success will depend on its ability to secure appropriations and legislative authorities from Parliament while avoiding disaster in Question Period, committee hearings, and the routine debates of the House and Senate.

A prime minister has several ministers and other caucus officers to help manage parliamentary affairs. The principal officers are the chief government House leader, the chief government whip, and the government leader in the Senate, now called the government representative in the Senate. But managing parliamentary affairs involves many other officers, including a deputy house leader, a deputy whip, a parliamentary secretary to the house leader, several assistant whips, the chair of the national caucus, and, in Harper's case, a separate chair of the Senate caucus. The Privy Council Office also has a secretariat devoted to legislation and House planning to assist the prime minister with the non-partisan aspects of parliamentary affairs.

The chief government whip is probably the most misunderstood office on Parliament Hill. The incumbent is usually described by observers as being in charge of enforcing party discipline by strong-arming caucus members to support the party line, as if party discipline needed to be enforced. The mythology around the office adds this impression. The chief government whip keeps a framed horse whip in the office as a symbol of authority, and the Reform Party replaced title of "whip" with that of "caucus coordinator" when its caucus grew from one MP to 52 in 1993. But all this mythology is misleading. The framed horse whip is as useful to the chief government whip as the ceremonial mace is to the Sergeant-at-Arms. Most of the time, the chief government whip *is* the caucus coordinator. The whip makes sure MPs know when to vote and assigns office space to MPs. Outside observers sometimes read too much into the Whip's power to assign offices, thinking that toeing the party line can get you a better space. In reality, the job is a thankless one that inevitably makes caucus colleagues unhappy and jealous. Often, the whip has to intervene when MPs, who may have had little management experience before getting elected, go astray in hiring or supervising staff. MPs are human beings and have all the human excellences and weaknesses that crop up in the rest of the population. Some MPs are afflicted by substance abuse, tax problems, health issues, and marital crises, all of which can be compounded by the pressures of travel and public life. A good whip is an MP that other MPs trust to lend a sympathetic ear and take a case for special consideration to the prime minister.

I rarely saw any of the whips I worked with, either in opposition or government, try to "whip" members into line. Moreover, Eddie Goldenberg, in his account of Chrétien's 2003 election finance reforms does not mention the Liberal's Whip playing a part in holding parliamentarians' feet to the fire. Instead, he reports that he, Government House Leader Don Boudria, and Clerk of the Privy Council Alex Himelfarb overcame most caucus opposition to Chrétien's plan by simply increasing the size of the offsetting public subsidy to parties (2006, 381–5). Politics is a team sport and MPs are usually pretty clear about that when they arrive on the Hill. After the tumultuous time in the Canadian Alliance and PC caucuses between 1997 and 2003, there was little need to convince MPs that they could hang together or hang separately. The departure of Belinda Stronach to the Martin Cabinet put smaller caucus disputes into context and forged a united parliamentary team for years to come.

While the PMO chief of staff, I worked closely with Chief Government Whip Jay Hill. Jay and his wife Leah have become friends of mine and of my wife since we all left politics. I joined Jay in his office to try to persuade Bill Casey not to vote against the government in 2007, the only time Jay ever really had to try to enforce party discipline on an individual member of the caucus. Despite all the allegedly awesome powers of the chief government whip and the PMO chief of staff, we did not succeed in convincing Casey to support the government. Hill also took a few shots from Garth Turner in his account of his time in the Conservative caucus (Turner 2009). Jay worked with his caucus colleagues, tirelessly and compassionately, to overcome problems that made them less effective members of the team. He listened carefully to MPs, filtering out the normal carping of high-profile people in high-profile jobs from genuine grievances that had to be conveyed to the prime minister. Hill is a tough man who made a living the tough way before he got elected to the House in 1993. No one has ever served as a whip longer than Jay Hill. He cared about Parliament, cared about his colleagues on both sides of the House, and is an unsung hero of the Harper government's early years.

Parliament and Afghanistan

One issue that kept returning to our parliamentary agenda was the military mission in Afghanistan. By the time Harper took office, Canadian troops had taken charge of the NATO military effort in Kandahar province, a rough piece of the country and a focal point for Taliban planning. A few months into the Harper government, Canada and our allies launched a dedicated effort to destroy the Taliban presence in southern Afghanistan that culminated in early September 2006. "Operation Medusa," as the final effort was known, destroyed the Taliban's ability to bring massed forces together on the battlefield and drove them to adopt irregular, guerilla warfare tactics.

The Conservative election platform for the 2006 campaign, *Stand up for Canada*, included a promise to "Make Parliament responsible for ... the commitment of Canadian Forces to foreign operations" (2006, 45). The issue of parliamentary involvement in decisions to deploy Canadian troops abroad is a long-standing controversy (Lagassé 2015). The power to deploy the Canadian Forces has remained a "prerogative" power of the executive since Confederation, although Prime Minister King asked the House of Commons to concur in the deployment of Canadian troops prior to entering the Second World War. Over the years, the Reform Party had introduced several proposals to bring Parliament back into the decision-making loop; as Canadian troops deployed to Afghanistan all parties came to demand some parliamentary input into military missions. The practical impact of a parliamentary resolution would be slim when a majority government is in office but eventually proved to make matters trickier when Harper headed a minority government.

In spring 2006, Harper faced the decision of whether to extend Canada's deployment to Kandahar beyond winter 2007. He was determined to bring the matter to a vote in the House. He was well aware that to win the House's support for extending the mission, he would need to have some support from the opposition parties. He and I met with the Bloc leader, Gilles Duceppe, and Bill Graham, the interim leader of the Liberals. Despite their deep differences over Canadian federalism and most other policy issues, Harper and Duceppe had a good professional relationship and their private conversations were always productive and clear. I like to think Duceppe appreciated Harper's efforts to master the French language. They were alike in seeing themselves as outsiders to the country's dominant political and business leadership groups. We left the meeting with Duceppe anticipating we would have the Bloc's support for continuing the mission. The meeting with Graham was more nuanced. We knew Graham was in a weak position as an interim leader and that some of his caucus colleagues were deeply opposed to the mission. Graham was a former defence and foreign minister and a genuine internationalist, however. He clearly favoured carrying on, but it was far from clear how many of his Liberal colleagues would follow his lead in supporting the mission. Harper led a one-day debate on the future of the mission in the House, proposing to extend the mission until February 2009. The Bloc ended up opposing the mission, but Graham carried the majority of his caucus and the motion passed easily.

Any hope for any easy repeat of the 17 May 2006 vote in spring 2008 was killed off once Stéphane Dion became Liberal leader at the end of 2006. As Liberal leader, Dion took an increasingly critical line on the conduct of the mission and became convinced we were withholding details of the mission from Parliament. By summer 2007, it was clear we would face a difficult time securing parliamentary support for a renewal of the mission in 2008 unless we did something to change the political context. During that summer, the PMO and PCO planning exercises for the coming year separately floated proposals for a "red ribbon panel" or a "blue ribbon panel" to take stock of the mission and propose a path forward. Everyone thought that former Liberal Cabinet minister John Manley would be the ideal chair of such a panel regardless of the colour of its ribbon. Manley was out of politics and enjoying a "post-partisan" life, but followed developments in Afghanistan quite closely. He was known to be a hard-nosed policy thinker in the small-l liberal internationalist tradition. I met with Manley and once I assured him that Harper intended to appoint serious people to the panel and would not appoint anyone over Manley's objections – we were already had the five members who ended up on the panel in mind, and I shared that list with him – Manley agreed to serve.[2]

The story of the Manley Panel is its impact on the machinery of government in managing the Afghanistan mission is set out in chapter 4. Here, the focus is on the impact of the *Manley Report* on the parliamentary vote to renew the Afghanistan mission. The final report of the panel did not, initially, persuade Dion to support a reconfigured version of the deployment. There was a furious debate about the *Manley Report* inside the Liberal Party. At times I was drawn into those debates through backchannels. I was amazed at how weakly Dion was connected to his caucus colleagues and even to his own staff. Senior caucus and staff members, some with long political and government experience, had only the thinnest relationship with their leader. No matter what assurances we tried to give in public and in private, Dion always seemed suspicious we were trying to pull a fast one on him over the parliamentary vote.

When we guessed the time was ripe for a higher-level meeting, Harper invited Dion to his Centre Block office. Fortunately, he also invited Conservative House Leader Peter Van Loan to join the meeting and asked me to make sure Dion's staff invited Liberal House Leader Ralph Goodale as well. In public, Harper was starting to speak about how he might need to go to the public if the House could not settle on a future for the Afghanistan mission. He needed Dion's support to avoid an election. When the meeting began, I soon realized that the Liberal leader had not brought a position to the meeting, or even a starting point for negotiations. He started his part of the meeting by reading the passages in the *Manley Report* that were critical of our government's conduct of the mission. Harper readily conceded the criticisms that Manley had made, and asked Dion if he had any suggestions for improving Parliament's ability to track and debate the mission. Dion ignored the opening and kept on reading critical comments from the report. The more Harper tried to steer the conversation toward a discussion of the path ahead, the more Dion wanted to highlight the mistakes that had already been made. Eventually, Goodale stepped in to talk about how a motion to extend the mission might be worded and when the debate might be held. Goodale quickly worked out an agreement with the prime minister about next steps. By the time the parliamentary debate on the mission was held in March 2008, just before the NATO Summit in Romania, Harper had asked the Liberals to put their conditions for extending the mission on the public record and then, in a speech to the Conference of Defence Associations Institute, he agreed to all those conditions.[3] The motion he put to the House set 2011 as the end date for the mission. It also promised a better mix of diplomatic, development, and military efforts in Afghanistan (as recommended by the *Manley Report*), and struck a House committee to serve as a continuing forum for parliamentary discussion of the mission.

Any worry that getting Parliament's approval of the mission would limit political debate about it (Lagassé 2015) turned out to be groundless. When there is a minority government, a parliamentary motion to support a deployment will almost certainly be a confidence matter. Given that Dion's initial hard line on the mission forced the Harper government to regroup and commission the Manley Panel, the prospect of the parliamentary vote improved the government's oversight of the mission, but it did not stop the Liberals or anyone else from criticizing the mission in the House and elsewhere. When there is a majority government, the opposition parties will be free to oppose any proposed military mission and criticize the conduct of it without limit. Even when the result of that vote is a foregone conclusion because the government has a majority and is firmly behind the mission, the parliamentary debate forces both sides to state their positions in public. The government has to offer a justification of the mission. It will face questions about its strategy, the resourcing of the mission, and its coordination with allies. Where the outcome of the vote is not a foregone conclusion, there may have to be some give and take between the parties, give and take that still lets the opposition criticize the conduct of the mission later. The index of Hansard during the Harper government shows no shortage of debate, criticism, and commentary about the Afghanistan mission in Parliament.

I regret that Stephen Harper and Stéphane Dion did not develop a better personal relationship as party leaders. Politics is competitive, and we did our best to keep Dion away from power, but he could have had more impact along the way. During the Afghan vote discussions, I realized he has only one tool in his political toolbox – the polemical argument. He used that tool beautifully to point out the poor arguments in favour of Quebec separation in 1995 and 1996. In doing so, he drew heavily on arguments that Harper had advanced years earlier. Like all of Dion's political science colleagues, I was proud of his contribution to the debate. But his polemical skills left him unable to think through a path ahead for himself, his party, or the country in prosecuting the Afghanistan war. Churchill's polemical attacks on British policy in the 1930s made him uniquely qualified to lead the war effort once he became prime minister. Dion did not seem to be able to follow the same path.

Supporting the Prime Minister in These Four Roles

The special status of fiscal policy, foreign relations, federal-provincial relations, and parliamentary affairs is clear in the way the Privy Council Office is organized. Routine business of government that requires a Cabinet decision is shepherded through the Cabinet system by the economic and social affairs secretariats of PCO's Operations Division. The deputy secretary of Cabinet for operations coordinates this work. Government business that touches on these four special areas of prime ministerial attention is managed elsewhere in PCO. The Secretariat for Macro-Economic Policy keeps track of budget and fiscal policy and is usually located in PCO's Plans and Consultations

Division, the organization that also plans the agenda of Cabinet meetings chaired by the prime minister and coordinates the drafting of the Throne Speech. PCO has also long had a separate foreign relations secretariat or division to manage the prime minister's international agenda. This function is now under PCO's national security advisor. The federal-provincial relations work of the prime minister is usually managed by a separate unit in PCO or a deputy minister under PCO. PCO's legislation and House planning secretariat is not usually part of the Operations Division. While PCO and the Prime Minister's Office coordinate decision-making on all types of issues across the federal government, the prime minister is inevitably involved in these four areas of policy-making personally, and that means PCO and PMO will have a hand in supporting him. No budget, no major foreign initiative, no major federal-provincial effort, and no effort involving Parliament can proceed without a Canadian prime minister's involvement in the file. This is the case not because the prime minister or the prime minister's courtiers have gone out of their way to centralize power within the executive branch but because there is no other way for government to work.

These key levers – over the government's fiscal policy, its international and federal-provincial relations, and its management of its time in Parliament – give the prime minister important powers. But they leave wide discretion for ministers to initiate and embark on their own policy agendas. A minister's plans cannot disrupt the government's budget, its relations with other governments, or its management of Parliament without the approval of the prime minister. A newly appointed minister may hear from departmental officials that the department's enabling legislation has not been reformed in many decades. Before that minister decides the top priority within the portfolio is to overhaul that legislation and reform all the department's legal authorities, a check with the prime minister is not too much to ask. But during my time in PMO, I witnessed several capable ministers work on significant reforms they wanted to proceed with. Jim Prentice spearheaded and delivered a broad reform to settle outstanding specific claims. Jim Flaherty persuaded Harper to reverse himself on the taxation of income trusts. David Emerson oversaw a settlement of the softwood lumber trade dispute with the United States that lasted for more than a decade. Michael Fortier conceived of and delivered a program to sell and lease-back government office buildings as a way of recapitalizing and renewing them. Working within the prime minister's broad direction there is plenty for ministers to do.

4

Making a Cabinet

Savoie's argument about the centralization of power in the prime minister's hands downplays the importance of Cabinet as a decision-making institution. At some point in the past, according to Savoie, Cabinet "mattered," presumably because ministers made important decisions without thinking about the prime minister's views. But over time, in Savoie's memorable phrasing, Cabinet became merely a focus group for the prime minister and his senior advisors. Savoie concludes that debates within Cabinet and the actions of individual ministers no longer explain the key actions of the Canadian government. Ministers have no independent power bases that allow them to resist the encroachments of the centre of government. The prime minister is free to make and remake cabinet as they see fit and, unless a minister is a "courtier" to the prime minister, that minister is a nobody. As Jonathan Malloy, a political scientist, puts it, "Prime ministers hold complete control over the appointment of ministers" (2004, 207).

Savoie's argument is plausible. The prime minister does decide who sits in Cabinet, a power restricted only by the convention – and it is merely a convention, not a requirement – that a minister must either have a seat in Parliament when appointed or find a seat shortly after being appointed, and the prime minister assigns ministers to portfolios. But a prime minister really has fewer choices in selecting a Cabinet than meets the eye. There are very real informal constraints, and those constraints matter. In Canada, the main informal constraint on selecting a Cabinet is the need for geographic representation, and that constraint limited Harper's choices. The prime minister's power to assign portfolios is constrained as well. Prime ministers and their advisors put a lot of time into selecting ministers and structuring Cabinet business, making it hard to argue that Cabinet and ministers are irrelevant.

Cabinet Size

A prime minister's first choice when selecting ministers is to decide how large a Cabinet to appoint. Goldenberg (2006) gives us little insight into how Chrétien determined the size of his Cabinets. Kim Campbell notably appointed a small Cabinet, and notes in her memoirs that meeting her target of a small Cabinet meant that selecting ministers was like "solving a jigsaw puzzle" (Campbell 1996, 313). Mulroney's Cabinets grew larger over time, and Martin's Cabinet was very large when the parliamentary secretaries, who were all sworn into the Privy Council, were included. Harper began with a small Cabinet of twenty-seven ministers plus himself. He added a few secretaries of state who were not Cabinet members early in his tenure. By the end of his time in office, his Cabinet had become large. Cabinets do tend to grow as a government gets older in Canada (Lewis 2015). Over time a prime minister has to bring new talent into Cabinet. Moreover, as a government gains experience it finds more and more files that require the special political management that only a minister can provide.

What factors go into deciding how large a Cabinet to appoint? Years ago, the Salaries Act limited the number of ministers who could draw a ministerial salary, but the prime minister was freed from that constraint in the early 1970s. Harper wanted to show his government was more focused and would make more-timely decisions than Martin's had. So, before the 2006 election was called, he decided to have a small Cabinet, and his transition team prepared accordingly. But there are informal but real constraints on how small a Cabinet can be in practice. Again, the main constraint is geography. Prime ministers typically appoint at least one minister from each province, and if each of the small and medium provinces gets one minister it is hard to justify appointing only one minister from the larger provinces. The larger provinces all have regions that might need Cabinet representation. Moreover, if a prime minister wants active Cabinet committees that chew over issues and proposals before they come to the full Cabinet, those committees have to be large enough to hold a useful discussion. On the one hand, a prime minister can double up portfolios to reduce the size of Cabinet. Harper did just that in 2006 by assigning responsibility for the regional development agencies to ministers with other responsibilities. Prime Minister Justin Trudeau has put all these agencies under the minister of industry. Over time Harper found his original arrangement too restrictive, and Trudeau may come to that view as well. On the other hand, some portfolios are so demanding that a capable minister cannot be expected to take on many other responsibilities. The transport minister not only heads the Department of Transport, a complex department with many regulatory, economic policy, and national security functions, but also oversees dozens of crown corporations, port authorities, pilotage authorities, and bridge authorities. A highly capable minister would have trouble managing Transport along with another large portfolio. So, a prime minister is limited in how small a Cabinet to form.

Some observers speculate that having a larger Cabinet helps to enforce party discipline since it encourages more backbench MPs to "toe the party line" in the hopes of getting a ministerial appointment. The case for this speculation is far from proven and doubtful in any case. As J.P. Lewis shows, even a Canadian Cabinet as large thirty-nine or forty ministers is smaller, in proportion to the size of the lower house, than recent Cabinets have been in Australia, New Zealand, or any of the provinces (Lewis 2015, 15). Moreover, Cabinet positions are not the only remunerative and powerful positions at the prime minister's disposal, as we shall see in chapter 7. Proposals to loosen party discipline by limiting the number of ministers by legislation are almost certainly based on a misdiagnosis of the prime minister's powers.

Selecting Ministers

Once Harper had decided to appoint a relatively small Cabinet, he had only a few genuine choices to make in selecting ministers. In naming a Cabinet of fewer than thirty members the prime minister, in practice, has limited discretion. Simpson's argument, that, "Once elected, the prime minister shapes his government as he sees fit without the slightest formal check on his prerogative" (2001, 14) is true but beside the point. The informal constraints on the prime minister's prerogative matter. How so? What follows in my assessments of Harper's decisions and should not be taken as an explanation of his thinking. However, I was involved throughout the selection of ministers in 2006 and my assessments are informed by that experience.

Consider, first, the smaller provinces: the four Atlantic provinces, Manitoba and Saskatchewan. The decision to have a relatively small Cabinet meant Harper could only appoint one minister from each of them, and in those provinces his options were tightly constrained. The 2006 election returned three Conservative MPs from Nova Scotia: Peter MacKay, Gerald Keddy, and Bill Casey. Everyone understood that MacKay would be the minister from Nova Scotia. MacKay has strong political judgment and can get up to speed quickly on the ministerial-level issues in any field of public policy. He has a strong background in criminal justice policy and is a strong internationalist in foreign affairs. He gave up his position as leader of the PC Party to create the Conservative Party in 2003. Not only were Harper and the entire party indebted to him, but having won the leadership of a political party showed he had good leadership skills. As a former party leader, he had an overarching political perspective that only Harper and Stockwell Day, another former national party leader in the caucus, shared. Harper would have made a serious mistake if he had overlooked MacKay and appointed someone else to Cabinet from the Nova Scotia caucus. MacKay turned out to be a pillar of Cabinet and developed a global reputation for his judgement. He ended up as a possible candidate to be secretary general of NATO, and the Halifax International Security Forum was built on his international standing.[1]

Harper's options were similarly constrained in the other small provinces. Three Conservatives had been returned in New Brunswick: Greg Thompson, Rob Moore, and Mike Allen. Rob Moore had been a strong and loyal staffer in Harper's office before the election and eventually became minister of state, but in 2006 Thompson was the natural choice. He was more senior and experienced and had been the only MP from the former PC caucus to endorse Harper for the Conservative leadership. He was independently minded and had good political skills. In Newfoundland and Labrador, all three Conservative MPs had prior ministerial experience in provincial politics. However, Loyola Hearn had been a leading member of the former PC caucus; both Fabian Manning and Norm Doyle accepted Hearn's leadership of their contingent. Hearn was the natural choice from Newfoundland. In Manitoba, Harper had to pick one Cabinet minister from eight Conservative MPs. Both Brian Pallister and Merv Tweed had prior provincial experience and would have been good candidates for Cabinet. Pallister later became premier of Manitoba. But Vic Toews was the ideal choice and the natural choice for justice minister. He had served as Manitoba's Attorney General. As Conservative justice critic, he had written the criminal justice part of our election platform. Harper was fortunate that he had little choice but to appoint MacKay, Thompson, Hearn, and Toews to Cabinet.[2]

Harper was only slightly less constrained in selecting ministers from British Columbia. BC is a large province and merited more than one minister. Given how many Conservative MPs had been elected, Harper had to ensure adequate representation of BC's various regions. Stockwell Day, the former leader of the Canadian Alliance and former Alberta treasurer, was an obvious pick in his own right and the best choice from among the Conservative MPs elected from the interior of the province. Like MacKay, Day had demonstrated his skills by winning the leadership of a national political party and had gained the unique perspective that comes from such an office. Overlooking Day would have been as big a mistake as overlooking MacKay. Chuck Strahl, a leading light of the former Reform caucus and a smart, decent, level-headed man, was the natural choice from the Fraser Valley. On Vancouver Island, John Duncan had gone down to defeat in his riding. That left Gary Lunn as the natural choice from the island. Again, Harper was fortunate that he had little choice to appoint these three ministers from BC.

In Quebec, the choices were trickier. Quebec is a large province and every prime minister since Confederation has had several ministers from Quebec. Yet, we had only elected a dozen MPs from the province's seventy-five ridings. Once Harper decided he needed to have several Quebec ministers, his choices were again restricted. Lawrence Cannon had a high profile from his experience as a provincial minister, city councillor, public transit authority president, and private sector executive. He had written the party's Quebec platform. He had to be in Cabinet. Josée Verner had experience as a provincial political aide and had worked in Harper's office before the election. The Quebec City area had elected several Conservative MPs and Verner would hold the city's seat in Cabinet. Maxime Bernier was new to elected office but had a strong policy background and a good public presence. Jean-Pierre Blackburn was an experienced and capable politician from a traditionally "bleu" region. Those three were clear choices to fill out the Quebec contingent in the Harper Cabinet. In retrospect, Harper could have appointed Christian Paradis and Steven Blainey to Cabinet. Both were smart, hard-working politicians, and both eventually made their way into his Cabinet, but in early 2006 Harper's four choices seemed clear.

Harper had a more freedom to select ministers from Ontario. Jim Flaherty, John Baird, and Tony Clement had all achieved success in provincial politics and demonstrated strong political judgement. Clement had run a credible campaign for the Conservative leadership. The three of them also came from three of Ontario's six regions – the GTA, eastern Ontario, and the near north. Rob Nicholson, a leading presence in caucus, had served in the House during the Mulroney years and in Kim Campbell's Cabinet. He rounded out the obvious choices from Ontario. The other choices from Ontario were more difficult. In southwestern Ontario, Diane Finley had the combination of political judgement and prior management experience to make her Cabinet-level talent. Other MPs in the area might have been credible choices as well. In central Ontario, Harper had the choice of Michael Chong and Peter Van Loan. Chong went to Cabinet first, and when he resigned Van Loan was elevated quickly. Bev Oda and Gordon O'Connor had strong claims to be in Cabinet. Oda was an experienced broadcast executive, and O'Connor had written the party's defence platform. These four had lots to recommend them at the time and turned out to be capable ministers, but they were not obvious Cabinet choices in the way Flaherty, Baird, Clement, and Nicholson were.

Table 4.1: Level of discretion in naming Harper Cabinet, 6 February 2006

	Ontario	Quebec	Atlantic Canada	Prairies	Alberta	British Columbia	Senate
Little discretion	Jim Flaherty John Baird Tony Clement Rob Nicholson	Jean-Pierre Blackburn Maxime Bernier Lawrence Cannon Josée Verner	Loyola Hearn Peter MacKay Greg Thompson	Vic Toews	Jim Prentice	Stockwell Day Gary Lunn Chuck Strahl	
Some discretion	Diane Finley Bev Oda Gordon O'Connor						
Wide discretion	Michael Chong	Michael Fortier		Carol Skelton	Rona Ambrose, Monte Solberg	David Emerson	Marjory LeBreton
Future Choices	Peter Van Loan	Christain Paradis	Rob Moore	Gary Ritz	Jason Kenney	James Moore	

Source: author's calculations.

Filling the rest of the posts in his original Cabinet meant making genuine choices. In a Saskatchewan caucus with several talented MPs, he chose Carol Skelton. When Skelton retired, he replaced her with Gerry Ritz, who went on to be a long-serving Agriculture Minister. Eventually Lynn Yelich was also appointed to Cabinet. Andrew Scheer became a presiding officer of the House, then Speaker of the House, and later Conservative leader. Any of them could have been Saskatchewan's Cabinet minister in 2006. From the lower mainland of BC, Harper could have named James Moore to Cabinet, and Moore did eventually join Cabinet. In the first round, though, David Emerson was Harper's first choice. The Alberta caucus was rich in talent. In northern Alberta, he selected Rona Ambrose for Cabinet but could have picked James Rajotte, a strong Harper supporter during both leadership campaigns, or Rob Merrifield. Merrifield eventually served as a minister of state. In southern Alberta, Jim Prentice was a clear choice. He was highly regarded in the community and, to encourage conservative unity, he had given up his campaign as the PC candidate in the 2002 Calgary Southwest by-election that returned Harper as a Canadian Alliance MP. With Prentice an obvious choice, Harper then had to choose between Monte Solberg and Jason Kenney as southern Alberta's second Cabinet minister. He selected Solberg and made Kenney his own parliamentary secretary. That was a genuine choice. Kenney eventually became a senior Cabinet minister. Harper also made a genuine choice in appointing Senator Michael Fortier to Cabinet. Finally, there were many Conservative senators who aspired to be government leader in the Senate. Harper passed over several worthy options to name Marjory LeBreton to the post.

Harper could have opted for a larger initial Cabinet, but once he's decided on a smaller one his choices were tightly constrained. More than half of his initial Cabinet was composed of ministers whom, in my view, he had little choice but to appoint (see table 4.1). Breaking informal rules by overlooking or losing any of those "obvious choice" ministers would have created major political problems. He was fortunate that the first two ministers he lost – Michael Chong and Carol Skelton – were among the genuine choices he had to make. That ensured smooth transitions as a result of the losses. Replacing Maxime Bernier as foreign affairs minister was relatively easy given David Emerson's work at international trade, but replacing him as a Quebec minister was trickier. A month after Bernier resigned from Cabinet, Harper promoted Christian Paradis. Four months later, in the 2008 general election, Harper lost another Quebec minister, Michael Fortier (who had resigned in his Senate seat to run unsuccessfully as MP for Vaudreuil–Soulanges), and replaced him as a Quebec minister with Denis Lebel.

The decisions to appoint Fortier and Emerson were both controversial, and I knew it at the time. Fortier was spared public outrage when the Liberals decided to focus their attack on Emerson. Harper was determined to appoint Fortier, believing that the controversy and violation of Reform Party democratic principles in making a senator a minister were outweighed by the importance of making sure the region of Montreal had a seat at the table. Fortier had once run for the PC leadership and had co-chaired Harper's leadership campaign. Fortier also had a strong background in financial circles, something we were otherwise short of. Harper understood the risk to national unity if it ever looked like a right-wing Albertan was not being sensitive to the political context in Quebec. I supported his decision to recruit Fortier completely.[3]

The case of Emerson was bound to be more controversial. Emerson had just been elected as a Liberal MP in a riding that would not likely have elected a Conservative MP under any situation. When we found out that Emerson was open to serving in the Harper Cabinet, I was immediately sold on the idea of recruiting him. Harper never made Emerson's Cabinet position conditional on him crossing the floor or joining the Conservative Party. While it would have been awkward and unprecedented to have an MP from an opposition party caucus serving in Cabinet, it would have been a useful experiment in a minority government. Emerson brought Cabinet experience to a government with very little, and I was sure that recruiting Emerson would destroy the business-oriented wing of the federal Liberals in BC. Of course, I had been outraged a few months earlier when Belinda Stronach crossed the floor, but she had been deeply involved in creating the Conservative Party and Emerson had a less partisan background. Her insinuation that Harper had been a bully or unprofessional toward her really burned at me. We never put out a story about Emerson having been mistreated by Paul Martin or anyone else in the Liberals. I contented myself with that.

After I left the PMO, I found a long-forgotten article published under Harper's name but likely written by someone else.[4] The article claims the "parliamentary system itself need[s] to be fixed" by "disconnecting the executive (cabinet) and legislative branches of government." A prime minister should be free to appoint ministers who are not in Parliament to get the very best talent. US presidents, the article argues, have the advantage of being able to recruit talent for executive branch positions without regard to their success in getting elected. Cabinet's function, according to the argument, is "mainly managerial" and should be composed of "elite individuals." The legislature, by contrast should be representative. Perhaps some of this thinking lay behind the decision to name Fortier to Cabinet. But the article's argument is off target. It is essential to the principle of collective responsibility that almost every minister hold a seat in the House of Commons. At a minimum, they should be available for questions when the House meets. More broadly, backbench MPs allow ministers to govern on the understanding that they are all in the same boat at election time. Appointing Cabinet from among caucus members gives ministers the common political experience that they all face the voters together. MacGregor Dawson got it right seventy years ago when he wrote: "This homogeneity creates a much more efficient executive body, gives more consistent leadership, discourages internal dissension, and develops a stronger fighting organization to ward off the constant attacks of the Opposition" (1948, 266). An American Cabinet is not the same tight group that a well-functioning Canadian Cabinet is, and US presidents sometimes find it hard to achieve the unity of purpose among their Cabinet secretaries that a Canadian prime minister would take for granted among ministers. Cabinet is primarily a political rather than a managerial institution.

Loyalty and Ministers

According to Eddie Goldenberg, Chrétien's top considerations in selecting his ministers were ensuring party solidarity and protecting his own position from an internal challenge. The need for party solidarity arose from internal party divisions in the wake of the Liberal Party's 1990 leadership race and led him to name Sheila Copps and Paul Martin to Cabinet. This led Chrétien to ensure he had a certain number of loyalists at the Cabinet table: "it is a law of politics that a prime minister needs at all times a core group of loyalists in Cabinet who will defend him from mutiny. Chrétien called these ministers his Roman Guard – ministers who would be prepared without hesitation to lay down their political life in order to protect the prime minister against a potential Brutus" (Goldenberg 2006, 60).

In my estimation, Harper did not face these issues in 2006. In 2003, when the Conservative Party was created by a merger, it had all the ingredients needed for deep divisions. There were many factions – former PC supporters who had joined the Canadian Alliance, former PC supporters who had stayed with the PCs and backed Joe Clark, former PC supporters who had stayed with the PCs but not backed Clark, Canadian Alliance members who had consistently supported Stockwell Day's leadership, Canadian Alliance members who had supported Stockwell Day and then supported someone else, Canadian Alliance members who had never really accepted Stockwell Day's leadership of the party, young urban libertarians, young urban social conservatives, and more. Harper won the leadership of the new party by drawing support from many of these factions. Others coalesced around Belinda Stronach.

Long-time friends of Tony Clement's supported Clement along with some others who found both Harper and Stronach unpalatable. Stronach's decision to cross the floor and join the Liberals in May 2005 was the key turning point in the early history of the party. Some Liberal strategists no doubt thought that recruiting Stronach would deal the Conservatives a serious setback. Media reports framed the floor crossing as an indication of profound unhappiness with Harper's leadership. Even crusty veterans who should have known better portrayed Stronach as a victim of Harper's personality (D. Martin 2006). But, within the party, Stronach's move solidified Harper's position. She not only left her followers without a leader, but Harper's handling of her departure persuaded almost all of her followers that he had the right "stuff" to lead. Her betrayal of Peter MacKay gave an emotional, romantic overlay to the drama that heightened its impact. I was executive director of the party at the time. The phone calls and other messages pouring into the party office were overwhelming. People who had been cool to Harper's leadership were now all speaking from the same sheet: as of now, we have to win.

But there was more to Harper's position than the Stronach floor crossing. Although Goldenberg describes it as a "law of politics" that a prime minister must protect him or herself from internal threats, he must be exaggerating. I cannot imagine someone becoming leader of a political party and prime minister who needs a core group of loyalists willing to go to any length to protect him from an internal insurrection. Certainly, Harper had no fear of an internal insurrection in 2006. I cannot imagine he would have depended on others to defend him if he had faced an internal challenge. I doubt that most of Harper's first Cabinet would have hesitated to oppose him if they felt he was overstepping his bounds as leader or prime minister. His ministers stayed in politics because they were committed to public service and felt Harper was a strong leader. If they had ever changed their minds, I would have expected them to speak up or leave politics to do something else with their lives.

This allowed Mr Harper to appoint a Cabinet with a broad diversity of conservative viewpoints from centrist technocrats like Bev Oda to socially conservative Canada-firsters like Rob Nicholson and socially conservative internationalists like Jason Kenney and less socially conservative internationalists like Peter MacKay, to liberty hawks like Maxime Bernier and business liberals like David Emerson, from prairie conservative populists like Monte Solberg to young fogies like Michael Chong, from French Canadian nationalists like Jean-Pierre Blackburn to good government populists like Diane Finley. Every member of the Harper Cabinet was a thoughtful, independent person.

Assigning Ministers

A prime minister's choice over who sits in Cabinet may be tightly constrained, but with significant discretion in assigning ministers to portfolios. Even that discretion is not unlimited, however.

Take the example of the minister of finance. There are some character traits that a finance minister should have: tact and discretion in dealing with senior players in the financial markets and an ability to take politically astute positions on issues that crop up in all areas of federal jurisdiction. On the first count, finance ministers must be unusually circumspect among ministers when speaking in public, since their every word is watched by market traders around the world and a misplaced emphasis can move financial markets. On the second, the finance minister has to see how all aspects of the federal government's agenda fit together in order to form fiscal policy and be able to reconcile the multitude of financial pressures on the federal government into a single budget. The finance minister must also be able to work with provincial colleagues on decisions involving billions of dollars in transfer payments. Beyond these character traits, the finance minister must have or be able to earn a high level of credibility in the Canadian, American, and global financial communities. It was not a coincidence that Harper's two finance ministers were from Canada's financial capital, the Toronto area. Jim Flaherty had been Ontario's provincial treasurer. In 2006, the Conservative caucus had few MPs from the Toronto area. Of all Harper's MPs, Flaherty was probably the best placed to form relationships on Bay Street. David Emerson would have been a credible candidate for finance in a Liberal government but was too new to the Conservative Party to serve there for Harper. Jim Prentice could have served at finance and, if Bruce Carson's account is correct, was slated to go to finance in the Cabinet shuffle of August 2007. When Prentice left federal politics, he went directly to the executive suite of a major Bay Street bank. Michael Fortier could also have served at Finance, but it is difficult to have a finance minister from the Senate. Later, Harper selected Joe Oliver, who had spent most of his adult life working in the Toronto financial community, to succeed Flaherty in the portfolio.

Given the importance of fiscal policy and the role of the finance minister in making fiscal decisions, a prime minister should consider how to manage the career of a finance minister. Pierre Trudeau took one approach. He changed his finance minister, on average, every two-and-a-half years; none of them served more than four years (see table 4.2). By cycling ministers through the portfolio so often, Trudeau ensured that fiscal policy remained closely tied to his government's overall agenda. Over time, expertise in the finance portfolio was broadly distributed around the Cabinet table. No single finance minister is associated with Pierre Trudeau's government. Brian Mulroney and Jean Chrétien adopted a different model. They both choose to rely on a single finance minister for an extended period. When Michael Wilson's six and a half years in the role came to an end, the appointment of Don Mazankowski marked a major change in the government's approach to fiscal policy. Paul Martin's eight and a half years in the role defined the Chrétien government's fiscal policy, and his departure from the portfolio plunged that government into a political crisis. The longer a finance minister serves in the role, the more his personality and political priorities take precedence in setting fiscal policy.

Bruce Carson claims that Harper tried to move Jim Flaherty out of the finance role in the August 2007 Cabinet shuffle, after he had tabled two budgets, but relented after Flaherty refused the move (2014, 207–8). Harper appeared to confirm that story in his eulogy for Flaherty:

> I had Finance in mind from the beginning, but Jim was actually, somewhat surprised, somewhat reticent about the portfolio at first. Though, it's safe to say, it wasn't long before he decided he would never let go of it. (Harper 2014)

If Carson's story is true, it certainly illustrates the real but informal limits to a prime minister's ability to move ministers once a Cabinet is up and running. If Harper really did have to reverse course and leave Flaherty in place, that turned out to be a fortuitous decision. Flaherty's experience in the portfolio certainly helped the government and Canada navigate the global financial crisis in 2008 and 2009. He knew the key policy levers, he knew the essential players, and had strong ties to his international counterparts. Flaherty's 2009 budget, coming so soon after the misfire of the autumn 2008 economic update, was broadly accepted and well-designed. But there are reasons to imagine Flaherty stayed on at finance too long. Once the G20 took the lead in coordinating the global response to the crisis, the constant travel and pressure of the portfolio might have contributed to the decline in Flaherty's health. His January 2013 interview with Bloomberg Television from Switzerland did not convey an image of strength to the world. But there was more than a personal price in his long tenure in the portfolio. Flaherty announced that he wanted to balance the federal budget before he stepped aside, and balancing the budget became an overriding priority for the government in 2012–14. During its crucial years with a majority in the House, the Harper government focused ministers' attention on deficit-reduction plans and senior officials

Table 4.2: Tenures of Finance Ministers, 1968–2015

Finance Minister	Days in office
Edgar Benson	1,378
John Turner	1,321
Donald S. Macdonald	721
Jean Chrétien	626
John Crosbie	273
Allan MacEachen	921
Marc Lalonde	659
Michael Wilson	2,407
Don Mazankowski	796
Gilles Loiselle	132
Paul Martin	3,132
John Manley	558
Ralph Goodale	787
Jim Flaherty	2,962
Joe Oliver	595

Source: author's calculations and data on members at http://parl.gc.ca.

focused theirs on managing within their frozen operating budgets. Even as the economy slowed, Flaherty and then Oliver delivered budgets that showed no deficit before the 2015 election. The focus on restraining spending certainly had Harper's approval. But if the Harper government had added a year to Flaherty's timeline for a balanced budget and set a looser fiscal policy in 2012 by, say, boosting infrastructure spending, the resulting projects would have been coming online by the 2015 election. If Harper had been prepared to tolerate a small deficit in 2015–16, it would have been harder for Justin Trudeau's Liberals to make the case for deficit-financed infrastructure in that autumn's campaign. Allowing any minister's career plans to determine government policy is never wise; allowing it in the Finance portfolio is especially bad.

Another portfolio where the prime minister faces constraints is the case of the justice minister. With only one brief exception, every justice minister since Confederation has been a lawyer. Lawyers are well represented in the House of Commons, and that ordinarily gives a prime minister many choices for the post. However, Harper's first Cabinet only had seven lawyers – Vic Toews, Rob Nicholson, Peter MacKay, Tony Clement, Jim Flaherty, Jim Prentice, and Gary Lunn. Given that Flaherty was already slotted for finance, Harper only had six lawyers to choose from in filling the justice portfolio. Over the next ten years, three of them served in the post. Toews had written the criminal law part of the 2006 Conservative election platform and had the strongest understanding of the reforms needed in the field. He was the natural choice to go to justice first. Later, as Toews's criminal justice legislation piled up on the Order Paper of the House, Harper moved former house leader Rob Nicholson into the portfolio to get some of those bills passed. Later still, when the government's agenda needed a reboot, Peter MacKay, who had good instincts on criminal justice reform and had worked as a crown counsel before entering politics, rounded out Harper's choices for the role.

A final set of special cases where a prime minister usually feels constrained is in naming ministers for the regional development agencies. Every region of Canada now has a regional development agency devoted to spreading federal money around its worthy economic development projects. There were four such agencies in 2006, and the Harper government created two more – one for southern Ontario and for the north. Each agency needs a minister and, until the Justin Trudeau government was elected, each agency was headed by a minister from that region. When Harper decided on a small initial Cabinet, he assigned these agencies as secondary responsibilities for ministers who had other portfolios as well. MacKay was the minister for the Atlantic Canada Opportunities Agency as well as minister of foreign affairs and then national defence. Clement was minister for FedNor as well as his other portfolios, and so on. Eventually, Harper decided to change his approach and each of the agencies got a dedicated minister. Trudeau has named an Ontario minister to head all these agencies, but over time he, too, may decide he needs dedicated ministers for each one.

Firing Ministers

On the morning of 26 May 2008, I was in my office in the Langevin Block, across from Parliament Hill. Around lunch time, my executive assistant, Lanny Cardow, interrupted to tell me I was needed in Centre Block. "Something about Bernier and secret documents he left at his girlfriend's apartment," he said. I was out the door in seconds, and as I left I asked Lanny to make sure there was someone from the Machinery of Government Secretariat in PCO available to work late that night. The Machinery of Government Secretariat plays the central role in changing ministers, and a Cabinet shuffle requires a public servant who is qualified to administer oaths to be in attendance. Suddenly, I caught myself and realized I had become quite accustomed to the routine of a Cabinet shuffle. That morning, I had arrived at work with every confidence that Harper's Cabinet was a settled group of ministers.

Before lunch was over, changes were coming. By the time I reached the Prime Minister's Office in Centre Block, Bernier and a staff member were meeting with Harper. I was told that Bernier was resigning, although if he had not offered his resignation he would almost certainly have been fired. Harper handed me the documents that Bernier had left at his girlfriend's apartment and asked me to look them over. They were all marked with security classifications but the content was pretty innocuous. When Bernier left, I asked Harper whom he intended to name as his new foreign minister. He had already settled on David Emerson, who was already trade minister and chair of the Cabinet committee on Afghanistan.

It is difficult, if not impossible, to predict ahead of time how successful someone will be as a minister, or how successful a minister will be in a given portfolio. Prior success outside of politics does not seem to predict who will do well as a minister. Prior success in municipal politics does not seem to predict it either. Prior expertise in a policy area is as much a hindrance as a help. Some people with precious little prior experience of any sort become good ministers. But some people just do not make good ministers. They may show poor political judgement or have difficulty making decisions. They may not be able to explain what they are doing to an audience of their fellow citizens. Accountability in government means that, sooner or later, a prime minister has to fire a minister for poor performance. Mulroney fired ministers. So did Chrétien and Pierre Trudeau. A prime minister who often fires ministers might be a good indicator of the centralization of power within the executive branch. How often did Stephen Harper fire ministers?

Determining when a minister has been fired is difficult. Ministers have lives outside of politics and may voluntarily leave Cabinet for many reasons. Sometimes politicians really do want to time with their families. Prime ministers do not usually advertise when or why they have decided that a minister must leave. When ministers commit serious errors, they usually resign before the prime minister has to fire them. There are few moments like the ones on *The Apprentice*, when the boss says, "You're fired."

Fifty-two individuals served in Harper Cabinet.[5] Of those, twenty-five departed before the Conservatives were defeated in 2015. Table 4.3 lists the departures and the circumstances involved. During Harper's first period in office, Michael Chong and Carol Skelton both resigned voluntarily. Bernier resigned in a situation where he might have been fired. In 2008, David Emerson and Monte Solberg retired rather than seek re-election; Loyola Hearn and Michael Fortier were then defeated at the polls. Following the 2008 election, Gary Lunn was moved from minister of natural resources to minister of state (sport) and Gordon O'Connor from minister of national revenue to minister of state and chief government whip. A prime minister does not appoint as chief government whip someone in whom he has lost confidence, so O'Connor was not fired. Lunn's assignment was a demotion, although his new post gave him responsibility for overseeing the Canadian team headed to the Vancouver Olympic Games. During his second period in office, Harper lost Greg Thompson due to illness, Jay Hill, who accelerated his announced retirement from the House after a long parliamentary career, and Jim Prentice, who left politics for a senior position in the private sector. In 2011, Chuck Strahl and Stockwell Day retired rather than seek re-election; Lawrence Cannon, Jean-Pierre Blackburn, and Josée Verner were then defeated at the polls.

Harper's third period in office saw more complex Cabinet changes. Keith Ashfield and Peter Kent left Cabinet due to illness. John Duncan went from Aboriginal affairs to become a minister of state and chief government whip; again, not an indication that Harper had lost confidence in him. Peter Penashue, like Bernier, resigned before Harper might have fired him. Vic Toews retired but was later appointed to the bench. Jim Flaherty resigned from politics in a well-advertised retirement that he, unfortunately, never got to enjoy. The three other departures are harder to explain. John Baird resigned from politics and media reports were not clear on why he did so. It is hard to imagine he was fired given that he was widely regarded as a top ministerial performer. Media reports indicate that Harper was taken by surprise by news of Baird's retirement, something that indicates Baird retired a voluntarily. Marjory LeBreton left Cabinet when her portfolio, government leader in the Senate, was dropped from Cabinet. She reached the mandatory retirement age for senators shortly thereafter. The last part of her tenure in Cabinet was overshadowed by a series of scandals in the Senate. Emails released during the trial of Senator Mike Duffy indicated a serious breakdown of relations between Senator LeBreton and Harper's political aides, but there is no indication that Harper had lost confidence in her abilities. It is more likely that Harper decided to move her out of her post as part of a broader Cabinet shuffle because of her pending retirement from the Senate.

Finally, Bev Oda resigned from Cabinet and left politics altogether one year after the 2011 general election. Her departure came in the wake of news stories about her ministerial expense account and controversy over how she indicated she did not agree with a recommendation from her officials about a piece of departmental business. Did Harper fire her, or did she simply grow weary of life in federal politics? I hope it was the latter. After I left government, when I worked in the international development sector, I watched Oda's work as international cooperation minister. She was an attentive minister and closely tracked all the major files in her department. Two of her courageous

Table 4.3: Departures from the Harper Cabinet

Minister	Date of Departure	Explanation
Michael Chong	November 2006	Resigned on principle
Maxime Bernier	May 2008	Resigned over mishandling of documents; later named Minister of State, May 2011
David Emerson	October 2008	Did not run for re-election
Monte Solberg	October 2008	Did not run for re-election
Gary Lunn	October 2008	Named Minister of State (Sport); later defeated 2011
Gordon O'Connor	October 2008	Named Minister of State and Chief Government Whip
Loyola Hearn	October 2008	Defeated
Michael Fortier	October 2008	Defeated
Greg Thompson	January 2010	Resigned; later did not run for re-election 2011
Jay Hill	October 2010	Resigned from House
Jim Prentice	November 2010	Resigned from House
Stockwell Day	May 2011	Did not run for re-election
Chuck Strahl	May 2011	Did not run for re-election
Jean-Pierre Blackburn	May 2011	Defeated
Josée Verner	May 2011	Defeated
Lawrence Cannon	May 2011	Defeated
Bev Oda	July 2012	Resigned from House
John Duncan	February 2013	Named Minister of State and Chief Government Whip
Peter Penashue	March 2013	Resigned following reports of campaign spending problems; resigned seat and defeated seeking re-election
Keith Ashfield	July 2013	Resigned citing illness
Marjory LeBreton	July 2013	Resigned, post removed from Cabinet
Peter Kent	July 2013	Resigned citing illness
Vic Toews	July 2013	Resigned from House
Jim Flaherty	March 2014	Resigned from House
John Baird	February 2015	Resigned from House

Source: author's calculations based on media reporting.

decisions – to focus Canadian development aid on a small number of countries and issues, and to "untie" Canadian aid money, removing the requirement that it be spent on goods and services from Canada – were well-received in the regular, comprehensive assessments conducted by the Organisation for Economic Co-operation and Development (Organisation for Economic Cooperation and Development 2012). She managed the shift of development projects in Afghanistan after the *Manley Report* without incident. The problems with her travel expenses, while her responsibility of course, reflects staff work not her inattention to procedures. Oda has ample reason to be proud of her work in the portfolio.

Of the fifty-two ministers to serve in his government, it is hard to find a clear example of Harper firing a minister outright. Bernier and Penashue resigned before Harper likely would have had to fire them. Oda left after, on balance, a good record in Cabinet. Harper was remarkable for keeping ministers rather than cycling through them. This record, if coupled with the possibility that Flaherty stared down Harper to stay at Finance in 2007, hardly indicates a centralization of power within the executive. Indeed, it suggests that even under a strong prime minister, ministers, once appointed, are reasonably secure in their posts. They may not be subject to the threat of being fired as often as we might expect.

Cabinet Organization and Cabinet Business

Governing from the Centre launched many snappy phrases – academic soundbites – into the political vocabulary of the country. None is as pithy as the one phrase Savoie borrowed from that unnamed Liberal Cabinet minister: that Cabinet is nothing more than a focus group for the prime minister. Or, as Rathgeber puts it, Cabinet is not deliberative but "ornamental" (2014, 99). These phrases are pithy, yet misleading.

First of all, a good focus group, when carefully assembled and properly led, is a useful way to test out ideas. It lets the group leader see how people arrive at their views, how they defend them against challenges, and how strongly they hold their views. A good focus group is a structured conversation with texture and depth among people who share certain views or backgrounds about an issue that matters to them. Any truly strategic discussion among, say, two dozen people might look like a focus group as people test ideas and arguments with each other. There is no reason to worry if the most useful part of a Cabinet meeting is an open-ended discussion that seems like a focus group. You cannot run a collegial government without regular, serious strategic discussions among ministers. Secondly, there is no reason to think we would be better governed if the full Cabinet hashed out every decision made in the Government of Canada. Full Cabinet only meets for a few hours each year. Its committees meet for a few hours more. Cabinet has to confirm thousands of decisions each year on behalf of the Government of Canada. These decisions are the formal business of Cabinet agendas, but most are routine and some are highly technical. If ministers and officials have done their homework and secured the approval of other ministers ahead of time, why hold a full discussion around the Cabinet table? Ministers are responsible for these decisions collectively and individually, and they are accountable to Parliament and the public if a controversy arises about them. But Cabinet should focus its time on more important discussions.

It is a better use of time to let ministers reflect on the political and strategic challenges facing the government. The prime minister gets the opportunity to hear from ministers and to probe their political insights. Ministers are, after all, smart people whose jobs give them different perspectives on government. Goldenberg's funny stories about Chrétien's efforts to involve his Cabinet in formulating the political and budget priorities of his government are instructive and point to the limits of what can be expected from a collective discussion. But ministers should share a general idea of the state of the government's fiscal situation and the country's economy. They should have a chance to air their political sense of the country. Cabinet is, after all, collectively responsible to the House of Commons and the country. Forming a collective view of the political challenges facing the government is an essential Cabinet function. It cannot be delegated to public service officials or to anyone else. These kinds of discussions, at times, might feel or sound like a focus group. The prime minister and colleagues might probe each other's views and test them against their own impressions. This is the nature of any discussion about the strategic challenges of any organization. When a Cabinet meeting is setting a path for the government's future, it is doing the critical work of the political executive work of, and it is not clear to me that Cabinet would be making better use of its time reviewing the details of a recent report of the Auditor General or the communiqué of a federal-provincial ministerial meeting.

Cabinet and its committees meet for only a few hours each year, so most of the work of Cabinet is done outside of formal Cabinet meetings. When the finance minister meets with each of his colleagues before a federal budget to discuss the fiscal state of the government and the plethora of spending and taxing proposals that concern each minister, that is Cabinet in action as much as anything that goes on in a formal Cabinet meeting. When the industry and heritage ministers meet to reach common ground on reforms to Canada's copyright law, that too is Cabinet in action. If the reforms they recommend to Cabinet meet with the approval of the prime minister and the rest of Cabinet without much debate, or with only a perfunctory debate, they have done their colleagues and the country a service by letting Cabinet focus its attention on more contentious and more difficult decisions. So, it is not quite enough to say that "Cabinet has become a focus group" and therefore conclude that Cabinet therefore is not important, or that power has been centralized in the hands of the prime minister and a few courtiers. The time of Cabinet and its committees is valuable. If ministers manage issues with their colleagues without needing a discussion at the Cabinet table itself, that is nothing but good time management.

Since the end of World War II, prime ministers have established Cabinet structures, committees, and informal rules of procedure. A prime minister can ask ministers for advice on how to structure Cabinet and its business, but only a prime minister can decide whether Cabinet will have committees, how those committees will be organized, and whether every decision that belongs to Cabinet must be on the agenda of a full Cabinet. Decisions about the operation of Cabinet can influence what decisions are ultimately made.

For example, John Manley's Independent Panel on Canada's Future Role in Afghanistan (2008) made many recommendations about improving Canada's military, diplomatic, and development efforts in that country. It recommended that Canada extend its military deployment in the dangerous Kandahar area and remain there until conditions on the ground improved enough to begin withdrawing. It also recommended that the mission could not be managed by the separate efforts of government departments working in parallel. A coordinated effort was required, and the panel urged Harper to lead the effort through a Cabinet committee acting with the support of a single task force of officials. "Fulfilling Canada's commitment in Afghanistan requires the political energy only a Prime Minister can impart," the panel concluded (28). In response to the panel's report, Harper struck a Cabinet Committee on Afghanistan and formed a special task force within PCO to support the committee. He named David Emerson, at the time minister of international trade, to chair the committee and Ambassador David Mulroney to head the special PCO unit. These decisions forced department officials and military leaders to bring key issues to ministers for Cabinet-level decisions and forced ministers to devote more attention to Afghanistan than they otherwise would have. Military, diplomatic, and development efforts became more centrally coordinated, and that influenced how the government managed Canada's exit from Afghanistan. If the committee had been structured differently under a different chair and with a different official supporting its work, different decisions would have been made.

Decisions about Cabinet structure and operations have a great impact on how well the government can make timely decisions and on the amount of time individual ministers must spend in Cabinet meeting instead of running their departments. Martin had a complex structure for his Cabinet with many committees and an unstructured decision-making process. Harper took advice from his transition team chair, Derek Burney, on Cabinet structure and ended up with an operation like Mulroney's.[6] He had monthly meetings of the full Cabinet to discuss the government's overall political direction and to make Order-in-Council appointments. Other decisions were delegated to one of two executive committees of Cabinet – the Operations Committee, which Harper did not attend, or the Planning and Priorities Committee, which he chaired. These committees met weekly when Parliament was in session. Each minister was a member of one of the executive committees, with the chair of the Operations Committee belonging to both. Three standing committees of Cabinet were the normal first stop for any substantive recommendation that needed Cabinet approval. The economic ministers met once a week as a standing committee, as did the social ministers and the foreign affairs and national security ministers. Treasury Board, the only statutory committee of Cabinet, also met once weekly. Over time, ad hoc committees like Emerson's on Afghanistan were added to the mix and other standing committees were formed. The standing and ad hoc committees were kept as small as possible. Each minister had a two-hour meeting of one of the executive committees each week, as well as a two-hour meeting of a standing committee. The chair of the Operations Committee would be busier since that position required attendance to two weekly executive meetings. Ministers were therefore free to run their departments and attend to the business of a regular parliamentarian on Monday and Thursday mornings, and two afternoons after Question Period, each week. The more the full Cabinet meets and the more Cabinet committees there are, the less time a minister has to run a department or attend to other business. Adding early morning and evening committee meetings to the agenda leaves ministers with little time to meet anyone other than their fellow Cabinet ministers and is a good way to ensure they get quickly out of touch.

Making Cabinet Work

A prime minister has core responsibilities that cannot be fully delegated, over fiscal policy, foreign affairs, federal-provincial relations, and parliamentary affairs. These are the key levers of prime ministerial leadership. Prime ministers can also reserve any decision or any file for their personal attention, but the fiscal, foreign, federal-provincial, and parliamentary priorities of the government must be determined at the centre and form the nucleus of prime ministerial leadership. Cabinet ministers, as a group, cannot and, if asked, generally will not settle these priorities themselves, and I suspect that dynamic has not changed since 1867. A prime minister can and should use Cabinet in a way that might look like a "mere" focus group when setting these priorities. Ministerial input is important. But the decisions are the prime minister's alone.

Within these strategic boundaries, ministers have broad legal and informal powers and tremendous workloads. The daily work of ministerial orders, agreements, procedures, and consultation unfolds. Ministers acting together have orders in council, other regulations and instruments, and endless other decisions to make. Some of the real political and governmental work of tending to these responsibilities goes on at formal meetings of Cabinet and its committees. Most of it, just like in every other organization, goes on during informal meetings, telephone calls and quick chats between ministers, their officials, and their staffs. That, too, is Cabinet in action, and there is so much ministerial business to conduct that no prime minister, even one assisted by the ablest PCO and PMO staff, can keep track of all of it. Ministers have to keep in mind the government's overall priorities and boundaries, as set by the prime minister, just as every other organization has an overall direction and priorities. They and the prime minister and all the members of the government caucus will be held accountable, after all, at the next election. But all those considerations still leave a lot of room for ministerial decision and innovation.

Sometimes, a course of action cannot be approved at the minister's level or even at Cabinet level. There are some kinds of decisions a prime minister, even with a united Cabinet and served by the most capable help, cannot make without the concurrence of Parliament. Levying taxes, spending public money, creating offences and setting penalties for them, and creating new powers for or changing the existing powers of ministers, departments, agencies, and other arms of the government requires legislation, and legislating requires Parliament. For the last generation or two, we have told ourselves that Parliament is dead. But is that right?

5

The Executive Branch and Parliament

If Cabinet Is Dead, Parliament Is Long since Buried

Parliament is Canada's much unloved institution. Public policy experts overlook it. Former MPs express only frustration and disappointment about it. Journalists mostly ignore it. Walter Bagehot (1961 [1867]) praised the British House of Commons as a place of real debate and listed it as one of the "efficient" institutions of the UK government. But in Canada, at some point after 1867, it seems that everyone just concluded that Parliament had become what Bagehot called a "dignified" or purely symbolic institution. Today, most observers agree that Canada's Parliament is dead. Some ideologues say the Harper government killed it. Other observers say Parliament was dead by the time Pierre Trudeau is supposed to have dismissed MPs as "nobodies." Those with longer memories say Parliament died during the Great Pipeline Debate of 1956. Or that Parliament died during the rise of party-line voting, something that we tell ourselves shows that party discipline and the whips have won out over "true" democracy.

In *Governing from the Centre*, Savoie has very little to say about Parliament. The book's index has only two entries under "Parliament" and one under "parliamentary government." He quotes a former senior official of the Privy Council Office that "Parliament is about assigning blame and not much else" (341). He surmises that, because Parliament is all about assigning blame, it forces the executive to focus on avoiding blame. Opposition parties and the national news media, working together, force government to contort its processes and contribute to the centralization of power. He notes that "students of parliamentary government" are increasingly concerned about "a shift towards a presidential form of government" (105).

Savoie's view of Parliament is widely shared by academic observers and journalists. The academic contempt for Parliament is blunt and long-standing. Journalists, even the ones assigned to the Parliamentary Press Gallery, pay little attention to Parliament aside from Question Period, throne speeches, and budgets. In the House of Commons, the visitors' galleries are often occupied by tourists and school groups. The gallery reserved for the press rarely has a soul in it. In 1998, the *National Post* began its life with a page devoted to Parliament. Paul Wells was assigned to write a daily British-style parliamentary sketch, and when the House was not sitting Wells would telephone MPs to discuss issues of the day and run their answers verbatim, creating a simulacrum of parliamentary debate. It was a great feature and made good use of Wells's style. Unfortunately, when Wells moved to other responsibilities at the paper the *Post* dropped the sketch column. As the *Post* evolved, its parliamentary coverage dwindled. Today, its tiny Parliamentary Bureau has little time to cover the House. Other parliamentary bureaus are similarly stretched.

All of which is a shame. While political observers have been ignoring Parliament, assuming it was dead, Parliament has in fact been enjoying a renaissance. From 2004 to 2011, during the seven years of minority governments, no one could take the verdict of the House of Commons for granted. House votes mattered. The confidence function of the House was always in play. But even during the majority governments, Parliament was more than just a rubberstamp for legislation proposed by the executive branch. Parliament has played a role – and an independent role – in determining which government bills got adopted and which did not. Moreover, on occasion parliamentarians who are not in Cabinet have been able to formulate their own legislative agendas and see them adopted. Parliament could play an even more vigorous role. The Reform Act, passed in 2015, was an effort to invigorate the role of MPs even more, although chapter 7 will argue the Reform Act was not well thought through. A better way to invigorate Parliament would be to revisit the House of Commons' role in reviewing the Cabinet's spending requests – the estimates and appropriations bills. But before turning our attention to the new parliamentary renaissance and prospects for expanding it, let us revisit the reasons we have come to think that Parliament is dead.

The Elements of the Argument

The argument for Parliament's irrelevance is so common that any well-trained student or close observer of politics can recite it almost by heart. A prime minister who heads a majority government is a near-dictator. The opposition can do nothing to thwart a majority government's legislative agenda. Parliament, in such circumstances, knuckles under to the will of the executive branch. Parliament is only "matters" when there is a minority government or when the government faces a hostile majority in the Senate. And even in those circumstances the prime minister can threaten an election to bully the opposition into letting the executive branch have its way.

This dark state of affairs is the result of undue party discipline, especially in the government caucus. Government backbenchers are trained seals, under the control of their party leader. This undue party discipline is, in turn, an unintended consequence of the decision Canada's major parties made a century ago to have their leaders selected by delegates to party conventions rather than by members of their parliamentary caucuses. Until 1919, in the case of the Liberals, and 1927, in the case of the Conservatives, caucus members selected party leaders and party leaders were therefore constantly accountable to caucus members. MPs and senators had influence over their leaders. But since the move to leadership conventions, caucus members cannot hold their leader to account. The recent trend to selecting leaders through a mass vote of party members has made the situation even worse. Chapter 6 will take up this part of the argument. Finally, a prime minister decides which government MPs to appoint as ministers, parliamentary secretaries, committee chairs, house officers, caucus officers, and so on. Each of these posts comes with a stipend and other perks. Some come with a car and driver. Ambitious MPs know not to challenge the prime minister if they want to ascend to higher office. These levers together make party discipline in Canada rock solid, far more solid than party discipline in other Westminster systems and certainly far more solid than party discipline in the US Congress.

This imbalance of power, particularly the prime minister's control of the government caucus, apparently makes Parliament a dead letter. The institution is, at best, a sort of Electoral College, the place where seats are totalled up to see who gets to be prime minister and who gets to be opposition leader. The House of Commons, in this view, has only one role, to be the confidence chamber. The daily shenanigans of Question Period and the annual pageantry of the Throne Speech or Budget Day produce news for journalists to cover, but the other daily proceedings of Parliament are not even interesting to journalists. Parliamentary debates are dry speeches composed from talking points issued by party leaders and their offices. The results of parliamentary votes simply formalize foregone conclusions. Why would a citizen bother to pay attention to that?

Samara, a Toronto-based democratic reform think tank, underscored this dreary picture in in a 2014 report on the views of eighty former MPs (Loat 2014). That report, *The Tragedy of the Commons*, depicts the life of an MP in almost desperate terms. MPs, according to Samara, have to be "coerced" into running for Parliament and therefore see themselves as perpetual outsiders from the political process. They first encounter politics through the murky waters of riding-level nomination races. Once elected, they see the critical business of Parliament being done behind closed doors in caucus or committee rooms. Power is centralized in leaders' offices, and because of this MPs are reluctant to speak out against party leadership fearing they will be demoted, kicked out of caucus, or put out of the running for a Cabinet promotion. The first-hand accounts of these eighty MPs are alarming and reinforce the idea of parliamentary dysfunction verging on death.

Since everyone knows that Parliament is dead, scholars rarely produce studies of Parliament. Sixty years ago, R. MacGregor Dawson wrote in his classic textbook *The Government of Canada* (1957) that Cabinet and the majority caucus in the House were so closely connected that they were "virtually" identical. Responsible government, he suggested, seemed to have "suffered a strange and alarming inversion; the Cabinet is no longer responsible to the Commons; the Commons has instead become responsible to the Cabinet" (431). J.R. Mallory, in his 1974 textbook *The Structure of Canadian Government*, was more categorical: "In a purely formal sense, Parliament makes laws, but *everyone knows* that the laws are drafted and decided on within the executive. Parliament is expected dutifully to ratify them" (emphasis added). The executive branch "controls the House of Commons rather than the reverse," and the House might be becoming a "sort of constitutional vermiform appendix" (1984, 270–1). Allan Kornberg and William Mishler, in their 1976 study of Canadian legislatures, declared that "The Canadian Parliament is a good source of examples for anyone who wants to demonstrate the decline of Parliaments" (x). Ron Landes, in the popular textbook *The Canadian Polity*, was also blunt: legislatures in Canada and elsewhere have "declining decision-making power"; they do play a role in "legitimating executive actions and representing the public in the governing process" but not much else (1983, 151). Jackson and Jackson's *Politics in Canada*, first published in 1986, tried to argue that Parliament was still a relevant part of the political process: legislatures "have multiple functions," it said, but the authors could not offer an example of Canada's Parliament playing an active legislative or deliberative role (2001, 295).

Canadian scholars have produced a few new titles on Parliament in the last generation. C.E.S. Franks's *Parliament of Canada* (1987) provided a comprehensive description of the House of Commons and Senate, but did not delve into the legislative or deliberative functions of Parliament. David Docherty's *Mr Smith Goes to Ottawa* (1997) gave us new insights into the work of parliamentarians, the trajectories of parliamentary careers, and the "folk-ways" of the institution. David Smith's fine multi-volume work on Parliament drew on the institutional features of its constituent parts to inject a Canadian perspective on global issues of democratic theory. The UBC democratic audit series devoted a slim eponymous volume to legislatures, also written by Docherty (2005). Of the many roles that the House of Commons could play many roles, these scholars generally concede it functions as a confidence chamber. Like a northern form of the US Electoral College, the House is where seats are totalled to see who has won an election. When there is a majority government, the confidence function matters little once the election returns are confirmed. When no party wins a majority of seats, the House plays its confidence role more frequently.

These studies generally downplay Parliament's deliberative and legislative functions. A 2009 literature review commissioned by the Library of Parliament concluded that "over roughly the last decade, scholars have not shown much interest in Parliament's organization and operations" (Sutherland 2010, 49). It found that "few academic authors execute finer grained empirical work on … important components of parliamentary democracy or … procedural tracks, including appropriations or supply." There is very little work on parliamentary committees or the significance of their work (51). No one studies the debates and procedural rules of the House of Commons to see if members exert independent influence on government legislation since this is assumed never to happen. Nor are there many studies looking into whether parliamentary debate has shaped the fate of individual bills.

Democratic Reform

This consensus about Parliament's death did not go down well with political leaders. And with good reason. The more everyone talked and acted as if Parliament was dead, the more actively elected officials in Parliament felt obliged to find ways to reinvigorate the institution. This eventually spawned a "democratic reform" movement in Canadian politics. Political leaders began to see advantage in promises to revive Parliament and our democracy. Direct democracy, a group of techniques that were initially intended to bypass Parliament, was a staple of Preston Manning's rise to prominence and the Reform Party's initial political success (Flanagan 1995). Establishment political figures responded to Manning's success by framing democratic reform in parliamentary terms. When Paul Martin won the Liberal leadership, he highlighted what he called a "democratic deficit" in Canada. Too much political power, he argued, depended on "who you know in the PMO." After he left the Chrétien Cabinet, he developed a series of proposals "aimed at reducing party discipline … strengthening parliamentary committees, giving MPs a role in overseeing government appointments, and creating an independent ethics commissioner" (Martin 2008, 245). Coming from a former finance minister and the scion of a great political family, these arguments seemed particularly frank and urgent.

In its first election campaign, the Conservative Party felt it had to outflank Martin on democratic reform. Its first election platform (Conservative Party of Canada 2004) mimicked Martin's plans by also promising reduced party discipline, stronger parliamentary committees, and a role for MPs in overseeing government appointments but also promised elected senators and fixed election dates. Its second platform repeated these promises (Conservative Party of Canada 2005–06). In his early years in office, Harper made moves to reform the Senate and advanced government legislation to allow new senators to be elected. In September 2006, he told senators that the status quo in the upper house was not acceptable to either his government or the Canadian public. "Years of delay in Senate reform must come to an end, and it will. The Senate must change and we intend to make it happen." He argued the case for bicameralism. Canada, he told senators, needs a Senate that provides "sober and effective second thought … [and] gives voice to our diverse regions." To play that role the Senate had to have "democratic legitimacy."[1] But in his later years, when his government was forced to respond to the 2008 global financial crisis, Harper's interest in Senate reform waned. Eventually he felt compelled to ask the Supreme Court whether his reform plans were constitutional, and the Court abandoned its traditional deference in matters of constitutional reform (Morton 2015). Harper ended up dropping the issue altogether and left office with his ambitions for Senate reform disappointed (Brodie 2014).

But the democratic reform agenda continues to be renewed. Conservative MP Michael Chong ignited a short interest in empowering MPs with his 2015 Reform Act, a subject that will be tackled in chapter 7. Later that year, Justin Trudeau was elected on a platform that revisited the reform theme. He repeated the promises made by Martin and Harper to reduce party discipline, make parliamentary committees stronger, and give MPs a role in overseeing government appointments. He also promised a more relevant Question Period. And, most importantly, he promised to end the "first past the post" electoral system. Since being elected, his ministers have been consulting MPs about ways to improve House committees and expand parliamentary reviewing the spending estimates.[2] Treasury Board President Scott Brison issued a discussion document on the estimates and financial reporting to Parliament (Treasury Board Secretariat 2016).

But Is Parliament Really Dead?

It is hard to reconcile the idea that Parliament is dead with the day-to-day realities of life on Parliament Hill. When I left academia and started work on Parliament Hill, I was shocked to discover how much time and effort party leaders devote to parliamentary debates and tactics. Parliamentarians work around the clock when Parliament is in session to prepare for debates in the House and the Senate. Every party has a cadre of MPs and senators who are knowledgeable about parliamentary procedure and can advise how to maximize their political opportunities in parliamentary debate. Some of the longest serving staffers on the Hill are the parties' procedural specialists. MPs generally turn out for votes in the House of Commons, and rules that allow the party whips to defer votes now mean votes are generally scheduled in the late afternoon on Monday, Tuesday, or Wednesday when it is easier for every MP to participate. The fact these rules have been implemented indicates how much these votes are valued by MPs themselves. Parliament, at least for those who work there, seems to be very much alive.

On the government side, many MPs – the party officers – work full-time to manage the government's business in the House: the government and deputy government House leader, the House leader's parliamentary secretary, the chief government whip, and several assistant whips. A smaller team of senators manage government business in the Upper House. All these officers have offices of parliamentary affairs staffers to support their work. The Prime Minister's Office and all other ministerial offices have parliamentary affairs staffers as well. Within the public service, the Privy Council Office has the Legislation and House Planning Secretariat. Most departments have a legislature affairs section or directorate too.

All these parliamentary affairs staffers ensure ministers and parliamentary secretaries are ready for Question Period and appearances before parliamentary committees. But their work extends beyond Question Period and committee testimony. Cabinet regularly monitors the status of government legislation in the House of Commons and the Senate. Ministers find they must devote their time and energy to getting their bills passed and spending estimates approved. That involves devising strategies and tactics to get their business through the House, the Senate, and their committees. Party officers meet daily with the opposition parties to see which parts of the government's legislative agenda can get through Parliament quickly. In the days leading up to the Christmas and summer parliamentary breaks, the party officers run back and forth between the opposition parties and the prime minister in a rush of negotiations over the fate of government bills. The objective of these

Figure 5.1: Sitting days of the House of Commons, 1968–2015

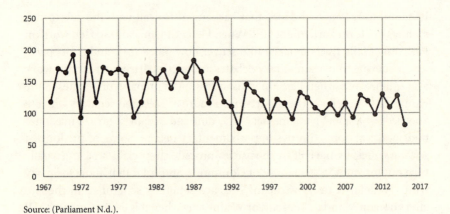

Source: (Parliament N.d.).

negotiations is an all-party agreement to let the House to rise early in exchange for all-party consent to waive some government bills through the House and get them off to the Senate. The Senate then typically sits a few days longer to pass those bills before senators rise for their break. Considering that most of this work goes on in public, it is astounding it attracts so little attention from journalists and scholars.

Moreover, if Parliament is dead – if all the key decisions are made within the executive – why does the executive bother investing so much time in managing its parliamentary agenda? After all, Parliament only sits when it is summoned into session by the executive branch. And Parliament only sits until it is prorogued or dissolved by the executive branch. If Parliament is a dignified rather than an efficient part of Canada's constitution, presumably a prime minister should summon it to meet only rarely and then only for a short time. After all, the Queen's Privy Council for Canada – a dignified institution created by the BNA Act – only gets summoned into session once every few decades. And summoning Parliament into session forces the government to prepare for the daily risks of Question Period.

One reason Parliament meets more frequently than the full Privy Council is the constitutional requirement that Parliament must sit at least once each year. The drafters of the British North America Act thought that annual sessions of Parliament were so important that section 20 of the BNA Act guaranteed them until 1982.[3] The drafters of the Charter of Rights and Freedoms thought that annual sessions were important enough to make it one of the Charter's democratic rights.[4] A prime minister who refused to summon Parliament for 366 days would be acting unconstitutionally. It is not quite clear how that democratic right would be enforced against a prime minister in that circumstance (Beaudoin 1982), but the issue is, and is likely to remain, moot. Parliament has always met more than once per year. Between 1968 and 2014, the House of Commons met an average of 131 days per calendar year – just over half the working days in a year (see figure 5.1). On almost every one of those days, the prime minister and Cabinet subjected themselves to Question Period. They gave the opposition parties free access to the news media and exposed themselves to all sorts of political risks. Why does the executive branch have Parliament meet so much and so often if Parliament is dead? Why not summon Parliament into session as little as possible?

What Cabinet Needs from Parliament ... and What Parliament Needs from Cabinet

The executive branch can make many decisions on its own, as we have seen in earlier chapters. Individual ministers can issue ministerial orders. Ministers acting together can issue Orders-in-Council. But if a prime minister and cabinet could only use ministerial orders and Orders-in-Council they would not be able to govern the country for long. The executive branch needs Parliament if it wants to make the wheels of government turn.

First, and most importantly, Parliament holds the power of the purse. The executive branch cannot raise taxes or spend public money without Parliament's approval. This ancient constitutional principle long predates the establishment of responsible government. Tax laws are massively complicated. They need to be amended and updated constantly. Spending authority requires constant replenishment as well. In a typical year, the government brings five appropriations bills to the House and the House votes on these bills on three separate occasions. From October 2013 to June 2015, the Harper government brought ten separate appropriations bills before the House (see table 5.1). In addition to this financial business, Cabinet needs Parliament's concurrence on other kinds of legislation. Some government bills grant authorities to ministers, Cabinet itself, and other government institutions. Some create offences and set penalties for committing those offences, or impose obligations on people, communities, corporations, or other organizations. Government bills also have to establish recourse for failing to meet those obligations. Since 1867, Cabinet has needed Parliament often enough that it has never failed to meet the requirement for an annual sitting. The courts have never had to sort out how to enforce the requirement, and likely never will.

When the executive needs to secure Parliament's approval for a decision, what impact does that have on the decision-making process? If something cannot be done by ministerial order or order-in-council – if it can only be done by legislation – what changes? These questions need a functional answer. When the executive branch needs legislation to make a decision, it expands the decision-making process beyond ministers to include two additional actors. The first is the governing party's own backbenchers – the members of the government caucus who do not sit in Cabinet. Cabinet must approve government legislation before it is tabled in Parliament, but the minister responsible for the legislation usually must also secure the approval of their caucus colleagues before the bill can be tabled. The second is the parliamentary opposition. Since 2003, the parliamentary opposition has included at least three parties in the House of Commons and often a handful of independent MPs, plus one party in the Senate, and a number of other senators.

Both of these actors – the government backbenchers and the opposition parties – want something in return for agreeing to transact the government's business, namely time. They both want time to consider and debate government bills. They will find some government bills agreeable and may decide to expedite them through the House if the government offers something in exchange. They will also find some government bills objectionable but, for strategic or tactical reasons, will decide to expedite them to avoid drawing attention to the government's efforts. And other government bills will be objectionable for reasons that make it worth dragging out parliamentary debate. When the opposition parties drag out debate, they slow down the government's progress and give themselves time to mobilize public opinion on the issue. Mobilizing parts of the voting public against parts of the executive's legislative agenda can, if done properly, build an opposition party's electoral support in the next election.

Government backbenchers and the opposition parties also want time in Parliament to raise other issues and concerns that are not on the executive's agenda. The executive's agenda never exhausts the number of federal issues that might be germane. For MPs, private members' bills, private members' motions, members' statements, adjournment proceedings (the "late show" held at the end of the parliamentary day in the House), Question Period, "take note" debates, emergency debates, and the debates in response to the Throne Speech and the annual budget are "free time."[5] MPs can raise almost any issue they wish during these parts of the House schedule. Some free time is more structured than others – take note debates and emergency debates are only held when the parties agree to hold them and speeches usually have

Table 5.1: Appropriations bills of the Forty-First Parliament, 2nd session, 16 October 2013–2 August 2015

Fiscal year	Appropriations Bill	Date adopted by House	Estimates	Value
2013/14	C-19	9 December 2013	Supp Est B	$5.4 billion
	C-28	24 March 2014	Supp Est C	$0.4 billion
2014/15	C-29	24 March 2014	Interim Supply	$24.8 billion
	C-38	10 June 2014	Main Estimates	$61.5 billion
	C-39	10 June 2014	Supp Est A	$2.5 billion
	C-45	3 December 2014	Supp Est B	$2.9 billion
	C-54	24 March 2015	Supp Est C	$1.8 billion
2015/16	C-55	24 March 2015	Interim Supply	$25.8 billion
	C-66	8 June 2015	Main Estimates	$62.4 billion
	C-67	8 June 2015	Supp Est A	$3.1 billion

to stick to the issue at hand, while adjournment proceedings, the Throne Speech, and budget debates are truly free time for MPs. Some free time gets more news coverage than others. Take note and emergency debates are held in the evening after most journalists have closed shop for the day, while member' statements are made in the valuable fifteen minutes before Question Period, when journalists and other viewers are tuning in.[6] But any time an MP raises an issue that might be interesting to voters back home on the floor of the House of Commons, that MP can get special print runs of Hansard to send to constituents. A capable MP will feature comments made on the floor of the House in the quarterly "householder" report that gets sent to every house in the riding. Something said in the House has a status that a local speech or media interview does not have.

Both government backbenchers and opposition MPs want time to debate government business and to raise these other issues, although for different reasons. Few government backbenchers are content to pass government legislation without an opportunity to make a speech on the issue, even if only to show their constituents that they play a role in the parliamentary process. Backbenchers also want to show they have their own agendas. The chance to make a member's statement is a chance to trumpet the achievement of a local school's sports team or the good work of a local community group, and these schools and groups are then usually happy to remind their parents and members that the local MP is paying attention to their achievements.

Government backbenchers highlight issues from back home during the government caucus's turn in Question Period. And every government backbencher has an issue that can be framed as a private member's bill, whether the prime minister and Cabinet are interested in that issue or not. In these respects, government backbenchers and opposition MPs have similar interests.

Challenges of Opposition

Opposition parties, although not necessarily individual opposition MPs, have an additional interest in using parliamentary debates strategically to oppose the government. If an opposition party leaders feels the party is vulnerable debating a piece of government legislation, the leader may decide to allow government legislation to pass without much debate. In 1983, soon after Brian Mulroney became PC leader, the Trudeau government introduced the Canada Health Act. The bill proposed outlawing extra billing for essential medical services by doctors and provincial governments. Mulroney later described Trudeau's move as throwing "the medicare grenade into our midst." (Mulroney 2007, 280). No doubt several PC MPs wanted to oppose this measure since it reached into provincial jurisdiction, solidified government control over health services, and would eliminate the most effective incentives for reducing demand on the healthcare system. But Mulroney did not want to be portrayed as an enemy of Canada's medicare system and forced his caucus to avoid what he saw as a political trap; or, as Mulroney puts it in his memoirs, "I reminded my [sic] members, most of whom were viscerally in favour of a free market, of the tough position the party was in" (ibid). There was no time to amend the Act before the next election. He told PC MPs to endorse the bill as is. "Then," he said, "when we become the government and we want to change something, we will."

In 2004, Stephen Harper did the same when he rushed to announce the new Conservative Party would agree to the first budget of the new Martin government even before Finance Minister Ralph Goodale had finished presenting the budget to the House. Several Conservative MPs, hearing the budget proposals for the first time, might have wanted to oppose the budget. But Harper wanted to focus his party's attack on the growing Sponsorship Scandal and decided to take the drama out of the budget debate. Martin's budget disappeared from the news headlines the next day. Note that in both these cases, Mulroney and Harper faced a majority government. There was no risk of either the Canada Health Act or the Martin budget failing in the

House. But both Mulroney and Harper decided to use the time of the House to focus the public's attention on other matters. Subsequently Mulroney went on to win a majority government and Harper reduced Martin to a minority government.

When facing a majority government, opposition MPs are free to oppose the government and its parliamentary agenda at every turn. The very structure of responsible government is liberating to opposition parties in that situation. By indulging their reflex to oppose, our system of government encourages opposition parties to engage in costless adversarialism, and although it is easy to be cynical about costless adversarialism no one would want to live under a regime that discouraged adversarialism in politics. But from 2004 to 2011, during the extended period of minority governments in the House, adversarialism was not costless; it had consequences for opposition parties. Minority government empowers opposition parties to topple the government and therefore constrains opposition parties at least as much as it constrains the government. The leader of an opposition party facing a minority government must carefully manage the level of adversarialism in that party. In a minority Parliament, an opposition party that falls into the "classic Opposition party mentality" where "everything is black and white" (Goldenberg 2006, 26) eventually has to explain why it allows the government to remain in power. In a minority parliament, those on both sides of the House must learn the discipline of power.

Measuring Parliament's Legislative Impact

So far, this chapter has offered some reasons to suggest that Parliament matters. Rigorous readers will want better evidence. One simple and surprising indicator of how much Parliament matters is to calculate the proportion of government bills that get through Parliament and to royal assent. This crude indicator is easy to calculate. How many government bills are introduced in each session of Parliament? How many of them are adopted by the House and the Senate and then assented to by the governor general?

If Parliament is truly dead, a majority government will simply ram its legislation through Parliament. Only the legislation of a minority government will face a risky ride on the Hill. But a moment's review of our crude indicator of legislative success shows this is not true. Figure 5.2 shows the rate at which government bills got royal assent in each session of Parliament since the thirty-sixth began in September 1997. The calculations exclude appropriations bills, which always pass, and bills introduced in the last two sitting weeks of

Figure 5.2: Fate of government legislation by Parliamentary session

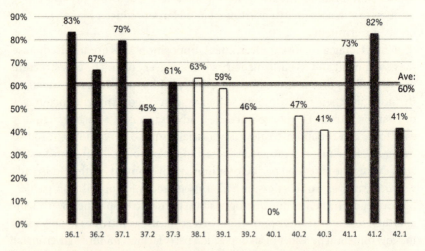

Note: Parliamentary sessions with majority government shown in black and sessions with minority government in white. The first session of the forty-second Parliament is based on calculations through the end of June 2017 and may therefore be unrepresentative.

Source: author's calculations based on (Clerks of the Senate and House of Commons and Library of Parliament N.d.); appropriations bills and bills introduced in the last two sitting weeks of a session are omitted.

a session, which are often tabled to permit consultations between sessions. It shows that only 60 percent of government legislation gets royal assent (and in sessions of Parliament that last longer than a few weeks, only about 70 percent of government bills gets royal assent). In other words, between one quarter and one third of government bills routinely die on the order paper when Parliament is prorogued or dissolved (Baker 2010). Majority governments get their legislation through Parliament more readily than minority governments, but the differences are not stark.

Cabinet, in other words, fails to get between one quarter and one third of its legislation enacted into law. A prime minister does not dictate government legislation to Parliament, even if the prime minister heads a majority government.

Admittedly, this is a crude measure of Parliament's impact. Not all government bills are created equal. Some propose major and pressing reforms to public policy or appropriate billions of dollars in spending. Others advance technical changes or amendments that are not time sensitive. But every government bill tabled in Parliament has some kind of rationale and an attentive public waiting for it to pass. Every government bill has a minister who wants it to pass. Every government bill has already passed through the hands of one or two Cabinet committees, been picked over by central agencies, and agreed to by the prime minister. If Parliament is a dead letter, if a prime minister heading a majority government can simply ram bills through Parliament without much effort, why do so many bills die on the order paper? Something is going on that has not attracted the attention of Savoie, the political science textbook authors, or most journalists? Parliament seems to be alive. And if Parliament has a blocking impact on a third of government bills, maybe it has an impact on the bills that pass.

The Battle for Time

The simple reason that so much government legislation dies on the order paper is the shortage of parliamentary time. Time is the most precious commodity that Parliament has. The executive can work on a multitude of tasks at once. Each chamber of Parliament can only work on one issue at a time. The chambers allocate that precious commodity in their procedural rules – the Rules of the Senate and the Standing Orders of the House of Commons. The Rules of the Senate and the Standing Orders have two purposes: they set the sitting hours of each chamber, and then they divide control over those hours between Cabinet and on the rest of the chamber.

Look at the Standing Orders of the House of Commons for the forty-first Parliament. In a normal week, the House would sit for about thirty-four hours. That time was divided up as shown in figure 5.3. Only about 65 percent of those thirty-four hours was allocated to government business – the time when Cabinet can conduct its business. The rest of the week's hours – members' statements, Question Period, or private members' business – were controlled by government backbenchers and the opposition parties. Moreover, under the Standing Orders governing the business of supply (in other words, the rules governing how the House deals with the spending estimates and appropriations bills), Cabinet must let the opposition parties determine what is to be debated on a certain number days each year. "Supply days" take place about one day per sitting week and government business is not transacted on those days. As table 5.2 shows, supply days take up about 20 percent of the House's sitting days. When supply days are added to the equation, only about half the sitting hours of the House are devoted to debating proposals from Cabinet.

Figure 5.3: Typical Parliamentary week

Hours	Monday	Tuesday	Wednesday	Thursday	Friday
10:00 – 11:00		routine proceedings		routine proceedings	government orders
11:00 – 11:15	private members' business	government orders		government orders	statements by members
11:15 – 12:00					oral questions
12:00 – 1:00	government orders				routine proceedings government orders
1:00 – 1:30					
1:30 – 2:00					private member's business
2:00 – 2:15	statements by members	statements by members	statements by members	statements by members	
2:15 – 2:30	oral questions	oral questions	oral questions	oral questions	
2:30 – 3:00					
3:00 – 5:30	routine proceedings government orders	government orders	routine proceedings government orders	government orders	
5:30 – 6:30		private members' business	private members' business	private members' business	
6:30 – 7:00	adjournment proceedings	adjournment proceedings	adjournment proceedings	adjournment proceedings	

Source: adapted by the author from O'Brien 2009.

Table 5.2: Supply days

Parliament and session	total sitting days	supply days	supply days per five sitting days
35.1	278	42	0.76
35.2	164	24	0.73
36.1	243	43	0.88
26.2	133	23	0.86
27.1	211	36	0.85
27.2	153	28	0.92
37.3	55	10	0.91
38.1	159	26	0.82
39.1	175	29	0.83
39.2	117	20	0.85
40.1	13	0	0.00
40.2	128	22	0.86
40.3	149	27	0.91
41.1	272	46	0.85
41.2	235	42	0.89
Total	2,485	418	0.84

Source: data kindly provided by the Office of the Clerk of the House of Commons.

Time Allocation

When a majority government has a bill that it decides it must pass, it can push the bill through the House using a procedure called time allocation. Time allocation has a long procedural history in the Standing Orders of the House of Commons (O'Brien 2009). In its current version, Cabinet can invoke time allocation unilaterally,[7] but using time allocation this way is time-consuming. Once the House has taken up a bill, at any given stage of debate, a minister may rise and give oral notice that the government intends to move time allocation. If no other party agrees to time allocation, a thirty-minute question-and-answer session follows. The minister may then move time allocation, at the earliest, at the next sitting of the House. The motion sets out how much time will be allocated to that stage of debate, but the minimum time is one sitting day. This process can be repeated at each stage of debate. If no amendments are adopted at the report stage, the government may move a single time allocation motion to cover both the report stage and the third reading. If the opposition digs in its heels at second reading, the government needs almost an entire parliamentary week to pass a bill with time allocation.

Using that much time to pass a government bill forces Cabinet to make difficult trade-offs in the rest of its legislative agenda. A government that legislates by time allocation limits the number of bills it can get through Parliament. A government that simply wants to maximize the number of bills it gets through Parliament will eventually reach a compromise with the opposition parties to allow expedited passage of some of its bills. But a government may not always want to maximize the number of bills it gets through Parliament. If it is in the government's political interests to polarize the House on an issue, it will usually avoid using time allocation. Giving the opposition parties time to mobilize also gives the governing party time to mobilize its supporters. In 1983, the Trudeau Liberals no doubt hoped to mobilize supporters of the Canada Health Act around their party with a long debate. This is precisely the dynamic that Mulroney was trying to avoid by having his caucus expedite the bill through the House.

In its last session of Parliament, the Harper government was criticized for resorting to time allocation on more than one hundred occasions. But it is not clear that this use of time allocation maximized the amount of government legislation that got through the House. Nor is it clear that it paid off politically for the Conservatives. Consider Bill C-51, the Harper government's anti-terrorism legislation. This bill was introduced shortly after the 22 October 2014 jihadist attack on the National War Memorial and Parliament Hill's main building, the Centre Block. The attacker was finally felled in a hail of bullets at the end of the Hall of Honour, Centre Block's main corridor, just as the Conservative and NDP caucuses were meeting in committee rooms that open onto the Hall of Honour. MPs and senators, including Cabinet ministers, were held for hours while security forces searched Centre Block for other threats. The attack revealed serious and long-standing holes in the security arrangements for Parliament Hill and left a heavy mark on everyone in the building that day.

Bill C-51 had been in the works before the attack. It was originally intended to fix gaps in Canada's national security legislation identified by two commissions of inquiry and several court decisions. When the bill was tabled on 30 January 2015, it not only closed these gaps but also proposed to create a criminal offence, advocating terrorism. While parliamentarians, successive governments, and others had long debated how to introduce a measure of parliamentary oversight of Canada's national security and intelligence agencies, Bill C-51 was notably silent on the topic. With civil liberties and other groups feeding on the revelations of Edward Snowden and the prospect of a federal election in a few months, the government knew its bill would face controversy.

The Harper government decided to pass the bill at all stages using time allocation. While the public will never know what kind of negotiations went on between the parties over Bill C-51, they must have been difficult. The NDP leapt to oppose Bill C-51 on traditional civil liberties grounds, attacking the government for overreacting to the attack on Parliament Hill. NDP leader Thomas Mulcair even refused to call the incident a "terrorist attack," a term Harper began using in the immediate aftermath of the event. After an internal party debate, Liberal leader Justin Trudeau decided his party would support the bill but promised to amend it if elected. This was an effort to take the middle ground between the polarizing positions of the government and the NDP.

The legislative history of the bill was short. Introduced and given first reading on 30 January 2015, the bill was called for debate at second reading three weeks later on 18 February. The government immediately gave notice of a time-allocation motion and scheduled two further days of second reading debate on 19 and 23 February. The bill was referred to the House Committee on Public Safety and National Security. That Committee held ten days of hearings in March and reported the bill back to the House, with amendments, on 2 April. The government then slated the bill for report-stage debate on 24 April and 4 May, giving notice of time allocation on 24 April. Bill C-51 was debated at third reading on 5 May and passed using time allocation on 6 May. In all, the government devoted seven days of floor time and ten sittings of committee time to the bill. In addition, the Senate's Committee on National Security and Defence devoted five meetings to a "pre-study" of the bill in March and April. Bill C-51 eventually passed the Senate and was given royal assent before Parliament was dissolved for the 2015 general election. Given how much time the Conservatives devoted to issues of national security in that election, it is not clear why they thought it was a good idea to pass Bill C-51 with time allocation. A longer debate might have served their political interests by giving them time to mobilize public support for the legislation. Maybe they were worried that, with the NDP rising in the public opinion polls that spring at the expense of the Liberals, the NDP would use a longer debate to polarize the electorate and peel more swing voters away from the Liberals. Given the level of Conservative support at that stage, the government's only hope for re-election was to push Liberal-NDP swing voters into the Liberal camp. The Conservatives could also have debated the bill, mobilized public support, and left Bill C-51 to die on the order paper. This would have let them turn the election into a referendum on the legislation. They tried to do precisely that with Bill C-53, The Life Means Life Act, which proposed to end the eligibility for parole from some Criminal Code offences that carry a sentence of life imprisonment. The bill was called for two days of debate at second reading in the last few days the House sat before the election but never came to a vote. Perhaps the Conservatives were worried that the Liberals' difficult position on the bill would lead to a collapse in Liberal support during the campaign.

Regardless of the electoral calculations around Bill C-51, using time allocation meant using seven days of the precious sitting time of the House of Commons to ensure it was passed before the election. With the Liberals winning a majority government in the subsequent election, Trudeau is now free to make whatever amendments he wishes to make on whatever political schedule he finds convenient. Given that an election was in the offing when Bill C-51 was being debated, it is possible that any other government legislation would have had an easier ride through the House. But the Harper government chose to give up seven days of House time to the bill, a decision that meant giving up seven days of parliamentary attention to another issue.

Trudeau's government made a remarkable effort to upset the balance of forces in the battle for time and the use of time allocation in May 2016. The so-called Motion #6, put down on the Notice Paper by House Leader Dominic LeBlanc on 17 May, would have given Cabinet control over how many days the forty-second Parliament sat that spring and how late into the night each day's sitting lasted (House of Commons 2016). It would have blocked the opposition parties from using several tools otherwise at their disposal for chewing up the time of the House of Commons to block the progress of government bills. While it is normal for the government house leader to negotiate the accelerated consideration of government bills in June each year, Motion #6 would have set a new precedent in unilateral government changes to the procedural rules of the House and deprived the opposition of its only tool for derailing the legislation of a majority government. If Motion #6 had been adopted, the government would have been able to get its legislation through the House without any of the trade-offs involved in using time allocation. Instead, the Trudeau government could have simply forced the House to extend its sitting hours and shut down the opposition's procedural options. Motion #6 was withdrawn shortly after it was introduced when Trudeau was involved in a physical altercation on the floor of the House.

The efforts of the Trudeau government to change the Standing Orders did not end with Motion #6, however. A year later, the government published a discussion paper on changes to the rules of the House of Commons and tried to restart negotiations with the opposition parties (Office of the Government

House Leader 2017). The discussion paper raised the possibility of shorter time limits on speeches in the House, shortening the time taken up by voting in the House through the use of electronic voting technology, limits on debate in the House committees, reducing the prime minister's appearance in Question Period to once per week, and eliminating Friday sittings of the House by extending sitting hours on the other days of the week. Taken together, the options floated in the discussion paper would certainly have improved the efficiency of the House as measured by the amount of government legislation that could be passed, but they would have stripped the opposition of its most valuable means of dragging out debate and forcing Cabinet to make decisions about which bills it really needed. After the opposition parties joined forces to delay the negotiations the government lost patience with the matter and dropped most of the proposals. The Trudeau government will have to rely on time allocation and take into consideration the trade-offs involved (Chagger 2017).

Parliament's Legislative Agenda

The House of Commons spends most of its time debating the executive branch's legislative agenda; as we have seen, this is a real, not just a symbolic, function. Opposition parties use procedural tools to influence which items from the executive's agenda get expedited to royal assent or delayed long enough that they die on the order paper. Certainly, the executive can use time allocation to push some of its bills get through the House, but it pays a price in doing so with the rest of its agenda. In short, the House is a real legislative institution. It is an efficient institution, in Bagehot's sense. The House does make key legislative decisions. It does not simply pass the government's legislative agenda automatically and intact.

Moreover, there is more to the House's legislative role than debating the executive's legislative agenda. The argument that Westminster parliaments "do not initiate legislation; rather they pass or defeat legislation that originates with the cabinet" (Docherty 2005, 19) is overstated. Private members (that is MPs who are not Cabinet ministers or presiding officers) also introduce their own legislative proposals. Private members' bills, like government bills, can propose new laws or amendments to existing laws. Private members' motions are more flexible. They can ask the House to express a view on an issue or order an officer of Parliament, a member, or committee of the House to take some kind of action. Some private members' business tackles uncontroversial and ceremonial issues. They name particular days after worthy people or causes, establish national animals, or rename a member's electoral district after redistribution. In other cases, private members' business can have a more substantial impact on public policy. These latter items of business influence the relationship between the executive and legislative branches. These proposals pass more often that observers generally acknowledge.

The history of private members' business in the House is enough to end the idea that backbench MPs played more important roles during some long lost golden era of parliamentarianism (Chong 2017, 11). Since the mid-1980s, the House has taken many steps to make it easier for private members' business to be debated and be voted upon. Procedural reforms undertaken since 2000 have produced a blossoming of private members' business. These reforms indicated how much importance MPs place on private members' business, regardless of which party forms the government. We are probably living in the golden era of Parliament right now. Backbench government MPs and opposition members now have broad opportunities to influence public policy independently of the executive's legislative agenda. The separation of powers and checks and balances between the executive branch and the House of Commons has probably never been this vigorous.

A Short History

Since Confederation, private members' business has given MPs an opportunity to devise their own legislative agendas. Until 1962, private members' business took precedence over government business on certain days of the week. Since 1962, the House has taken up private members' business for one hour on most sitting days. House records show, however, that the Standing Orders regulating private members' business have changed many since 1867, especially in the last thirty years.

From 1867 until 1962, the Standing Orders of the House of Commons gave priority to private members' business on certain days of the week. However, during these years the House kept reducing the amount of time it actually devoted to private members as successive governments found the remaining days of the week were "inadequate for the passage of their own legislative programs." Starting in 1906 and for nearly five decades thereafter, "virtually all the time remaining for private Members" (Robertson 2005, 2) was turned over to the government legislation through special and sessional order. This left government backbenchers and opposition MPs with little time to develop their own legislation. In 1955 the House made an effort to ensure eight days in each annual House session would be reserved to private members' business, but even those eight days proved to be too burdensome on the government's agenda. In 1962, the House abolished private members' days altogether and moved to the current system of reserving one hour to private members' time each sitting day. Even so, after forty hours in a parliamentary session, private members' time was reduced to a single hour on only three days per week. Eventually, private members' time was capped at forty hours per year.

The trend for government legislation to squeeze out private members' time would not change until the Mulroney government took office. Two House committees, the Lefebvre and McGrath Committees, spent three years reviewing the role of the House of Commons and the place of the private member. The final report of the McGrath Committee proposed a number of reforms to the House with three objectives: "to restore to private members an effective legislative function, to give them a role in the formation of public policy, and in so doing, to restore the House of Commons to its rightful place in the Canadian political process" (McGrath 1985, 1). On the balance between government legislation and private members' business in the House, McGrath's report was blunt: "The House does not attach any great importance to private members' business as it is now organized." It noted that few MPs took advantage of the opportunity to propose or debate private members' legislation, "and this is largely because private members' bills and motions rarely come to a vote" (40).

In the wake of the McGrath Report, the House adopted several reforms to expand the opportunity for private members' bills and motions. The first reforms came in 1986. That year, the House decided to focus the time set aside for members' business on only a few items at a time. These items, referred to as the "order of precedence," were selected every few months at random from bills and motions submitted by government backbenchers and opposition MPs. In addition, the House decided that six (and later ten) items from the order of precedence would be guaranteed an up or down vote after they had received five hours of debate. Finally, the House took steps to protect the daily hour of private members' time against encroachment by government legislation. In 1990, the House made a further decision to shorten the amount of debate before an item of private members' business automatically came to a vote from five hours to three. The House also changed the draw for the order of precedence so that members' names rather than individual bills and motions were drawn, giving MPs more control over which of their legislative proposals was debated in the House. In 1994, the House removed a "major constraint" on private members' legislation (Robertson 2005) when it relaxed the money bill rule and allow a bill to be debated, although not passed, if it involved spending money or raising taxes. Finally, in 1998, the Standing Orders were amended so that, after Parliament was prorogued, items on the order of precedence would be reinstated to the stage they had been at the end of the previous parliamentary session.

Another major round of reforms designed to expand the opportunities for private members' business began in 2002. An insurrection in the government caucus had forced Prime Minister Chrétien to commit to a retirement date. During his remaining months in office he pressed ahead with a major overhaul of political finance law that was profoundly unpopular in his own caucus (Goldenberg 2006, 383). By February 2003, further reforms to private members' business became urgent "as the opposition parties were engaged in various delaying tactics in the House to pressure the Government" into addressing the matter (Robertson 2005). With both the government backbenches and the opposition in revolt, the Chrétien government agreed to more changes in the rules governing private members' business. The Standing Orders were amended to guarantee each private member one opportunity every four years (the life of a majority parliament) to have a bill or motion voted upon by members, and to reduce the length of debate on those items from three hours to just two.

Finally, the money bill rule was further loosened in a speaker's ruling of September 2006. Following the election of the Harper government earlier that year, Liberal MP Pablo Rodriguez had introduced Bill C-288, a proposal to force the new Harper government to "fully" implement the Kyoto Accord. The estimated price tag for this move was $10 billion. A year earlier, a speaker's ruling had taken the cautious view of private members' business and the money rule: "Where it is clear that the legislative objective of a bill cannot be accomplished without the dedication of public funds … the bill must be seen as the equivalent of a bill effecting an appropriation."[8] But on Bill C-288 the speaker ruled that a private member's bill could commit the government to "objectives" if it was vague about the means of achieving that objective and still respect the money bill rule.

Stepping back from the precise details of each reform, the trend of reform over the course of more than forty years is clear. Whereas once, private members' bills were rarely successful, now most private members have an opportunity to get a bill voted upon before they have to face re-election. The House made news in 1964 by adopting rookie Quebec MP Jean Chrétien's private member's bill to change the name of Trans-Canada Airlines to Air Canada. But over the past ten years, private members have passed dozens of private members' bills (see figure 5.4). Since 1984, even in the face of strong party discipline on government bills, private members' have had more and more leeway to formulate and advance their own legislative agendas. By 2015,

Figure 5.4: Successful private members bill by Parliament

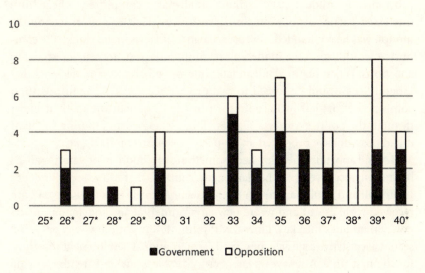

Note: * denotes minority government.

no one could report, as McGrath did, that members did not "attach any great importance to private members' business."

Private Members' Business and the Government Agenda

The new rules on private members' business have let backbench government MPs and opposition MPs challenge and, in at least one case, disrupted the sitting prime minister's political priorities. In 2012, Conservative backbencher Stephen Woodworth used his turn in the order of precedence to challenge Harper's election promise not to reopen the issue of access to abortion. Woodworth was cautious in approach. His private member's motion proposed striking a special committee of the House to reconsider the Criminal Code's declaration that a child becomes a human being when it has "completely proceeded, in a living state, from the body of its mother."[9] Harper declared he would oppose the motion, and Gordon O'Connor, the chief government whip, argued against the motion in public (Fitzpatrick 2012). The issue must have been a difficult one behind the closed doors of caucus. Some government MPs voted with Harper and almost all the opposition MPs to defeat Woodworth's motion. His motion garnered the support of eighty-six Conservative MPs, including eight of Harper's Cabinet colleagues and two of his ministers of state. Two pro-life ministers were absent. Considering that the motion was substantively milquetoast – striking an all-party committee to hear from interested parties is not a draconian measure – Harper's effort to stop the motion was heavy-handed. Given the balance of views in the House, the committee would not have made any recommendations to restrict access to abortions. When Justin Trudeau later one-upped Harper and declared that Liberal MPs would be forced to cast pro-choice votes in the future, their combined effort left little room for pro-life Canadians to air their views through the political process (Payton 2014). Woodworth's motion might, if it had passed, have produced an all-party consensus on the issue.

Beyond abortion, there has been something of a boom in private member's business in recent years. In the Harper government's first two years, Rodriguez's Kyoto bill and Paul Martin's on the Kelowna Accord (Bills C-288, 292) both received royal assent and wrote new environmental and indigenous affairs policy mandates into law. Liberal MP John McKay got Bill C-293 passed; it set out a legislative mandate for Canada's international development programs for the first time. A few years later, NDP MP Alexandrine Latendresse's bill passed, mandating bilingualism for appointees to certain high profile federal offices. Joy Smith, a Conservative, successfully piloted two bills on human trafficking through to royal assent; opposition MP Maria Mourani added a third. Larry Miller used his turn on the order of precedence to enact a legislative ban on bulk water exports. When Brian Storseth's turn came, he successfully had a provision of the Canadian Human Rights Act that restricted freedom of expression removed from the law books (C-304). Russ Hiebert had a bill passed to impose certain transparency requirements on labour unions.

In 2008, by the time the Harper government was re-elected, it was becoming clear that, in some cases, contentious private members' bills were easier to get through the House than contentious government bills, provided a majority of members supported them. Since a private member's bill was guaranteed a vote after only two hours of debate, private member's bills could speed through the House faster than a government bill could even with the use of time allocation. After Harper won a majority in the 2011 election, the forty-first Parliament saw a massive increase in the number of successful private members' bills – thirty-one in total, including twenty-seven bills proposed by government backbenchers and four by opposition MPs. Given the huge increase in the number of successful private members' bills from the government benches, an observer might be tempted to suggest that the Harper government was using private members' time to advance parts of the government agenda. But twelve of those Conservative bills amended criminal justice legislation and were referred either to the Justice or Public

Safety Committees. The time those committees spent dealing with those bills came at the expense of the government's own substantial agenda of criminal justice bills. During my time in Ottawa, I regularly witnessed the Government House Leader pleading with government backbenchers not to introduce justice-related private members' business so as to keep the Justice Committee focused on the government's justice bills. It seems more likely that as complaints from the Conservative caucus about the amount of control being exercised by "the boys in short pants" from the Prime Minister's Office leaked into news reporting, the prime minister and his Cabinet colleagues had to acquiesce by giving government backbenchers more leeway with their own legislative agendas. Nonetheless, the now speedy procedure for handling private members' bills has raised questions about whether the wide opportunities it opens up provide enough time for deliberation by MPs.[10]

Forty years ago, a textbook could claim that Parliament's legislative function was "purely formal" and that "everyone knows that laws are drafted and decided on within the executive" (Mallory 1984, 270), but that is certainly no longer the case today. The reform movement that began with the Lefebvre and McGrath committees has borne fruit. Private members, for the first time since Confederation, can not only propose their own bills, they can get see them enacted into law. The government's legislative agenda predominates, but Parliament can and does develop its own legislative agenda. McGrath got his wish. Private members now exercise an independent and often effective legislative function. They have a distinct role in the formation of public policy. And that has gone a long way toward restoring the House of Commons to its rightful place in the Canadian political process

Restoring the Power of the Purse

The McGrath Report inspired a generation of parliamentarians to invigorate the legislative role of the House. Private members can now each draft one bill every four years and have it voted. They play a bigger legislative role than ever before in Canada's history. In the last parliamentary session of the Harper ministry, a record number of private members' bills were piloted through Parliament. It is hard to imagine that record legislative output being bettered. In fact, the Trudeau government has already said it will repeal some of those bills. The tide might already be turning against McGrath's legacy. The next step to invigorate the House will need to go beyond its legislative role. Chong's Reform Act aimed at the wrong target. Laws cannot change the balance of power within parties. Instead, the next step to invigorate the House should focus on the power of the purse.

Table 5.3: Private members' bills passed, forty-first Parliament, second session

Bill	Subject	Government or Opposition sponsor	Committee	Reinstated from
C-462	Disability Tax Credit Promoters Restrictions Act	Government	Finance	41st 1st
C-217	Criminal Code (mischief relating to war memorials)	Government	Justice	41st 1st 40th 3rd
C-444	Criminal Code (personating peace officer or public officer)	Government	Justice	41st 1st 40th 3rd
C-394	Criminal Code (criminal organization recruitment)	Government	Justice	41st 1st
C-489	Criminal Code and the Corrections and Conditional Release Act (restrictions on offenders)	Government	Justice	41st 1st
C-501	National Hunting, Trapping and Fishing Heritage Day	Government	Heritage	41st 1st 40th 3rd 40th 2nd
C-483	Corrections and Conditional Release Act (escorted temporary absence)	Government	Public Safety	41st 1st
C-442	An Act respecting a Federal Framework on Lyme Disease	Opposition	Health	41st 1st
C-428	Indian Act (publication of by-laws) and to provide for its replacement	Government Affairs	Aboriginal and Northern Development	41st 1st
C-525	Canada Labour Code and other Acts (certification and revocation – bargaining agent)	Government	Human Resources	41st 1st
C-266	Pope John Paul II Day	Government	Heritage	41st 1st
C-479	Corrections and Conditional Release Act (fairness for victims)	Government	Public Safety	41st 1st

C-247	Main point of contact – death of a Canadian citizen or resident	Opposition	Human Resources	41st 1st 40th 3rd
C-452	Criminal Code (exploitation and trafficking in persons)	Opposition	Justice	41st 1st 40th 3rd
C-591	Canada Pension Plan and the Old Age Security Act (pension and benefits)	Government	Human Resources	
C-555	Marine Mammal Regulations (seal fishery observation licence)	Government	Fisheries	41st 1st 40th 3rd
C-627	Railway Safety Act (safety of persons and property)	Government	Transport	
C-586	Reform Act	Government	Procedure and House Affairs	
C-377	Income Tax Act (requirements for labour organizations)	Government	Finance	41st 1st

Source: LegisInfo data at http://parl.gc.ca.

The power of the purse is an ancient one in our system of government. The English kings needed Parliament's consent to taxes long before they needed it to enact laws. The earliest colonial legislatures in North America had the same right to grant taxes to colonial governors. Responsible government was instituted in Canada in part to tame the legislature's power of the purse. Durham recommended both responsible government and the money bill rule, envisioning a separation of powers over fiscal policy and a potential for checks and balances. Only Cabinet can propose to increase taxes. It must secure Parliament's consent. And only Cabinet may propose expenditures. It must likewise secure Parliament's consent. The literature on parliamentary procedure is full of grand claims about the House's power to grant spending authority, or "supply." Standing Order 80 of the House of Commons declares that:

All aids and supplies granted … by the Parliament of Canada are the sole gift of the House of Commons … [I]t is the undoubted right of the House to direct, limit, and appoint in all such bills, the ends, purposes, considerations, conditions, limitations and qualifications of such grants …

Furthermore, as the main procedural manual of the House puts it, "The direct control of national finance, has been referred to as the 'great task of modern parliamentary government'" (O'Brien and Bosc 2009: chapter 18, quoting Redlich 1969 [1908], 160). But parliamentary reality has fallen short of Durham's ideal. The sharp declaration in Standing Order 80 does not describe parliamentary practice. Approval of the government's fiscal plans is a confidence matter. Government MPs are obliged to support its tax and spending plans. When facing a majority government, opposition parties are free to oppose them, but when facing a minority government even the opposition must make way for the its fiscal plan or risk an election. The business of supply, the part of the House agenda where Cabinet asks for Parliament's approval to appropriate and spend public money, is a parliamentary afterthought. If supply is a "gift" of the House, it is Parliament's version of giving an iron on a wedding anniversary.

As we saw earlier, the Cabinet presents its spending plans in three requests each year. The "spending estimates" for each department are referred to a standing committee of the House. The committee can decide to do nothing. In that case, the estimates are "deemed reported" to the House on a certain date. The committee can also decide to scrutinize the estimates. It can call the minister and departmental officials to answer questions. In theory, it can reduce or reject the estimates, but if the House agrees with the Committee the fate of the government is in peril. So, in practice, Cabinet's spending estimates are approved by committees and the House without amendment. Given the inevitable outcome, busy MPs do not spend much time on the estimates. Committees rarely devote more than one two-hour meeting to the job each year.

Parliament's bit role in the business of supply is no secret. Jack Stilborn, a long-time Library of Parliament analyst, puts it this way: "Dissatisfaction among parliamentarians with the form and substance of Parliament's role concerning the estimates dates back virtually to Confederation" (Stilborn 2006–07, 7). Robert Marleau, a former clerk of the House, has argued that the Commons has "almost abandoned its constitutional responsibility of supply" (quoted in Savoie 2013, 39). Savoie lambastes Parliament's work on the estimates in his only lengthy treatment of Parliament (2013, chapter 2). But Savoie implies that there was a "golden age" of parliamentary scrutiny of the estimates in the past. This is not correct. Parliament's control of public finances was slipshod before 1867. The United Province of Canada did not have a way to ensure public spending was authorized by Parliament until 1864. Until then, Parliament often passed appropriation bills after a fiscal year had ended (Ward 1962a, chapter 2). In the early years of Confederation,

Canadian government departments often circumvented the power of the purse. They either borrowed from commercial banks or relied on governor general's warrants and reported to Parliament afterward (Stilborn 2006–07, 22). When these problems were resolved, parliamentary debates on appropriations were neither cool nor rational. The estimates were usually debated by the whole House sitting as the Committee on Supply. Committee procedures were usually chaotic. MPs hardly debated the estimates themselves. Instead, they raised questions about scandals and partisan missteps until, at the last minute, just before the government's spending authority expired, they approved the estimates in a flurry of debate. When government spending plans were simple, MPs could question ministers on the line items in the estimates. But as the reach of government and the scale of public spending expanded in the 1950s and early 1960s, the estimates process did little to satisfy anyone.

Dissatisfaction with Parliament's performance finally drove MPs to reform the business of supply in the 1960s. In 1968, the House adopted three reforms that persist to this day. First, the House moved the scrutiny of the estimates to its standing committees. Committees, it was hoped, would provide deeper oversight of spending and give the House more time to debate legislation (Stilborn 2006–07). Secondly, to avoid last-minute appropriations votes, the House adopted the "deemed reported" rule. Appropriations would be approved on a predictable schedule. Finally, the House gave twenty-five sitting days each year – supply days – to the opposition parties so they could pick the subject of debate. In 2001, a further reform let the Opposition Leader pick two departments whose main estimates would be reviewed by Committee of the Whole during evening sittings. Together, these reforms gave the opposition more control over the Commons' agenda and reduced the time available for government business. In exchange, Cabinet got an assurance that the House would approve the spending estimates on a predictable schedule.

Committee scrutiny of the estimates never lived up to these hopes. One problem was the quantity and quality of information sent to Parliament. MPs complained that the estimates were difficult to understand. Any outsider who has ever tried to work with the estimates would be quick to sympathize. Savoie relates the story of Shawn Murphy, the former chair of the House Public Accounts Committee, urging Treasury Board officials to insert blank pages into their documents to see if MPs would notice. The financial reports tabled in Parliament, Murphy complained, were "too complex, too voluminous, and too convoluted to be of any use either to parliamentarians or to anyone else" (Savoie 2013, 37). In the mid-1990s, the Improving Reporting to Parliament Project tried to improve the quality of information available to the House. The estimates and other documents moved away from "primarily quantitative outputs (cases heard, brochures issued, etc.)." Instead, departments began reporting "higher-level outcomes that show how departmental activities make a difference to citizens" (Stilborn 2006–07, 23). Departments also produced two new reports: the annual Report on Plans and Priorities (RPP) sets out future goals and plans; the annual Departmental Performance Report outlines progress against past goals and plans. But, if these reports are measured against the standard that government financial reporting "must be intelligible to the layman who sits in Parliament" (Ward 1962, 22), they have largely failed. Parliamentarians still say that these reports are "excessively bureaucratic, and especially vague about areas where performance has fallen short" (Stilborn 2006–07, 24). Committee members, it must be said, "have yet to exploit their powers to foster improvements" in financial reporting.

Savoie claims there is now "broad agreement" that these reforms "made things worse" (2013, 45). There is good reason to be dissatisfied with how committees handle the estimates. In the 2000s, according to Stilborn, committee hearings on the "involve[d] wide-ranging and relatively partisan exchanges over political priorities and the policy directions of departments, minimal attention to the substance of the estimates, scattered and unsystematic questioning … [and] predictable votes in support of the estimates as proposed by the Government" (2006–07, 24). Yet, today's opposition parties would never agree to undo the 1968 reforms. Giving up supply days in favour of more debate on government legislation and no additional influence over government spending makes for an unattractive exchange. Parliamentary scrutiny of the estimates might not have improved, but the reforms give the opposition more control over the parliamentary calendar and allow committees to decide whether to put their scarce time into scrutinizing legislation or the estimates.

Since the mid-1990s, the business of supply has been studied many times. In 2002, the Institute for Research on Public Policy reviewed the matter and listed many ways Parliament could improve, especially in assessing program performance. The Gomery Commission recommended increasing staff support for committees and better efforts to relate estimates to individual programs, seemingly with the hope that better parliamentary scrutiny could head off future scandals like the Sponsorship Program. The House created a separate Committee on Government Operations and Estimates to serve as a permanent forum for reflecting on the business of supply. The Committee has issued several comprehensive reports. Many of these studies have harshly criticized the "deemed reported" rule. Some studies have criticized the structure of the estimates and the fact that the estimates, the annual budget, and the annual public accounts are impossible to reconcile. Yet, even with a mounting collection of studies and proposals, the House has yet to force reforms to the business of supply that could match the comprehensive reform private members' business that followed the McGrath Report.

Savoie sees many reasons to be hopeless about the estimates. Proper scrutiny is time-consuming for MPs. It might lead to MPs raising awkward questions about ministerial performance. Under the confidence convention, MPs cannot change to the estimates without imperiling the fate of the government (2013, 43). Parliamentary committees, he writes, are like the full House of Commons; they operate in a "highly partisan environment. Scoring political points matters more than having reasoned debates about public policy" (52). But Stilborn warns that invigorating the power of the purse cannot depend on a "bureaucratic-rational conception of the role of the Parliament that remains largely detached from the real world of politics" (2006–07, 27). Parliament is a partisan institution. Parliament's committees will not usually escape Parliament's partisanship. If we hold the scrutiny of the estimates to the standard of "reasoned debates about public policy" we are bound to be disappointed. If the McGrath Committee had held itself to that standard it would not have made any progress at all.

Parliament Is Back

As Tom Hockin, a political scientist with experience in Cabinet, put it more than thirty-five years ago:

> Complaints about the "decline of Parliament" seldom identify that historical moment, that state of grace and perfection from which decline has occurred. It is difficult to trace a fall from grace if a parliamentary Garden of Eden is not identified. (1979, 8)

Notwithstanding frustrations about Parliament's scrutiny of the estimates, Parliament matters, and Canadians are ill-served by those who continue to assert that it does not. Parliamentary debates may not all be terribly interesting to watch, but Parliament's ability to delay legislation is a strategic tool for the opposition parties and forces the Cabinet to make difficult decisions about legislative priorities. Parliament sits a lot, and MPs on both sides of the House expend an enormous effort to gain maximum political and policy advantages out of that time. Caucus meetings matter, and I regret that so few Canadians get to witness their deliberations. Securing the unity of the party caucus in parliamentary votes is a central concern of party leaders. In the wake of the McGrath report, parliamentarians can and do develop their own legislative priorities. The confirmation bias that Canadians have applied to the argument that the prime minister is all-powerful blinds us to the dynamics of these developments. If Parliament matters, maybe Cabinet actually matters, too.

6

Managing a Government Agenda

Cabinet is at the head of the government, and Cabinet is composed of a prime minister and Cabinet ministers. "Cabinet minister" is a double-barrelled title. It speaks to the two roles Cabinet ministers play. "Cabinet" is an institution of government, like Parliament or the Supreme Court. It is a decision-making body with powers set out in legislation and the Constitution of Canada. A political science textbook may have a diagram or organization chart with a box labelled "Cabinet." "Ministers" are individuals. They share some traits. They (usually) hold a seat in Parliament, and most have been elected to the House of Commons. They are usually from the same political party. They all have the confidence of the prime minister. Yet, despite these similarities, each Cabinet minister has a personality and a unique point of view. Each minister has a set of life experiences and a set of political concerns or priorities that motivated them to enter politics. Some are long-time partisans with years of political experience. Their points of view are enriched (or limited) by long service in the political trenches. Others have short political resumés but are accomplished in other walks of life. A few are young enough to be new to responsibility of any kind. There are ministers with highly sophisticated views of the role of government, and others with a more basic understanding. Some are used to working as part of a team. Others are not.

When ministers form a Cabinet, do they become ciphers who buckle under to the power of the prime minister and a few prime ministerial courtiers? Well, most of them follow the prime minister's lead most of the time. That, after all, is what makes Cabinet government function. But we should be careful not to assume that ministers suddenly become marionettes when they join Cabinet. The personalities and experiences they bring to the Cabinet table give them their own views and their own abilities. The ones who sit in the House of Commons have been elected to Parliament by voters back home. If they represent swing ridings – constituencies that regularly change hands from one party to another – the very fact that they got elected means they probably have some political smarts and personal toughness. If they represent safe ridings, they probably won a highly competitive race for their party's local nomination. That kind of race requires stamina, will, and an ability to motivate hundreds of people to turn out to support you at a nomination meeting. The senators in Cabinet hold secure seats until they turn seventy-five, better protection than a tenured university professor has. Cabinet ministers are not pushovers. They are tough, smart people. Moreover, they hold their primary positions – in the House of Commons or the Senate – regardless of the prime minister's view of their abilities. MPs are not hired or fired by the prime minister. They are selected by voters back home in their ridings. Senators, once appointed, cannot be fired by the prime minister. Cabinet ministers therefore have to be handled in a more collegial way than the Savoie thesis would suggest.

A government must be about more than the sum of the ministerial priorities and local concerns of Cabinet ministers. Local concerns matter, and a government must attend to them, but even the most parochial citizens know that the country is bigger than their county. Even the most entrenched special interests realize, even if only dimly, that the success of their interest depends on the broader success of the country. The rent-seeker must have rents to seek and will sense when those rents are in peril because of government inattention. If a prime minister or Cabinet minister comes to a local chamber of commerce lunch and only speaks about the local road that have been paved or number of CPP and OAS cheques that were mailed to the town that month, local voters usually feel cheated and may even be alarmed that the government does not have a broader grasp of the country's political situation. Cabinet ministers who speak to the annual meeting of the most diligent, focused, and successful special interest – say, dairy farmers, or chartered bank executives – will find the audience shocked if they only extol the government's defence of their interests in international trade negotiations or trumpet some regulatory change to the compositional standards for cheese that secures their preferential access to the domestic market. After all, the livelihoods of dairy farmers and bank executives depend not only on the preferences they get from government but on the continued success of the country and its domestic market. They want to know: what the government is doing to ensure the success of our country into the future? How strong will our market be tomorrow? While protecting my domestic preferential access, has the government secured free access to other markets for, say, Canadian grains or lentils? Yes, you are protecting my privileged position as a deposit taker in Canada, but have you have helped my friend in the insurance business gain access to emerging markets? Citizens wants their interests protected, but every citizen no matter how strong their own interest, also has enough pride to want the country well governed.

Democracy means a government only remains in office if it is able to secure the consent of the citizens for its work. And a government must be able to satisfy the broader concerns of the citizenry in order to earn that consent. Citizens want to hear about more than the hundreds or thousands of ministerial priorities being pursued in their names. Speaking to those broader concerns is the role of the government agenda. A government – any government – has to strive to do more than just pursuing the priorities of two- or three-dozen ministers and their departments. This turns out to be a challenge, and to understand why we first have to understand that Cabinet ministers have dual roles.

Cabinet Minister: The Dual Role

SIR HUMPHREY: Prime Minister, can't you persuade the Chancellor? He's your cabinet colleague, after all.
HACKER: That's the point. I need help from someone who is on *my* side.
– "The Smoke Screen," an episode of *Yes, Prime Minister* (BBC)

A minister (short for "minister of the crown") is, formally, an individual invited to advise the Crown on the exercise of its official powers. Some ministers are made heads of a department. So, the minister of finance is head of the Department of Finance and the minister of justice head of the Department of Justice. Each minister who heads a department has a deputy minister and, under them, a department of public servants to support their work. Other ministers who are not strictly speaking heads of departments, like the minister for trade or the minister for international development, still work with a group of public servants who may look and act like a department. The minister for international trade is usually "styled" the minister of international trade and has a deputy minister of international trade to work with. The machinery of government behind the scenes is a little more complex but the minister of international trade is much like the minister of justice. A third type of minister is supported by a division or branch of a larger department. The government house leader, for example, relies on the staff of the Legislation and House Planning Secretariat of Privy Council Office to be the equivalent of a department, and a deputy secretary of Cabinet usually fills the role of the House Leader's deputy minister. A minister is rarely "stranded" without some group of officials to direct.

Most ministers are given formal powers and obligations in legislation, and most of these powers can be exercised by a minister acting alone. The minister in charge of the Department of Indigenous and Northern Affairs, for example, has many powers under the Indian Act. Section 17 of that act gives the minister the power, "whenever he considers it desirable," to amalgamate First Nations bands when a majority of their members ask for an amalgamation and to create new bands if requested to do so. The Indian Act gives the minister dozens of other powers. The transport minister has powers under the Canada Marine Act to establish and amalgamate port authorities. The *Table of Public Statutes and Responsible Ministers* sets out every legislative authority assigned to a federal minister and is updated constantly by the Department of Justice. As of summer 2017, the English version of the document runs to more than 500 pages (Department of Justice 2017). Almost every minister has formal powers to allocate funds, sign contracts, manage relationships with other governments, and allocate countless scarce resources – people and time – to government tasks. These powers mean every minister is at the centre of an ecosystem of power, influence, and advocacy. In addition to the dozens, hundreds, or even thousands of departmental officials devoted to their work, every minister also has political aides whose immediate career prospects are tightly tied to that minister's performance. Departmental officials can be counted upon to whip up a briefing or policy proposal on any passing fancy the minister may have. Political staff defend and advance the minister's political interests. The material accoutrements of a minister are comfortable. Everywhere they go wearing the mantle of their portfolio, ministers are important people.

Those powers also bring "stakeholders" for a minister to meet and consult. Stakeholders are mostly rent-seekers – representatives from corporations, associations, or other pressure groups who want something from government. They have a proposed policy they want to advance, a privileged position to protect, a contract to secure, or some other advantage that needs attention from government. These organized interests see the minister's powers as a way to advance or, or at least impede the retreat of, their interests. Stakeholders do what they can to add to the importance of ministers, making a great fuss to their members when they secure a meeting with ministers, issuing fawning media releases when ministers make decisions, and in turn inviting ministers to address gatherings of their members. Every portfolio also has journalists or other purveyors of information watching them. Some portfolios are still on the "beat" of reporters from the major news outlets. Others are on the beat of journalists who file for specialized trade publications, or someone who publishes a hobbyist newsletter, or someone writing for one of the online "verticals" that has emerged to fill the demand for around-the-clock coverage of every nook and cranny of government. In short, all ministers have an "interested public" or a "policy community" following their work, and every minister wants to be covered and covered positively by the media that follow them. That drives the need for announcements to be made, interesting places to be toured, and appointments to be named. When a prime minister creates a new portfolio, even one with a small or narrow scope, and names a minister for it, a new ecosystem of power soon emerges. The ecosystem will ensure the minister develops a political agenda to suit the role.

Most ministers find the agenda of their portfolio fulfilling, and they devote themselves almost entirely to it. Most have little time or inclination to think about the broader government agenda or even the country that lies beyond their portfolio. Goldenberg relates many examples of Chrétien's efforts to involve his ministers in planning his government's broader agenda. At the end of Chrétien's second year in office, he asked Goldenberg and Policy Director Chaviva Hosek to interview Cabinet ministers for an hour or two at a time, to discuss what the government's priorities should be for the rest of the mandate. He and Hosek found that "most Cabinet ministers were so busy with their own departmental responsibilities that they had given little serious though to what the overall priorities of the government should be" (Goldenberg 2006, 104). Goldenberg writes he was not surprised since, when he worked as an aide to Chrétien during his time as a minister in the Trudeau Cabinet, Chrétien "always focused on his own departmental responsibilities and rarely talked to me or others about the overall agenda of the Trudeau government" (ibid). The portfolio easily becomes the primary identification of most ministers. Harper also held unstructured "political discussions" during meetings of the full Cabinet, during Cabinet retreats, and often when he chaired meetings of the Planning and Priorities Committee. Not surprisingly, most ministers spoke to their departmental priorities and, if pressed, could speak about their province or region. Few can speak about the broader agenda. Some are former party leaders (Stockwell Day, Peter MacKay, Stéphane Dion). Some had prominent roles in provincial politics that gave them the ability to see past their portfolios (Jim Flaherty, John Baird, Tony Clement, Loyola Hearn, Norman Doyle, Fabian Manning, Vic Toews, David Emerson, Ralph Goodale, Jim Carr). But, on the whole, the main pressure on a Cabinet's attention is away from the centre, not toward it. Cabinet is a centrifugal institution. Left to their own devices, ministers will drift off to tend to portfolio responsibilities rather than overarching government-wide ones.

It is good for ministers to be focused on their portfolio. Every portfolio has challenges and demands. The work of government departments and agencies matter to millions of Canadians every day. The Department of

Fisheries and Oceans might not have a big impact in Toronto or Calgary, but it is a complex portfolio and its work influences the fate of dozens of communities and the livelihood of thousands of people. Transport Canada, and the agencies and Crown corporations in the transport minister's portfolio, reach into every corner of Canada and every sector of the Canadian economy. It also has important responsibilities for Canada's national security. Immigration, agriculture, veteran's issues, public pensions, federal policing – these are all government responsibilities that need attention from ministers, and citizens should expect ministers to focus their attention on them. But as *Cabinet* ministers, these individuals are *all* supposed to be part of a team, namely the prime minister's governing team. They eventually develop their own agendas for their portfolios, but to pursue these ideas they need resources or decisions, and to get those means they need team buy in and at least the acquiescence of the prime minister. A good prime minister will have something for each Cabinet minister to do, even if it is just to manage the portfolio well without causing trouble. Major initiatives that really matter to the government agenda must be handed to the most capable ministers, and those ministers have to deliver on those initiatives in a way that is faithful to the agenda.

In his eulogy for Jim Prentice, Stephen Harper related a story about the most capable ministers getting the most difficult jobs. He had made Prentice his environment minister just ahead of the inauguration of President Barack Obama, with the hope that Canada and the US could forge a "comprehensive regulatory approach to energy and the environment" under the new administration. In a telephone conversation, Obama asked Harper to send someone down to Washington early to look at the options. Harper replied that he was sending Prentice, and added: "I think you guys will like him. He's probably the most capable guy that I've got." Obama, in Harper's telling, responded "That's great Stephen, I promise not to tell your other guys you said that" (Harper 2016). Obama was new to leadership at the time of the conversation but would eventually learn that no one sitting around the Cabinet table is misinformed about who the most capable Cabinet ministers are.

So, how does a prime minister, who is, after all, just one person, ensure that two- or three-dozen Cabinet ministers are working as part of the governing team? After all, even the fictional British prime minister Jim Hacker complained that, when facing his Cabinet, he felt he had very few people on "his" side of most debates. His fictional permanent secretary for health Sir Ian Whitworth exaggerated when he said "It would be different if the government were a team but in fact they're a loose confederation of warring tribes." But if the dominant pressures of a Cabinet are centrifugal – drawing ministers toward their portfolios and away from Cabinet and the prime minister – how does a prime minister impose centripetal forces? How does a bigger, broader government agenda get formed?

Part of the answer to this essential question of prime-ministerial leadership comes from the exercise of the four special policy powers that a prime minister can never fully delegate outlined in chapter 3. The prime minister must be involved in fiscal policy because there is only so much money available to the federal government and fiscal decisions cut across every portfolio of government. Most portfolios eventually involve international or federal-provincial issues, and the prime minister's special involvement in these areas will help ensure ministers are working on the government's agenda. The prime minister's role in managing the government's parliamentary time also means monitoring the legislative plans of every minister. A prime minister also has some influence over how ministers spend their time and can require them to spend time on government-wide thinking at meetings of the full Cabinet and Cabinet committees. But to do more in forming a Cabinet team requires more careful thought about the fundamental dynamic of ministerial life.

As chief of staff, I saw ministers, their political staffs, their department officials, and their attentive publics – what I have called their portfolios – as natural allies in pulling ministers closer to their departments and away from the agenda of the government as a whole. Following Goldenberg, I see the prime minister as the only one who can truly craft an agenda for the government as a whole. In crafting and then implementing the political dimension of that agenda, the prime minister is supported by his political staff in PMO. When nonpartisan public service support is appropriate, the prime minister is supported by the officials in PCO. PMO is quite small. There were about eighty staffers in PMO when I was chief of staff. Given that about twenty-five or thirty were assigned to Harper's travel and scheduling needs or responding to the roughly two million pieces of correspondence he received each year, there were about fifty-five involved in planning, policy, speechwriting, issues management, and communications. PCO has far more resources, so in my view a wise prime minister should rely on his PMO staff only for things that cannot be done in PCO. PMO and PCO are partners, in my view, in ensuring there is an overall government agenda and that it is being pursued by ministers and their portfolios. If a prime minister has an agenda to pursue – in other words, if the prime minister aims to be successful – his closest allies in ensuring that agenda is pursued are PMO and PCO. If he cannot rely on his PMO and PCO, he is effectively alone facing his ministers and their portfolios. It was therefore always important, in my view, that PMO and PCO be on the same page about what the government was trying to accomplish, and that they both be on the prime minister's page. When PMO and PCO sent different signals to ministers, officials, departments, and political aides, the government tended to freeze up. When PMO and PCO sent the same signals, the Harper government could and did move quickly. PMO and PCO have different roles and different strengths. But they both serve as the prime minister's tools to thwart the natural, centrifugal forces in Cabinet and to bring government together under a single agenda.

After I retired as chief of staff, my successors brought a different view of the fundamental dynamic at the heart of government. They tended to see the political side of the government – the prime minister, Cabinet, PMO, and ministerial political staff – as natural allies, and the permanent team of Ottawa – the public service and the attentive publics of the various portfolios – as another group of natural allies. PCO, in this view, has more in common with line departments than with PMO, and PMO has more in common with ministers and their staffs. This view of government is rooted in the same view of democratic accountability as mine – that the government is a single team and is accountable to Parliament in the near term and the voters in the medium term. But it is based on a different view of the mechanics of governing. The shift may explain Jonathan Craft's observation that Clerk of the Privy Council Kevin Lynch, during most of my time as PMO chief of staff, "worked effectively" with me, and that "Political-administrative relations were, however, contentious and strained" under my successor (2016, 78). I am sure that, looked at a different way, political aides I worked with would say relations between PMO and ministerial offices were smoother after June 2008.

It still peeves me that outside observers with no first-hand experience rely on the fictions of movies and television programs to understand the personal dynamics of politics. The original *Yes, Minister* and *Yes, Prime Minister* series were full of acute insight, and I remain a fan of them. Other shows too often portray a political leader's senior aide as a psychopath in a perpetual state of rage storming around the halls of government screaming obscenities at lesser mortals or planning outrageously cynical plots to deceive. One newspaper account, perhaps inspired by some Malcolm Tucker-like character, reported that as Harper's chief of staff I "frequently reduce[d] ministers to tears." The account relied on a single anonymous source. I do not recall making anyone cry in the job and always tried to treat elected officials with respect. A PMO chief of staff cannot be a pushover; the job entails delivering tough news. But the idea that I could push ministers around and make them cry is hard to take seriously. As Graham White puts it: "Even assuming the accuracy of the insider's claim – that the tears were said to flow 'frequently' strains credulity – it is well to recall that, like the denizens of *Animal Farm*, some ministers are more equal than others. It would seem a very safe bet that, among the ministers who were not reduced to tears by Ian Brodie would be the likes of heavyweights such as Jim Flaherty, Jim Prentice, John Baird and David Emerson" (2015, 238). A safe bet, indeed. I would add to that list that names of other tough ministers I worked with, which amounts to basically all of them.

The Strategic Agenda

In setting up the Prime Minister's Office for Stephen Harper, I was keenly aware that the government would need to deliver on many of the initiatives that we had included in our platform (with others being, understandably, impossible to deliver on in with a minority government) and on other initiatives that Harper would select for some kind of action while still managing issues that arose along the way. The maxim about the urgent crowding out the important is true in politics as in every other walk of life. I therefore decided early on to organize the Prime Minister's Office in a way that focused some people on the strategic initiatives and others on day-to-day issues management. Patrick Muttart, our best strategic thinker, headed a strategy department and Keith Beardsley, an experienced hand with Mulroney-era experience in government as well as years of experience on the opposition benches, headed issues management. The government's agenda, then, had two parts: the strategic agenda and the issues-management agenda. The emerging scholarly fields of political marketing and the study of party "brands" are in their early days (Marland 2016; Delacourt 2013). As these fields of inquiry develop, they will have to distinguish between the government's strategic or pro-active agenda and its issues-management or reactive agenda. These two sides of a government's agenda come from different sources, pose different challenges to those in government, and therefore are handled with different techniques or modes of operation. Pursuing the strategic agenda and managing issues both involve political branding and are informed by political market research. But they are different strands of work entirely.

The government's strategic agenda should be front and centre as much as possible. The government has to decide what it wants to do, craft policies and communications plans that try to accomplish those objectives, and show visible, consistent progress toward them. Tone and language convey how important each part of the strategic agenda is to the government. The strategic agenda should be faithful to what was promised to the voters. It takes months or years of effort to get properly drafted, well-considered legislation to House, spending or taxation measures into a federal budget, or ministerial announcements out the door. Ministers, officials and political aides devote hundreds or thousands of hours to crafting the substance of these initiatives. Harper was adamant that the communications around these initiatives be as professionally and properly crafted as the substance was. Patrick Muttart had persuaded Harper's staff to use a single form, a "message event proposal," to summarize the thinking and arrangements for a pre-planned communications effort while we were in opposition and during the 2005–06 election campaign. One innovation that we brought to government in 2006 was to carry forward the discipline of these MEPS. When applied to the government's strategic agenda, MEPS reflected an annual government plan that was approved by the PM, communicated to ministers and departments through regular mandate letters, and then translated into Cabinet and Cabinet committee agendas by PCO.

The MEP – a tool for planning ministerial and eventually broader government communications events or products – was a simple form that asked someone planning a ministerial or other public event or document to summarize, in a page or two, the purpose of the event, the intended audience of the event, and the various ways in which the event was going to be supported with media releases, website material, and so on. Every organization needs a method of ensuring it is communicating clearly and effectively with the public on a timely basis. We had used the MEP form as a management tool to plan our work in opposition and during the 2006 election campaign. When it worked well, it made sure a large team of people who were in touch with the public had thought through why they were doing what they were doing. The alternative to careful planning in any organization is chaos, and chaos in political or government communications is asking for trouble. When we first asked public service officials to work on MEPS with us, many of them welcomed the clarity of process and expectation that resulted. They understood that basic professionalism in communications is a fundamental expectation in any large organization, and officials who complained about the discipline and professionalism we expected had trouble explaining why it was better for them to go public and "wing it." Officials who pride themselves on the elaborate planning and expertise that go into legislation or policy decisions should welcome the same planning and expertise going into communications. The MEP was not a way to prevent information from becoming public or to inhibit transparency with the public. But transparency and communications, especially when done on behalf of the Government of Canada, should not be chaotic.

When I was chief of staff, the Harper government had an annual planning cycle. It began in May and June with preliminary discussions of the year to come. The Government of Canada and the Conservative Party conducted market research to understand the public mood, the public's priorities, and our successes and failures in securing the consent of Canadians to our work.

PMO and PCO consulted broadly inside the government and outside to prepare options for the coming year's agenda. Harper typically convened a Cabinet retreat and asked ministers to reflect on how much progress had been made over the previous year as well as on special challenges for the coming year. In late June or early July, the prime minister might issue mandate letters to his ministers asking them to prepare specific policy plans over the next twelve months. This allowed departments and ministers to use the summer months of July and August, when Parliament is not sitting, productively. The next stage in the annual cycle usually came in September with the return of Parliament. If Parliament had been prorogued, the return of Parliament meant PMO and PCO drafted a Throne Speech for the governor general, and PMO would draft a Commons speech for the prime minister. Together, they would serve as a public announcement or launch of the government's strategic agenda for the year. If there was no throne speech, we would find another opportunity for Harper to give an agenda speech. In October or early November, Flaherty would provide a formal economic update to the country to set out the themes for the following spring's budget and start the budget consultation season. In autumn, Harper also typically attended a major international summit, either under the auspices of NATO, the Commonwealth, or the Francophonie. January and February were usually devoted to making the final decisions regarding the government's budget and launching that budget with Flaherty's budget speech. Finally, in June, the cycle closed with the prime minister attending a G8 summit.

When planning for the 2007–08 cycle, for example, we knew there would be several issues to confront. International credit markets were beginning to see serious crises. In Canada, this led to a crisis in the asset-backed commercial paper market. These crises were slowing investment decisions around the globe, an early indication of a slowing economy. Back home, our criminal justice bills were stacked up in the House of Commons behind a backlog of work at the House Justice Committee. These were the major outstanding items from our election platform. The informal parliamentary mandate for the mission in Afghanistan would need to be renewed even as the leader of our main parliamentary partner on that aspect of our agenda, Liberal leader Stéphane Dion, was raising tougher and tougher questions about the mission in public. The post-Kyoto approach to climate change remained a constant challenge domestically and internationally. And, finally, we faced the constant threat of a return to the polls since the opposition parties could vote non-confidence in our government at almost any time.

Our spring consultations and the Cabinet retreat of June 2007 confirmed these issues as our main considerations. Over the summer, officials and political aides began drafting an autumn Throne Speech, and as Harper travelled across the country he began asking provincial premiers for their assessments of how their economies were managing. He shuffled Cabinet in August, the shuffle that Bruce Carson claims was to see Jim Prentice move to Finance and Jim Flaherty move to Industry. As it turns out, Flaherty stayed at Finance and Prentice moved to Industry. New mandate letters went out to all ministers, allowing PCO to plan the Cabinet agenda through the first part of 2008. In October, Harper named former Liberal deputy prime minister John Manley to head an independent panel to review options for the mission in Afghanistan. Harper obviously hoped that naming a prominent Liberal to lead this effort would eventually mean finding a way to convince Dion to support the renewal of the mission, but the panel was also an opportunity to review the mission and look at options for its future. October also saw the reading of the Throne Speech and the tabling of the Tackling Violent Crime Act. That Act was a comprehensive collection of criminal justice reforms, and Harper set down a marker about the bill, warning that if it was not passed within a few months he would consider it a loss of confidence in his government and call an election. Flaherty released his autumn economic update on 30 October 2007, announcing a massive fiscal stimulus for individuals and businesses. He announced the reduction of the GST from 6 percent to 5 percent, effective January 2008, and a multi-year plan to reduce the top corporate tax rate from 22 percent to 15 percent. Finally, in November, the prime minister signed onto a Commonwealth Summit statement on climate change. As the economic situation continued to darken, Harper invited the provincial premiers to a pre-budget dinner in Ottawa and announced a Community Development Fund of $1 billion to support communities hurt by international economic developments. The Manley Panel reported out, leading to a resolution of the informal parliamentary mandate for the Afghanistan mission the following month. The February budget expanded on the pre-budget dinner with the premiers by announcing the Tax-Free Savings Account, phasing out certain tax incentives for oil sands development, special measures to retrain older workers, and a plan to subsidize innovation by auto manufacturers with operations in Canada. The Manley Panel report helped set the stage for Harper's participation in the April 2008 NATO summit in Bucharest. In June, the budget passed the House, averting the last threat of a spring election. The G8 Summit produced a serious climate change statement. I retired as chief of staff at the end of June, and planning for autumn began anew.

Issues Management

Of course, it is not possible to foresee all the political issues that will arise over the course of a year in politics. Governments make mistakes. Money is misspent. Dumb comments are made. Reporters dig up stories, and most of them are not flattering to the government's efforts. Opposition parties are not foolish. They make hay of issues. Question Period is often uncomfortable for the government. The prime minister and ministers need answers or comments on these issues or, if answers are not available, at least something to say. The answers that the prime minister and ministers make about issues should be consistent across the government. Nothing makes a government look incompetent like different people giving different answers to legitimate questions. Reporters and opposition MPs see when a government does not have its story straight. They exploit – and should exploit – any inconsistency or imprecision in the government's answers to questions. Political accountability is rough justice, but it is usually justice.

The speed of media reporting has accelerated in the past two decades, and the internal speed of government communications is struggling to keep up. When I was chief of staff, we could still manage issues around a daily media cycle. The PMO issues management team started its work early in the morning. Keith Beardsley and his core staff were usually in the office at 4:30 or 5:00 AM, and there was always an issues management shift working late into the night, when the media cycle ended. Public servants who started their work days at 8:30 could find three or four hours of PMO issues-management work sitting on their desks or in their email accounts when they arrived at the office. Just trying to find out the facts of an issue that is likely to be raised in Question Period or a press conference is tough, tougher than any outsider can imagine. Public servants and others are typically cautious when the Prime Minister's Office or a minister's political aide comes asking for the facts behind a story in the news cycle. They want to be absolutely sure they are providing the correct information. But assembling and verifying facts well enough to be absolutely sure the prime minister is getting the correct information is time-consuming. Getting answers from lower-level officials means running the risk of getting only part of the story. Getting answers from higher-level officials means running the risk of missing important details or waiting hours or days for the entire story to become clear. In 2006, coming up with a solid set of facts in response to a news story that broke at 5:00 AM in time for Question Period at 2:15 PM was challenging. Doing that for the dozens of news stories that broke each day in the national news and all the local news from coast to coast was an exhausting undertaking best left to political aides who did not hesitate to drive hundreds of people to the limits of their work abilities every day. Doing it when the daily news cycle has been replaced by an hourly or minute-to-minute cycle is nearly impossible.

The best fictional depiction of the challenge of getting the full picture of a political situation in government is in the six-part CBC television program *Snakes and Ladders* that originally aired in 2004. It depicted the life of a political aide through the eyes of a young woman who was just out of university and arrives on Parliament Hill to work for the minister of the fictional Department of Minister of Human Resources and Government Services. Her minister backed the losing side in her party's most recent leadership race and now fears her own political staff are working with the prime minister's chief of staff to destroy her political career. The new staffer has no time to learn the ropes of life on the Hill, and must, in the description of tv.com, "chart her way through the world of hidden agendas, scrums and damage control – while trying to find some time for dating." (I do not believe that any of my PMO staff had time for dating.) The miniseries introduced many of the pitfalls of political life, and the plot of each episode was driven by the same dynamic: the amount of time it takes to figure out what is really going on in government. Most people whom you ask for a fact give you a response that is shaded by what they think you want to hear and their own interests. Ask several people for the same fact and be prepared to get contradictory answers. People who have never served in senior government roles sometimes find it hard to understand how difficult it is for a powerful official to uncover quite simple facts, and therefore the great value of loyalists who will be plain in telling you the state of the world.

Issues management, when done properly, has one clear purpose, and that is to move an issue off the public agenda as quickly as possible. If an issue has arisen because of a serious problem in government, it will take time to figure out the scale of the problem and the possible set of solutions let alone the best solution. Implementing the solution might take years. None of that can be done properly if the issue is the lead question in Question Period for days or weeks. The best way to destroy a government is to pull its attention away from its strategic agenda into hundreds or thousands of issues. A government only succeeds when it can successfully manage issues and keep its focus on its agenda. This is not a cynical exercise. Most voters will accept a reasonable explanation when things go wrong in government. When a minister or prime minister has made a mistake personally, it is best to apologize and take remedial steps. If public money has been poorly used, it should be repaid promptly. Good issues management resorts to "holding lines" – bland statements of fact intended to satisfy media or parliamentary questions while the search for a deeper answer goes on in the background – only when absolutely required.

One issue I found especially frustrating during my time in government was the allegation that Canadian soldiers were somehow complicit in the torture of Afghans detained on the battleground in southern Afghanistan. These allegations still resurface, years after they were first made. The original reporting in *The Globe and Mail* was sensational and caught us off guard. There were allegations made by a Canadian diplomat who had been posted in Kabul. Years of investigations followed. In early 2015, a group of MPs that included Stéphane Dion was given tens of thousands of pages of records about detainee operations in Afghanistan. That included the reporting of that diplomat from Kabul. The group found no substantiation of the allegations. A United Nations investigation jointly run by the UN mission in Afghanistan and the UN High Commissioner for Human Rights found all sorts of problems with the treatment of detainees in Afghanistan, but its only reference to Canada quoted a detainee saying Canadian detainees never complained of mistreatment (UNAMA 2011, 38). Exhaustive reviews have shown that Canadian soldiers fully respected international and Canadian rules when handling the detainees they captured in the midst of a brutal, indiscriminate insurgency. In a long set of battles that pitted ordinary Afghans trying to live their lives in an unforgiving corner of an impoverished country against zealots claiming a religious mandate for murder and destruction, Canadian soldiers and their Afghan military and police partners apprehended locals in the midst of planning or mounting attacks on civilians. In the wake of the terrible beating and killing of a young Somali man during the Canadian Airborne Regiment's tour of duty in 1993, the leadership and frontline troops of the Canadian Forces were especially sensitive to any allegations of detainee abuse. The "Afghan detainee" issue was a persistent concern to Harper, to me, and to many of our staff while I was chief of staff.

The Afghan detainee story began when news media began to report on documents secured by a University of Ottawa professor that suggested battlefield detainees taken by Canadian soldiers were being mistreated by Afghan interrogators. Like all stories about Canada's military mission in Afghanistan, this one broke at the beginning of the day in Ottawa, which was also the end of the day in Kandahar, the main Canadian military base in Afghanistan at the time. The Canadian Forces maintained a round-the-clock command post in Kandahar, but the night watch at a command post has a limited capacity to respond to questions from Ottawa, especially if night operations are being conducted. The military chain of command is designed to accomplish military objectives, not to respond to urgent questions from the Prime Minister's Office. PMO staff found out that the agreement between Canada and the Afghan government regarding the treatment of battlefield detainees had been negotiated by Canadian diplomats and signed by General Rick Hillier, who was by this point a particularly high-profile chief of defence staff. Canada had been forced to negotiate its own agreement on detainees when the International Security Assistance Force – the NATO-led force in Afghanistan – was unable to conclude a master agreement covering the entire operation.

Hillier and Defence Minister Gordon O'Connor had served together in the Canadian Army for years. Hillier had strong views about the future of the army and the Canadian Forces, as did O'Connor. Hillier was a media star – a plain spoken, gung-ho military leader from Newfoundland. O'Connor was not interested in being a media star. His initial responses to the Afghan detainee story were careful to a fault. Harper's follow-up comments were more definitive: that Canada handled detainees in accordance with international law and then handed them over to Afghan authorities pursuant to an agreement negotiated under the previous government. Canada exercised its rights to meet with these detainees once they were in Afghan hands. Canada's agreement with Afghanistan was sufficient. I believed, and still believe today, that that response was truthful and sufficient. If the government had left things at that, the Canadian Forces and the foreign service could have continued their difficult work in Afghanistan.

However, somewhere in the Government of Canada, someone decided that the detainee agreement needed to be renegotiated. Canada's right to follow up contact with detainees was not sufficient. Formulating a negotiating position and finding someone in the Afghan government to negotiate it with took time. Arranging teams that could track and follow up with every detainee our troops handed over to Afghan authorities took time. Proving that the new arrangements were not only better than the original arrangements but were acceptable to every international organization, human rights group, and interested bystander took time. The Afghan detainee story stretched over months. A diplomat who had been posted to the Canadian embassy in Kabul came forward with a different story, although, as mentioned above he did not report any such claims at the time he was in Kabul. In the end, nothing came of the Afghan detainee issue. But as the story dragged on, we ended up sending Canadian correctional services officers – people used to first-world prisons – to try to improve Afghan prisons that do not operate to first-world standards. A new detainee agreement was negotiated. New systems were devised and extra staff devoted to following up with detainees. I would never excuse a violation of international conventions or condone torture. Earlier in life I watched most of the hearings of the Somalia Inquiry and read most of the reports and books on the death of Shidane Arone. The very suggestion that Canadian troops conducted themselves illegally or improperly in Afghanistan is wrong, and it is well past time to put this issue to rest.

Another ready source of issues is the difficult business of the consular services provided by Canadian diplomats. Canadians think of themselves as mostly upstanding, law-abiding people who are welcomed as visitors around the world. The myth that American students stitch Canadian flags onto their backpacks to get an easier ride when travelling the world travels well in Canada. But against this self-image is the fact that Canadians get up to shady and sometimes illegal things overseas. Simply being Canadian is not a "get out of jail free" card when travelling abroad. When Canadians, through no fault of their own, find themselves in a war zone, no flag on their backpack will necessarily save them from harm. When a large number of Canadians are stranded miles from our shores in a war zone, Canada does not have the capacity to rescue everyone within hours. Instead, Canadian diplomats working for the consular services branch of government try, with few tools or advantages other than persuasion, to cajole foreign governments into treating our people fairly and do whatever is possible to extricate innocents. Unfortunately, the drama of the circumstances makes for compelling new stories. Even aside from times of war, when Canadians are caught up in a foreign criminal justice system, the federal government's legal obligation to withhold personal information about them lets Canadians who have been up to no good spread misrepresentations about themselves without repercussions. Since the government must abide by privacy rules, it usually cannot debunk falsehoods or partial truths spread by Canadians in trouble abroad.

Mass evacuations overseas are always disorderly and chaotic. The first demand for a mass evacuation that faced the Harper government was the exodus of Canadian citizens trying to get out of Lebanon during the Israeli-Hezbollah War of 2006. In July 2006, after Hezbollah had been shelling northern Israel for some time, Hezbollah increased tensions by launching a raid into Israeli territory, killing several Israeli soldiers and capturing two. Israeli Defence Forces launched a drive into southern Lebanon with the objective of destroying Hezbollah's ability to launch further attacks. As the Israeli effort continued deeper in Lebanon and reached the outskirts of Beirut, thousands of people living in Lebanon tried to escape. Those with Canadian citizenship sought help from the Canadian government, quickly overwhelming the small Canadian embassy in Lebanon. Given the hostilities, flying or driving out of Lebanon was dangerous if not impossible. Unlike Mediterranean countries and the US, Canada does not maintain a regular navy presence in the region, so consular services officials tried leasing civilian ships to get people out quickly. Many other countries were trying to do precisely the same at that point. At times, our officials would rent boats and then lose them to other countries outbidding us to rent anything that would float. No matter how quickly we got people out of Beirut, Canadian reporters always found someone with a Canadian passport who could not get through to the consular services offices, could not get an answer from the local embassy, and was waiting, without food or water, to leave Beirut. The House of Commons was not sitting at the time, so we avoided a daily Question Period barrage on the issue. But a daily Question Period would have let us respond to the mounting humanitarian mess in a structured way. Instead, government communications were chaotic as well. We were being lambasted for siding with Israel, lambasted for not doing enough to get Canadians out, and even taking flak from our own MP, Garth Turner, who blogged about "Canadians of convenience" being rescued even though some had not lived in Canada for several years. In the end, I remain impressed that 13,000 Canadians were moved out of Lebanon in the middle of a war with no one killed. That summer, hundreds of people, including my brother, worked around the clock to get them out. But, as an issues-management challenge, our only success came at the end of Harper's official visit to France in July 2006. He decided to empty his government airplane of journalists and staff and then flew to Cyprus to pick up more than one hundred evacuees and get them home. The effort – a very small part of a much broader evacuation – was widely and positively covered. Unfortunately, the Prime Minister of Canada is not always well-positioned to help out personally in the midst of the inevitable consular services issue of a mass evacuation.

In early 2011, after I had left government, a smaller number of Canadians were similarly stranded and desperate to leave Libya when the Gaddafi regime began to unravel. During that evacuation, a Canadian television news crew got access to the beach to provide nearly live footage of desperate, displaced people back to Canada. That, combined with the new ubiquity of Twitter and other social media made the issues-management challenge of the mass evacuation trickier and more immediate. One public servant called me to ask for guidance on how to deal with a PMO staffer who was sitting in his living room in Canada watching the CBC coverage and calling diplomats on the beach in Libya to demand updates on the Canadians being interviewed on television. That was an overreach by a zealous political aide and did nothing to help expedite the evacuation or roll back the issues-management challenge. Governments need to plan ahead, though, for the social media challenge of disasters and other emergencies like mass evacuations. The Canadian Forces have long made an effort to have photographers and camera crews in the field to cover their operations through Combat Camera. One of the fathers of Combat Camera – the fearless Jacques Fauteux – worked in the Prime Minister's Office after he left the Canadian Forces. More than a decade later, every government department needs a Combat Camera of its own to report back to Canadians on their work. Combat Camera should be part of every consular services operation so Canadians can see what is being done to help Canadians in desperate straits overseas.

In autumn 2007, the government took up another consular services case, this one involving a Canadian on death row. Nearly twenty-five years earlier, Ronald Smith, a Canadian citizen, had pled guilty and asked to be sentenced to death for his part in a double murder in Montana. American death penalty cases often end up in appeals for years. After Smith changed his mind and decided to contest his sentence, his case was reviewed many times by both the Montana state and US federal courts. As of autumn 2007, the sentence had been upheld. Despite the exhaustive judicial scrutiny of Smith's case, Canadian diplomats eventually intervened with governors of Montana as well as other state and federal officials asking for clemency. The main written intervention came in 1999 when Canada's consul general in Minneapolis wrote the Montana governor noting that while the Canadian government "does not sympathize with violent crime" or pass judgement on Smith's guilt or innocence, "The practice of the Department of Foreign Affairs and International Trade to seek clemency for Canadian citizens sentenced to death in foreign countries is based on humanitarian considerations."[1]

By the time his government was sworn in, Harper had put his personal views of the death penalty on the public record. During the 2005–06 election campaign, he noted that, while he was personally in favour of the death penalty, he did not plan to reopen the criminal law on the matter. Accepting the legislative status quo in Canada did not mean the Harper government would necessarily push for the abolition of the death penalty elsewhere, though. So, in March, 2006, I advised a senior official of the Department of Foreign Affairs to be careful about issues involving the death penalty and to seek guidance before committing the government to any particular position.

So, in autumn 2007, when someone mentioned that a reporter was asking about Canadian diplomats trying to have Smith's sentence commuted, I was surprised I had not heard about the case already. Harper quickly consulted Maxime Bernier, Stockwell Day, and Rob Nicholson, at the time the foreign, public safety, and justice ministers. They agreed that, while the government would ask for clemency in countries that did not adhere to the rule of law like the US does, we would no longer automatically do so for Canadians on death row in the US. When the new practice was announced, our most socially conservative MPs, pro-life people who opposed both abortion and the death penalty on principle, worried Harper might try to reopen Canada's criminal law. Once he assured them he was not changing his position, caucus concern abated. The new practice was, however, strongly opposed by public servants and foreign service officers. I appreciated that many of them also opposed the death penalty in principle and as the internal debate unfolded I always acknowledged that fact. Some officials wanted to know how we would decide when to seek clemency in the US and when not to do so. I think ministers might have welcomed advice from officials on that issue. But some of the objections raised to the new practice were ridiculous. How, some wondered, could we accept the death penalty in the US and then seek clemency for Canadians in countries with less rigorous judicial systems? It is not difficult for people working in the area to see which countries respect judicial independence and which do not. Eventually, Harper convened a large meeting of ministers and officials in his office to hear all the objections at once. A vigorous debate followed but none of the ministers nor Harper changed their minds as a result.

Nonetheless, one legal argument stood out from the others: that, under administrative law, we had a duty of fairness to Smith and should hear from Smith before changing the government's policy. I asked officials to find the policy statement that established the practice of asking for clemency in every case. Clearly, Canadian diplomats had long sought clemency in death penalty cases, as the 1999 Déry letter noted, for humanitarian reasons. But were those efforts simply initiatives of permanent officials or had there been a policy decision taken by responsible ministers? No one could produce a record of a policy decision. Since there was no evidence of a policy, the change in practice did not mean the government was changing its policy. Consular services are a matter of foreign policy, and there are good reasons for the courts to avoid subjecting foreign policy to judicial review and oversight. On the issue of the death penalty, the Canadian Charter of Rights quite plainly permits it. Section 7 is blunt: "Everyone has the right to life ... and the right not to be deprived thereof except in accordance with the principles of fundamental justice."

Smith's lawyers soon launched a legal challenge to the change of practice. Officials had advised strongly against the change, and I respected the fact that some people have a principled and religious opposition to the death penalty. I did not think it was either fair or prudent to entrust the defence of the case to the staff of the Department of Justice. I urged Harper to hand the case to outside legal counsel. After speaking with Rob Nicholson, he agreed to hand it to Code Hunter, a Calgary firm that Harper had worked with in the past. In the end, the Federal Court decided against the government. In ruling on the case, Justice Barnes relied on affidavits from a former Foreign Minister and a former diplomat to find that there was an official policy on clemency before 2007; no official record of such a decision had been found. The ruling claimed that Canada had a "principled objection to the death penalty" (27), even though the Charter of Rights specifically permits it. The ruling also claimed that denying clemency assistance is "hard to reconcile with Canada's international commenting to promote respect for international human rights norms including the universal abolition of the death penalty" (29). With respect to the Federal Court, Canada's international commitments should be determined by the government of the day. That, after all, is why we have elections. I understand that public servants, foreign service officers, and judges often oppose the death penalty on principled grounds. Harper and many Canadians support the death penalty on principled grounds as well. Mutual respect is required even as the government of the day determines Canada's practices. The Harper government responded to the Federal Court decision by seeking clemency for Smith. As of the timing of writing, Ronald Smith remains on death row in Montana.

Crafting and delivering a government agenda means delivering on the government's longer-term strategic agenda and the day-to-day or hour-by-hour issues management agenda. Good delivery on the strategic agenda can make up for many missteps in issues management. A government that only manages incoming issues will accomplish little and eventually run out of ways to justify itself to the voters. Cabinet government does not naturally tend to produce a government agenda, since the natural pressure on Cabinet ministers is toward the portfolio and away from Cabinet. But a government agenda must exist and be pursued, through a careful use of the prime minister's powers. Some matters must be settled at the centre, but that leaves plenty of room for ministers to be ministers.

7

Prime Ministers and Political Parties

Elizabeth May, leader of the Green Party of Canada, recently wrote that "In Westminster parliamentary democracy, political parties are not an essential ingredient" (2017, 17). She continued:

> I have often said that if I were to invent democracy from scratch I would not have invented political parties. Their existence is not a necessary, or even desirable, part of responsible government.

I am afraid that May is wrong on both counts. Political parties are a necessary part of responsible government, and of democratic politics in most places. They are also a very desirable part of responsible government.

Political parties, as May points out, are not mentioned in the Constitution Act, 1867. Nor are they mentioned in the US Constitution. But some of the leading lights of the American founding – James Madison, Thomas Jefferson, and Alexander Hamilton – were adept architects of politics parties. Madison and Jefferson founded the Democratic-Republican Party, while Hamilton was a leading light of the Federalists. The Fathers of Confederation were all deeply involved in party politics even as they drafted the Confederation constitution. Sir John A. Macdonald, George-Étienne Cartier, and their friends built one of the direct ancestors of today's Conservative Party. George Brown, a leading visionary of Confederation, led the Liberals in the first general election following Confederation. William Henry, one of the drafters of the Constitution Act, 1867, and a future Supreme Court of Canada judge, argued that "Party government must prevail in the new parliament. There must, as in all countries under responsible government, be a government and an opposition" (Ajzenstat et al. 1999, 266). The delegates to the Confederation conferences were selected from among the parties represented in the colonial legislatures, and they understood the central importance of political parties to parliamentary government in Westminster. Bagehot, writing at the time of Confederation, understood that "party organization is the vital principle of representative Government" 1961 [1867], 125). Everyone involved in drafting the Constitution Act, 1867, would have found May's allegations about the necessity and moral standing of parties hard to understand. And they would have insisted on the importance of having not just one political party, but at least two, one that becomes (temporarily) the government and the other (temporarily) the opposition in Parliament.

Political parties, as political scientists say, "structure" politics in our form of government. First, political parties organize Parliament. The leader of one of the parties becomes first minister. The leader of the largest party not supporting the government becomes leader of the opposition. Both those offices are formally recognized in our form of government. Other parliamentarians then play other roles according to which party they belong to, and they divide on the most important issues facing the country according to that party membership. Voters understand that parties matter, and so parties are the most important vehicles in fighting elections. Until the late 1960s, Canadian political parties were private organizations, and even though parliamentarians have used their legislative powers to regulate some aspects of their parties, Canadian federal parties remain largely private organizations. The Canada Elections Act sets out a basic structure that a party must have in order to compete in federal elections, but beyond that parties are free to structure themselves, select their own officials, recruit and nominate candidates, select leaders, and develop positions or strategies as they see fit. Parties need leaders, and one of the party leaders serves as prime minister. The governing party must therefore not only be able to restrain the PM; it must also be able to offer up a leader capable of being prime minister. The prime minister's role as leader of the governing party (or one of the governing parties) certainly helps in trying to understand the role.

Parties are also our reminder that politics is, by its very nature, a team sport. A leader without followers, as the saying goes, is just a person going for a walk. Even a skilled citizen with a superb idea is powerless unless that citizen can build a team by persuading other citizens to follow. This is part of the way – but only part of the way – we distinguish between a citizen with a superb idea and a kook. For a country rarely faces the problem of finding a political leader with followers. The challenge is to create a form of government that allows room for many leaders with many followers, all with divergent views. Politics is full of leaders like Papineau, who denigrate the importance of parties because they do not concede the legitimacy of divergent views. The genius of responsible government is to rest its legitimacy on its need for at least two teams, at minimum a party that is temporarily in government and a party that is temporarily in opposition. The US government, with its exquisite system of checks and balances, depends on the institutionalized competition between the branches of government, giving to those who administer each department "the constitutional means, and personal motives, to resist encroachments of the others," as Madison put it. "Ambition must be made to counteract ambition" (*Federalist* no. 51 in Hamilton 2001). Later, Martin van Buren argued that parties were not a perversion of the US Constitution but a "positive constitutional doctrine" that promoted the well-being of the regime (Ceasar 1978, 723). Non-partisan politics led to "personal factionalism and dangerous leadership appeals" (726), relying on "personalistic image appeal devoid of all principle" or "demagogic issue arousal" based on "sectional prejudices" (727). Responsible government relies on the institutionalized competition between parties. The constitution gives both government and opposition the constitutional status to pursue their goals. Parties and partisanship gives them the personal motives to use that status.

Measuring the health of our form of government therefore means understanding the health of our parties and understanding the balance of forces inside the various parties. The party is key source of power for its leader, especially if its leader is also prime minister. The leader must be able to lead, and that sometimes means holding the party together in the face of difficult political waters. But the party also has to be able to hold the leader in line. In this way, parties are an important a pillar of the Canadian regime along with responsible government, federalism and the Charter of Rights and Freedoms

The balance of forces inside our parties is often said to be out of whack, and that is an important part of the argument that a Canadian prime minister is overly powerful. The allegation that a prime minister holds too much power over the governing party is what supposedly turns a system featuring regular, free elections into a near dictatorship. Michael Chong and his colleagues write that "Question Period is how Ottawa really works," where debate is controlled by the small leadership teams that are "dominating our parties" (Chong et al. 2017, 1). Former Conservative MP Brett Rathgeber criticizes his former colleagues, writing that "members of the governing caucus think of themselves as part of the government, rather than [as] a check on the government" (Rathgeber 2014, 64). By controlling their parties, leaders control debate and shape policies. Peter Aucoin and his co-authors (2011) claim that the leadership of the governing party gives four tools to a Canadian prime minister that allows the centre of government to control the first minister's Cabinet and caucus colleagues. Together, they allow a prime minister to act independently of ministers and caucus backbenchers. First, a party leader, once selected, does not answer to MPs or party members. Until a century ago, party leaders were selected by their caucus colleagues and could be removed by them at any time. Prime ministers and government MPs were accountable to each other, limiting the prime minister's authority. Starting in 1919, first the Liberals and then, in 1927, the Conservatives moved away from caucus to select their leaders at national conventions. That reform is said to have severed the mutual accountability of prime ministers and caucus colleagues. Later, when parties began using even broader methods like direct votes of all party members, this connection was severed even more fully. The result was to eliminate the caucus' power to remove a sitting leader.

Secondly, since 1970, party leaders have had the power to certify their party's candidates for by-elections and general elections. This gives the leader control over who runs as the party's candidates. Starting in 1970s, when federal election ballots were allowed to list the party affiliation of candidates was allowed onto ballots, someone had to be authorized to determine who was entitled to the affiliation. To keep local returning officers out of the dispute, particularly when returning officers were named by the prime minister, party leaders were given the power to do so. Aucoin et al. cite the work of Samara in interviewing former MPs (2011, 2010) to claim that the power to name candidates is exercised on an ad hoc and arbitrary basis, although confusingly he also claims that prime ministers and party officials take very little interest in local nomination contests except to occasionally overturn the results. A party leader can also eject MPs from the party's caucus.

Finally, a prime minister has power to appoint caucus members to higher offices, effectively giving the centre further control over an MP's parliamentary career. The prime minister can appoint an MP to Cabinet or the post of parliamentary secretary to a minister. There is no longer a limit on how many ministers a prime minister can appoint. There is, contrary to Aucoin et al.'s claim, a limit on the number of parliamentary secretaries.[1] The prime minister also names MPs to House of Commons committees and picks the chairs of some committees. Finally, the prime minister can appoint an MP to a patronage position outside of the House – to the Senate, a diplomatic post, or some other Order in Council position.

The internal life of a political party is no cotillion. Every party has its own contests of friendships, enemy-ships, ideas, interests, and power. The balance of power within between shifting alliances of elite and rank and file members can be difficult for any outsider to understand. This is why merging political parties is such difficult work. The similar policy positions of the PC Party and Canadian Alliance did not make the early years of the Conservative Party any easier. Elite and grassroots members from both sides of the merger had to learn how to navigate the internal histories of the two organizations. After

Harper became Conservative leader, I became executive director of the party for almost two years. I struggled to understand how thirty-year-old battles over who would be twelfth vice-president of a federal or provincial PC youth wing could still resonate with savvy, serious Cabinet ministers in 2005. Some Conservatives with longer roots in the PC Party struggled to understand why old Reformers like me pointed to their long-forgotten youth wing battles as the reason we did not want a formal youth wing for the Conservative Party. But it is precisely the memory of these battles, and the friendships made and unmade during them, that sustains the will to continue on with political life at times when the fruits of the effort seem dim (von Heyking 2016). The dusty regimental standards that adorn so many Canadian churches and museums and the faded photographs on the walls of armories, military headquarters, and Legion halls from coast to coast keep alive the memories of bloody battles and play a role in unifying soldiers for battle. Recounting the memories of obscure political fights helps form political parties into teams as well.

Parties on the Hill: The Caucus

Writing anything about the government caucus in Canada is difficult. Caucus meetings are closed, and their proceedings are confidential. Parliamentarians usually maintain that confidentiality discussions zealously. For members on the government side of the House, membership in caucus brings privileged access to Cabinet ministers, including the prime minister; both MPs and senators feel pressure to maintain the caucus room as a zone for free discussion. It is easier to confirm what goes on in Cabinet, since most Cabinet documents become public after thirty years. Caucuses do not keep formal records of their business. Even after thirty years, caucus confidentiality is harder to penetrate.

I was honoured to be invited to attend several meetings of the Canadian Alliance and then the Conservative Party caucuses from May 2003 through June 2008. Prime Minister Harper asked me to attend all meetings of the government caucus once I became PMO chief of staff so I could follow up on issues that arose during the meetings. I also attended the Monday afternoon meetings of the caucus steering group – a weekly meeting with the chair of the government caucus and the caucus officers. I penned the first draft of Harper's opening remarks at caucus meetings, although he edited my drafts frequently and thoroughly. There is, however, no normal or fixed practice regarding staff attendance at caucus meetings. Chrétien did not usually invite his staff to attend caucus meetings. Instead, his parliamentary secretary briefed PMO staff on items of discussion that needed staff follow-up.

I wish more Canadians had the opportunity to witness the government caucus in action. The discussions and deliberations were serious, vibrant, and frank. The government caucus meetings I attended always started with the singing of the National Anthem. Harper followed, taking the podium for ten or fifteen minutes to recap his activities since the last caucus meeting and present an overview of the government's agenda. The other party officers then spoke. The House Leader would give a preview of the House agenda, and the Senate leader a preview of the Senate's work. The whip would let MPs know about upcoming votes and any changes to the procedural rules of the House or the administrative rules governing MP budgets and staffing. Then, the floor was open for about an hour of comments from caucus members. Ministers and senators rarely spoke during that hour. It really belonged backbench MPs. After the comments from the floor, ministers would be called on to introduce upcoming legislation or recently tabled bills. The prime minister closed with a few comments and, ideally, a rousing reminder of the caucus mission. I learned that Harper remembered every comment ever made in a caucus meeting. After caucus wrapped up, he would go over the interventions from the floor with me, telling me which ones needed follow-up and reminding me of any MP whose comments contradicted a position they had taken in caucus a week earlier, a month earlier, or even years earlier.

Attending caucus meetings restored my opinion of Canadian democracy each week. Caucus meetings freed MPs from having their comments recorded. Caucus confidentiality let them speak directly with Harper, other members of the government, and each other. Every week, caucus members spoke up for their constituents, the country, and their principles. They meted out criticism of and commendations for the government without fear of reprisal. It is an unfortunate paradox of modern democracy that our elected representatives have to be off the record to be so impressive. Many caucus debates are impressed on my memory. I cannot convey the details of these meetings owing to the confidentiality rule, but I hope the caucus members of the time will not mind if I convey the sense of one caucus meeting, held on 22 November 2006.

Bloc Québécois leader Gilles Duceppe had just given notice that he would ask the House to recognize that Quebecers formed a nation. He had hinted that such a motion was coming the previous spring, and Harper had publicly warned Duceppe not to set the precedent that the House of Commons could define Quebecers. When the motion finally came, some Conservative MPs were irritated at having to reopen the debate about Quebec's status in Confederation. Fifteen years earlier, the debate about recognizing Quebec as a "distinct society" in the Meech Lake and Charlottetown Accords had, after all, divided the PC Party and helped to mobilize support for the nascent Reform Party. Caucus members from Quebec spoke eloquently and passionately about the importance of the issue to them and their constituents. Harper announced he was planning to move his own motion to recognize that "les Québécois" form a nation within a united Canada. Those extra words – "within a united Canada" – satisfied most Conservative skeptics, and the government caucus rallied around his plan. One source reports that Harper ordered his members not to oppose the motion.[2] I do not recall that being case. A few days later, Conservative Cabinet minister Michael Chong resigned from Cabinet over the issue and was absent from the final vote, a sad memory of my time in Ottawa even a decade later. I knew it marked the end of Chong's chances of succeeding Harper. But the rest of the Conservative caucus embraced Harper's leadership on the issue, leadership that, when combined with his respect for limits on the federal spending power and his successful effort to resolve the fiscal imbalance, led to a decade of progress in Canadian federalism. Harper's role in undercutting support for the Bloc Québécois should be applauded. The Bloc took more than 10 percent of the vote in the 2006 election that Harper won, but less than 5 percent in the 2015 election at the end of his time in government.

I was rarely involved in managing problems within the Conservative caucus. I found most caucus members wanted to deal with other caucus members, not with PMO staff. The caucus officers worked closely with Harper to handle such problems. One exception was MP Garth Turner. After Harper's Cabinet was sworn in, Turner publicly criticized Harper's decision to appoint David Emerson to his ministry. Harper had accepted private criticism of his Cabinet choices but was unhappy to see Turner taking his criticisms public. He had me call Turner to remind him of the conventions of responsible government. If Turner could not see his way to supporting the ministry as a whole he would have to leave the caucus. The conversation was a heated one. Turner called back a few weeks later and arranged to meet with me and PMO communications director Sandra Buckler. I consulted with Harper and got his approval to offer Turner an olive branch. When Buckler and I finally sat down with Turner, the conversation was again memorable. "Garth has powers," he began, "and Garth's powers can be used for good or Garth's powers can be used for evil." I told him I knew he had long advocated constitutional protections for property rights in Canada. Our election platform had promised to enshrine property rights in the Charter of Rights and Freedoms. Harper let me offer Turner the chance to lead that effort. Would, I wonder, Turner use "his powers" to push the property rights amendment through Parliament? He demurred and asked for an opportunity to do something with a higher profile. I told him I thought that promoting a constitutional amendment, especially on an issue he had previously championed, was a pretty high-profile opportunity. It soon became clear that Turner was not asking for a particular role, and the meeting broke up without resolution. We had several property rights advocates in caucus, all of whom wanted to handle the constitutional amendment. Offering that job to Turner meant Harper was willing to disappoint the others to keep Turner engaged. I never saw Harper close the door on a caucus member he thought was interested in working with him. But Turner, like Stronach and Casey, just did not seem interested in working with Harper.

Is the balance of power within party caucuses out of whack? Does the power of appointment give a prime minister too much control over caucus members? A prime minister's ability name ministers, ministers of state, secretaries of state, parliamentary secretaries, and so on probably does afford the incumbent some power. Each of these positions come with a stipend to add to the pay of a member of Parliament and many come with money to hire extra staff. Some come with a government car and driver. A prime minister can also appoint caucus members to Order in Council positions, as ambassadors, agency heads, or judgeships and has the power to appoint MPs (or anyone else) to the Senate. But the number of appointments at the prime minister's disposal suggests that the appointment power's influence in enforcing caucus discipline is overstated. In 2006, at the beginning of the Harper government, 75 of the 123 MPs other than the prime minister received appointments from Harper; 39 percent were true backbenchers. In 2015, at the conclusion of the Harper government, 65 of the Conservative MPs 159 were "true" backbenchers. In other words, 41 percent of the MPs in the government caucus were not receiving a stipend to supplement their pay. Pick any point during the Harper government and a substantial number of MPs probably understood that they were never going to receive an appointment – never going to be a minister, parliamentary secretary or chair of a parliamentary committee chair. It is hard to see how the prime minister's power of appointment might help keep those MPs from thinking and acting as they please. Moreover, the historical record shows that party-line voting developed before the prime minister acquired much in the way of appointment power (Høyland 2015).

Since there are no dependable sources about debate within the government caucus, it is sometimes difficult to identify policy files where government backbenchers have had influence. There is little ammunition to rebut claims that government backbenchers are "trained seals" with no power. But a moment of reflection shows the implausibility of the idea that government backbenchers simply knuckle under to dictates from the prime minister

Figure 7.1a: Government caucus as of spring 2006

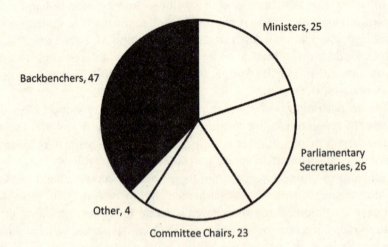

Spring 2006

Ministers, 25

Backbenchers, 47

Parliamentary
Secretaries, 26

Other, 4

Committee Chairs, 23

Figure 7.1b: Government caucus as of autumn 2015

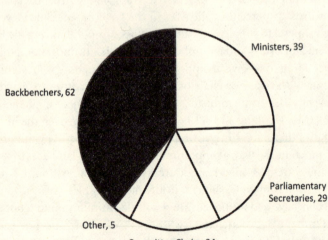

Autumn 2015

Ministers, 39

Backbenchers, 62

Parliamentary
Secretaries, 29

Other, 5

Committee Chairs, 24

and the executive branch. First, government backbenchers are in close physical proximity to Cabinet ministers and the prime minister when the House is in session. An ambitious MP could not possibly be that close to ministers and the prime minister without voicing views on public policy issues. Caucus members do not need to wait for formal caucus meetings to have influence. They mingle with ministers and the prime minister before and after Question Period in the government lobby, the cramped lounge behind the curtain on the government side of the House chamber. MPs sit with ministers during their long hours on House duty. Is it possible that backbench MPs and ministers spend that much time together without discussing politics? Is it possible backbenchers do not use that time to try to influence ministers? And is it possible that ministers, who have to testify before House standing committees and speak to their legislation at caucus meetings, do not know how backbenchers can make a minister's committee testimony or speech to caucus easier or more stressful? There are public hints at the influence of government backbenchers. Figures show, for example, that discretionary government grants for infrastructure and community groups go disproportionately to ridings held by government MPs.[3] That should not be surprising given that government MPs have preferential access to the ministers making the final decisions. If ministers favour projects in the ridings of government MPs, is that evidence of the impact of MPs?

Backbenchers have influence over weightier matters too. Take the Harper's government's Bill C-30, a legislative proposal to reform the rules around "lawful access" to the internet and other online communications. The bill, called the Protecting Children from Internet Predators Act, was introduced on Tuesday, 14 February 2012. It proposed to let law enforcement and other government agencies get certain information about online accounts from telecommunications companies and internet service providers without a judicial warrant. The caucus debate the next morning must have been interesting, since Conservative backbencher John Williamson later went on the record to criticize Bill C-30 for being "too intrusive as it currently stands." One media report mentioned that Williamson was only "one of several MPs" talking to the press about the bill.[4] Bill C-30 remained on the order paper for a year until, in February 2013, the government announced it would abandoning the effort. On hearing the news, Williamson went on the record again, saying that "[there is no justification in a free country with judicial oversight to force Internet companies to disclose information about their customers without a warrant. I'm satisfied … that our government will not be putting that measure forward again." According to media reports from the Hill, other government backbenchers had also complained about the bill, and the fact it was introduced in the House without time for caucus consultation.[5] Few bills generate such high-profile media commentary from backbenchers, but an observer must wonder whether other pieces of government legislation are abandoned or rewritten as a result of opposition or complaints from within the government caucus. After all, why would an ambitious and intelligent party operative like John Williamson otherwise leave a job like PMO Communications Director for elected life as a backbench MP if backbench MP were not a promotion?

In the next chapter, we will see how often government backbenchers and opposition MPs are able to get their own legislation passed into law. Short of that, a determined MP with a good public policy case can persuade the government to present legislation. Conservative MP John Cummins, who went on to lead the BC Conservative Party in provincial politics, was a persistent and persuasive advocate within caucus. Harper was fond of Cummins and always gave a sympathetic hearing to his policy concerns. In 2007, Cummins worried that court rulings were giving Canada Post too much power over international mail. Parliament has long given Canada Post a monopoly over delivering routine letters within Canada in exchange for the company delivering letters to all Canadian addresses for a single price. Court rulings handed down in 2005 and 2007 tried to reconcile the French and English versions of the Canada Post Corporation Act and extended the company's monopoly to international mail.[6] Those decisions undercut the business of some small Canadian firms called "international remailers" who work with European post offices to move letters in bulk from Canada to other countries at a lower price than Canada Post charges. Cummins repeatedly pushed Harper to do something to save these small firms from Canada Post's monopoly. The government eventually introduced Bill C-14 in October 2007 to restore the original understanding of Canada Post's monopoly.[7] Although the bill never passed, it was debated at second reading and gained the support of the Liberals.[8] Canada Post eased off on its efforts to squeeze the Canadian international remailers out of business.

But perhaps the greatest lever of influence available to government backbenchers comes from the confidence principle that is at the core of responsible government. On major issues, the government cannot allow itself to be defeated lest it be seen as having lost the confidence of the House. The division of the Commons into government and opposition, as we have seen before, leaves opposition MPs free to oppose the government as vigorously and consistently as they wish. The prospect of opposition MPs opposing the government at every turn means that the executive branch must have support from nearly every government MP at every turn. This dynamic is hard to document except by seeing holes in the government's legislative agenda where, one might imagine, the government caucus is deeply divided. No prime minister, given a choice, would lead caucus into a vote in the House of Commons that divides caucus members against each other. Note how reluctant Mulroney was to bring the issue of abortion to a vote in the House with Bill C-43 (Flanagan 1997) and Harper's unsuccessful effort to block a private member's motion on the question of when human life begins (see next chapter). Not every caucus member will be happy with every part of the government's agenda, but successful MPs see this as part of being a team rather than the central imposition of blind obedience (Rathgeber 2014, 82).

A party is elected or defeated as a team. The governing party and all its members of Parliament stand or fall as a group. They joined the party for a reason – either because they were attracted to its principles or its policy positions, or because they liked the prospects of its leader. Some people join parties quite early in life. The characters and habits and myths of the party become the characters and habits and myths that shape their own lives. MPs, despite all the cross-party friendships and temporary alliances that emerge, understand that everyone in the other parties is trying to defeat them and their colleagues. That fact makes for omnipresent pressures to act like a team.

Political Parties off the Hill

Political parties do more than shape political life on Parliament Hill. The major political parties have associations in ridings across Canada. Some have regional and provincial wings. They all have national offices. These non-parliamentary wings of the political parties influence our politics as much as the parliamentary wings do. Most candidates for election to the House of Commons are selected by party riding associations, and most leaders are selected by the non-parliamentary wings of the parties as well. The non-parliamentary wings may have policy development, volunteer development, and campaign planning roles. They also raise the substantial funds required to keep themselves running.

Another way in which party leaders, including prime ministers, are said to have upset the balance of forces inside parties is in their legislative power to approve who runs as a candidate under their party's label at election time. They are said to have too much power over the non-parliamentary wings of their parties. Aucoin claims that a leader's power to approve the candidates who run under the party's banner at election times is evidence of this imbalance of forces. Elizabeth May even claims that this power is the "key change" in our system of government (2017, 18).

Under the Elections Act, the power to approve candidates is actually one of the weaker formal powers of a party leader. It is not much of an exaggeration to say that the act makes a party the creature of the leader rather than the leader the creature of the party. For example, under the act, it is the party's leader who must apply to register the party with the chief electoral officer (s. 385) and the leader may withdraw that application (s. 386). Registration is critical for any political party since a party cannot accept donations or spend money until it is registered. The leader and two officers of the party may ask to have the party deregistered (s. 414). Similarly, a party riding association cannot register, and therefore cannot accept donations or spend money, without first submitting an application to register that is signed by the party leader (s. 448(2)). A party leader and two officers of the party can force the chief electoral officer to deregister a riding association (s. 467(2)). Short of creating or abolishing the party or one of its riding associations with the agreement of two officials of the party, a leader must agree to the appointment of the registered agent of his party (s. 405(1)). The registered agent then controls and accounts for all the money raised and spent by the party's national organization. The registered agent may then move national funds to local campaign accounts once an election is under way. And, informally, a party leader has the power to name the party's campaign manager.

These powers are far more influential than the formal requirement that a party leader sign the nomination forms of all the party's candidates, and they are well-known within the government caucus. An MP with a well-funded riding association may not need the national party's funds for a re-election campaign, but an MP or candidate with few local funds may feel that toeing the line will help secure financial assistance at election time. Even an MP with a well-funded riding association might want the prime minister or minister to drop by the riding for a fundraising event. These fundraising activities bring well-deserved scrutiny under the federal conflict of interest rules from the ethics commissioner, particularly since former Minister of Natural Resources Lisa Raitt was investigated in relation to a riding fundraiser (Commissioner 2010). Harper steered clear of Conservative fundraising events, but Justin Trudeau has been involved in several Liberal Party events. The campaign manager selected by the prime minister makes thousands of decisions about the governing party's re-election campaign that can help or hurt individual MPs and candidates. A prime minister usually wants to win as many seats as possible during an election, but every MP realizes that campaign decisions about where the leader's tour will travel, where other "surrogates" will travel, and where national advertising, telephone banking, direct mail, and digital marketing goes all matter to that MP's re-election campaign.

Fortunately, at Harper's insistence, the Constitution of the Conservative Party of Canada prohibits members of Parliament or senators (other than the leader), employees of parliamentarians including ministerial aides, and members of provincial or territorial assemblies from serving on the party's National Council (Conservative Party of Canada, 2016, s. 8(3)).[9] This puts decisions about party policy, riding-level organization, and the rules regarding the selection of party candidates in the hands of volunteer activists. Don Plett, for example, had to step aside as a member of the party's National Council and as its president when he was named to the Senate. A Conservative leader has the formal power to nominate the party's executive director, but that nomination must be approved by the National Council. Certainly, Harper, when he was Conservative leader, had a strong influence over the operation of the party, but its political and organizational affairs were run at a distance from its parliamentary wing.

Would Canada's political parties be better with more influence in the hands of volunteer activists and members? Perhaps. Unfortunately, since the Election Act was amended at the end of Chrétien's time in office to expand the regulation of party riding associations, it has become harder to maintain the influence of volunteer activists. Chrétien's political finance reforms gave national party offices new levers to police local riding associations and ensure they comply with the new financing regulations. Riding associations must now have registered financial agents between elections to ensure they comply with the law. Those financial agents are supposed to be volunteers, and yet they have heavy responsibilities under the law. The handbook for financial agents is sixty-three dense pages (Elections Canada 2017). Elections Canada has a comprehensive program for training and supporting local volunteers who take on the obligations of being a registered agent, but, as in every industry, new regulation brings the need for professionalization. Chrétien had good reasons to pursue his political finance reforms, and I support them. But they had consequences in squeezing out volunteer efforts at the local level.

Reforming Parties: Chong's Reform Bill

In the last year of the Harper government, Michael Chong's Reform Bill, an ambitious private member's bill, garnered media attention. In its original form, the Reform Bill was almost a direct response to Aucoin's criticisms of imbalance of power within political parties. The very name of the bill was intended to hearken back to the British reform acts, particularly the Great Reform Acts of 1832 that overhauled voting and election law in UK. But whereas the Great Reform Acts were intended to democratize British government, Chong's Reform Bill had a more limited aim: to rein in the power of federal party leaders, especially of the party leader that becomes prime minister. Chong's Reform Bill eventually squeaked through in a heavily amended form in 2015, just as the forty-first Parliament was drawing to a close. The final version of the bill was a weak legislative effort. It allowed the MPs (but not senators) in each party caucus to decide if they would like to elect their caucus chair, if they would like the power to expel and re-admit caucus members, and if they would like to empower 20 percent of their colleagues to trigger a review of their leader's mandate. The Reform Act came into effect following 2015 election. MPs in most of the parliamentary caucuses promptly decided they didn't want to take advantage of any of its provisions. So far, the Reform Act has had no practical effect on our system of government.

The original bill was a more ambitious effort. It would have turned control over local nomination contests to an official selected by the members of each party's riding association. Central party machines would have lost any influence over these contests, and party leaders would have to sign the nomination forms of the party's candidates. It would also have forced parties to allow as few as 15 percent of the MPs in their parliamentary caucuses to trigger a review of the party's leader at any time. And it would have set rules governing how a caucus member may be expelled or readmitted to a caucus and for the selection and removal of the chair of each caucus. Chong's defence of his original bill was explicit about the need to restrain the power of party leaders and echoed the arguments of Aucoin and others. He argued the bill would limit the control of party leaders over candidates and MPs seeking re-election by removing their power to certify who runs under each party's banner. He felt that the "unwritten rules" of Parliament have changed in ways that disadvantage ordinary MPs and put power in hands of party leaders. "The governance and power structure of these parliamentary parties are important because it is parliamentary parties, and not individual MPs, that directly control the agenda and activities of Parliament"; he also argued that "The role of the parliamentary party in reviewing the leader has been little used, and the rules opaque. This has weakened the accountability of party leaders to MPs.". His bill, he argued, would "rebalance power in Ottawa, putting a check on the power of party leaders, and by extension the PMO. By giving the people's elected MPs a greater say, these reforms will restore Canada's Parliament to the way it once successfully worked for decades in Canada. A greater diversity of views will be allowed and MPs will be able to vote more freely in the House of Commons, whether on principle or on behalf of their constituents" (Chong 2014, 17).

Although the original version of the bill was applauded by some observers, it was not well thought through. First consider the bill's impact on local nomination races. Readers who have never been involved in a local nomination contest would be astounded at the tactics employed by undesirable would-be candidates. Local nomination races are often brutal contests fought face to face. The bill would have put every hotly contested local nomination race in the hands of whoever controlled the local riding association at the time the nomination race began. Local party boards would have been able to hold their nomination races whenever they wanted, using whatever rules they chose to adopt. The earliest potential candidate for the nomination in a riding would only have had to stack the riding executive early in the electoral cycle, usually when a local party organization is at its weakest point, to be able to set the rules for the race and name the returning officer. The first version of the bill would have created an overwhelming incentive for candidates to organize early and use their dominance of the local organization to keep other candidates out of the contest. National party organizations would have been powerless to step in and level the playing field. This part of the Reform Act, if it had survived, would have generated a steady stream of court challenges from losing candidates across the country. Moreover, national party officers would have been powerless to reject candidates with serious criminal records, poor credit ratings, or public records of making incendiary comments. As Executive Director of the Conservative Party of Canada in 2004–05, including during the run-up to the 2004 general election, my staff and I, with the backing of the party's National Council, intervened in local nomination contests on all these grounds. The work that party staff do to keep wife-beating, drug-dealing goons from getting elected to Parliament is an essential public service. Parties are held to account, and should be held to account, for the candidates that get to use the party's name in elections. A candidate that has been deemed unsuitable by one party's officials can always run for another party or as an independent candidate.

Then consider the bill's impact on leadership reviews. Party leaders are now generally selected by thousands of party members in riding associations from coast to coast, including in areas where the party has not elected an MP. Each party's constitution has rules governing leadership reviews and these are updated from time to time by party members or delegates to party conventions. Chong's original bill would have set aside all those arrangements. In their place, it would have imposed a single rule allowing a small number of MPs to trigger a review, even (or especially) for the governing party.

Chong's case for his bill was hard to square with the recent political history of Canadian parties. A party leader has had to sign the nomination forms for every party candidate since 1970. That power has hardly been abused. How many times has a party leader, especially a prime minister, refused to sign the nomination papers of an MP seeking re-election? If party affiliation is going to appear on the ballot, someone has to certify who is entitled to have it. Turning this power over to someone who would likely be a supporter of the locally elected candidate removes a check and balance from the process. The cost of having a bad candidate running under a party's name is not born just by that candidate, either. Every candidate running for the party is hurt when bad candidates go off the rails. This is especially the case in new parties, and Chong's Reform Bill would have hit them particularly hard. Consider Tom Flanagan's experience keeping extremists out of the young Reform Party (Flanagan 1995). Or the impact of 2012 Wildrose candidate Allan Hunsperger's "lake of fire" comments, which helped that party lose control of its own campaign messaging in the final week of the provincial campaign (Flanagan 2014a, 185).[10] Chong's original bill imagined that every party has healthy riding associations in every part of the country. But given the regional nature of party support there will always be areas of the country with weak riding associations in every party. Far from enhancing local democracy, the nomination rules proposed in original Reform Act would have caused untold new problems. Chong lived through all of this history, but none of the lessons of this history made it into the original version of the bill.

When it comes to expelling caucus members, the considerations are similar to those governing the nomination of party candidates. In the autumn 2003, seven months before Chong was elected to the House and in the middle of the campaigns to have the Canadian Alliance and PC parties ratify their merger to form the Conservative Party, the Vancouver Sun reported comments by MP Larry Spencer calling for the recriminalization of homosexuality and raising concerns about a gay conspiracy to seduce young boys. Spencer left the Canadian Alliance caucus after the comments came to light but probably would have been expelled or suspended by his colleagues if he had not left. The comments of individual caucus members reflect on their colleagues. Chong was a caucus colleague of Garth Turner when Turner was suspended from Conservative caucus in October 2006. During his short time as Conservative MP, Turner regularly sniped at party leader Stephen Harper. Although his Wikipedia entry claims he was ejected from caucus by an edict of the party's leadership, this seems unlikely. Turner had criticized Harper's appointment of David Emerson to Cabinet eight months earlier. He was not suspended from caucus, however, until after he criticized his caucus colleagues for opposing more rigorous gun control, dismissing them as the "hats-and-horses" crowd.[11] While it is safe to say Harper did nothing to stop caucus from suspending Turner, I never saw him do anything to provoke or encourage the suspension either. Chong, who was a Cabinet minister at the time, did not raise any questions about the suspension – in effect an expulsion – at the time. He did resign from Cabinet five weeks later and did so over another issue. Chong also did not object when Bill Casey was ejected from the Conservative caucus for voting against the 2007 budget – a confidence motion.

His argument that the power of party caucuses to review their leaders has been little used fares even worse. Party caucuses do eject their leaders. As Flanagan (2014b, 19) notes, "It is not as if Canadian party leaders are hard to turn out of office." Jean Chrétien, once reputed to be in total control of his caucus, was deposed as party leader and prime minister by supporters of Paul Martin within his own caucus. "Caucus already has the ability to unseat a leader if enough members feel strongly enough about the issue," Flanagan writes, citing the PC caucus and Cabinet deposing John Diefenbaker and the Canadian Alliance caucus deposing Stockwell Day at the national level. The PC caucus certainly helped to topple Joe Clark as PC leader in 1983. A very different PC caucus toppled Clark a second time in 2002. Provincial politics provide many examples of caucuses toppling sitting premiers – Ed Stelmach in 2011, and Alison Redford and Kathy Dunderdale in 2014. Manitoba Premier Greg Selinger was nearly deposed by his caucus in 2014.[12] Canadian party caucuses seem to have no trouble deposing leaders when they need to do so. In recent Canadian history, the list of first ministers ejected by government caucuses is impressive.

For some Canadian observers, Australia's brutal "leadership spills" are an attractive way to make party leaders accountable to their caucus colleagues.[13] Under rules established by each party in Australia (not by Reform Act-style legislation), a caucus member may propose to declare the party's leadership vacant at any caucus meeting. If a certain number of caucus members agree with the call, the leadership is declared vacant and a new party leader is immediately elected by caucus. The original version of the Reform Act would have moved Canada in the direction of Australian-style spills.[14] Spills have triggered high profile, high-stakes moments of intense drama in Australia politics in the last few years. Between 2003 and 2010, both of Australia's major parties, the Liberals and Labour, subjected their leaders to frequent reviews while serving in opposition. But starting in 2010, a series of leadership spills were called in the government caucus, making the Australian prime ministership an unstable, revolving door. The Labour government was beset by a deep caucus divide over who should lead the party. Kevin Rudd, who had led the party to a landslide victory in the 2007 general election, was toppled by his deputy leader, Julia Gillard, in a June 2010 spill. In a general election held two months later Labour tied the Liberals and Gillard survived as prime minister only with the support of a few independent MPs and the sole Green MP. She then survived a spill triggered by Rudd in February 2012 and another by long-time Labour leadership hopeful Simon Crean a year later. Gillard was eventually topped by Rudd in June 2013, just months ahead of that September's national elections. Tony Abbott led the Liberals to a landslide victory in that campaign. Abbott in turn survived a spill in the government caucus in early 2015, only to be dumped in a second spill a few months later. He was replaced as prime minister by Malcolm Turnbull.

As the debate over Chong's Reform Act was unfolding in Canada, Australia's Labour Party moved to tame the spill. When Rudd returned to the Labour leadership in 2013, he pushed his caucus colleagues to reform the party's rules on leader's spills. The threshold for triggering a spill increased from 30 percent of caucus members to 60 percent when the ALP is in opposition and increased to 75 percent of caucus members when the party is in government. At the same time, Labour extended the length of any leadership campaign that follows a spill. Rudd argued these reforms would ensure "the prime minister the Australian people vote for is the prime minister the Australian people get."[15] Taming the spill did not save Labour in that autumn's election, but it reassured voters that the party could manage its own internal pressures without producing upheaval in the government as a result.

Finally, a closer study of the selection of political party leaders in Canada shows that caucus support matters when mounting a successful leadership campaign. Few federal party leaders are elected without widespread support in their party's parliamentary caucus, and the ones who are elected without substantial caucus support do not last very long. Chrétien and Martin both had broad support from caucus members when they became Liberal leader. Harper was far ahead of his rivals in caucus support for the Conservative leadership. So was Mulcair. By contrast, leaders with little caucus support, like Stockwell Day and Stéphane Dion, have trouble surviving leadership crises. In the recent Conservative leadership race, it was surprising to see Maxime Bernier, who had narrow support from caucus, come so close to winning but not a surprise to see Andrew Scheer and Erin O'Toole, the candidates with broad caucus support, also at the top of the ballot. Do members of Parliament exert influence over local party members in one-member, one-vote leadership races? Or are MPs simply very good proxies for grassroots party members? We need more research in the dynamics of these races to know for sure. But the idea that the move from caucus selection of leaders to leadership conventions and now one-member, one-vote systems somehow reduces the power of MPs over party leaders needs some reconsideration.

A few journalists speculated that the watering down of Chong's Reform Bill meant MPs had buckled to pressure from party leaders. But it is just as likely that both government and opposition MPs considered the bill and concluded there were good reasons to be cautious about it. The Reform Act eventually passed, with much ado about very little. Even its original form would have given a small minority of MPs the power to cause chaos in even a governing party. It would have had a terrible effect on political dynamics at the riding level. The great British Reform Bills of the nineteenth and early twentieth centuries are rightly remembered for enfranchising millions of people and cleaning up corrupt institutions of that country's government. Michael Chong's Reform Act could have been something similar in Canada if it had been better thought through.

The timing of Chong's original bill should also have raised eyebrows. It was introduced on 3 December 2013, merely five weeks after the Conservative Party's national convention in Calgary. Delegates elected by party members across the country spent hours debating amendments to the party constitution. Chong could have brought his proposals to change party nomination and leadership rules to that convention. He could have explained them to party activists and members with experience in hotly contested nomination races or leadership reviews. Those activists and members could have offered their views. If Chong had been persuasive, the Conservative Party would have been the test bed for the Reform Act, and the next few years would have either substantiated Chong's arguments or invalidated them. Instead, he ignored rank and file party members and enlisted his fellow MPs to set aside the wishes of party activists and members.

Parties, Partisans, and Partisanship

Responsible government is more than a mechanical contraption. It is more than a set of institutions and offices impersonally and automatically checking and balancing and administering. Responsible government shapes the minds of Canada's political leaders and Canadian citizens. Parties are sewn into its fabric. Just as the rules of hockey and football condition us to see these as team sports, responsible government conditions us to see politics as a team sport. The US Constitution conditions Americans to see the president and Congress at loggerheads. Our form of government pits team against team – government against opposition. Just as a casual sports fan may only be able to name one or two stars on a team, busy citizens who do not pay close attention to politics may barely be able to name the party leaders. Nonetheless, it is the team aspect of politics that makes it accessible to citizens.

It is the team spirit of politics that supplies the Madisonian "personal motivation" to make parties work. Parties need partisans, and partisans are citizens who are motivated, in part, by partisanship. Not every citizen is suited to being a partisan. Some people are just loners who prefer the unfettered liberty of living life alone or who find they make enough effort to be married, to work in a firm, or to contribute to a local club or church without needing to be part of a larger human enterprise. Others may feel so certain of their own righteousness that find they cannot make the kinds of compromises needed to work within a political party. To them, teams may seem like closed clubs or cliques. In a free country, citizens are free to join or not to join political parties. But people who cannot find a way to work with their fellow citizens will have little impact on the collective life of the community. To have impact, citizens must work with others, making compromises along the way. Partisanship is one way to empower citizens.

Canadians who watch hockey understand the dynamics of teamwork. They come to games expecting to see two teams in a competition. The know they will join cheering fans in the stands. They know they will see players on the bench shouting encouragement to teammates on the ice. In the middle of a game, a hockey arena is filled with loud, raucous celebrations of good plays and loud, raucous commiseration at bad ones. Some fans will let their sense of fair play escape them; they boo and hiss when a referee's call goes against their team. Other fans who want to be seen exercising greater self-control will tut-tut a bad call quietly. Playing the game well requires passion as well as skill. We should not be surprised, then, when Question Period and other political debates sound like a hockey game. Cheers and groans are the essence of team competition, on ice or on Parliament Hill. What kind of kill-joy wants a Stanley Cup game to be played in silence, with those in attendance only permitted to clap politely at the end of a period? The stuffy rules of civility at Wimbledon are not suitable to a Canadian sensibility. University professors, who are not usually known for making good team players or fans, struggle to understand how partisanship can make someone into a better citizen. For me, without partisanship, politics becomes the dull disengagement of a faculty meeting.

Good parliamentarians like Michael Cooper (Cooper 2017) are sometimes distressed when teachers and youth leaders say they will not take young people to see Question Period because they want to protect their charges from the juvenile behaviour that goes on between elected representatives in the House of Commons. This drives parliamentarians like Cooper to recommend reforms to make Question Period more civil or tame. Cooper proposes to end clapping and some heckling. With respect, though, this is the wrong approach. A wild, raucous Question Period is a wonderful teaching moment. Other countries settle their political disputes with civil wars or riots. The antics of Question Period are the worst way to settle political disputes, except for all the rest. Why not use Question Period as an opportunity to introduce young people to what is at stake in politics rather than trying to hide them from it? In Canada, people are free to disagree, and we disagree about matters big and small. What is at stake in the House of Commons is far more consequential than what is at stake in a hockey game, and we should expect people to be just as committed to their cause in the House as hockey fans are to their team in an important game. Yes, sometimes parliamentarians can be juvenile, just as hockey fans are sometimes juvenile. Sometimes parliamentarians lose their sense of decorum and drop the metaphorical gloves, just as hockey players drop their actual gloves at times. But if young people want to have an impact as citizens, it behooves us to teach them what is involved in organizing and motivating groups and political parties. Political parties need partisans, and we all need political parties whether we can imagine ourselves in them or not.

Unlike the US form of government, Canada presents citizens with a governing team – and a team that could become government. Americans get to see their political alternatives for election to the House of Representatives every two years, for the White House every four years, and for the Senate twice in every six years. In between, citizens can only guess what their choices might be at the next ballot, and when American candidates are finally nominated voters may find they have little time to compare them. Canadian citizens see their choices more clearly. At the next election, they will be able to re-elect the government or put one of the other teams in office. Every Question Period, every budget speech, every parliamentary debate, and every parliamentary committee hearing informs that choice by highlighting the role of the opposition and the responsibility of the government. Television talk shows devoted to politics reinforce the parliamentary context by featuring talk heads from the government and the major opposition parties. And at every turn, the governing party makes its argument for its re-election while the opposition parties make their arguments for the alternative. This gives voters a lot of material to work with in casting their vote. Citizens may want to be able to pick and choose individuals from among the parties to create a Cabinet, but our form of government presses the parties to become teams and forces citizens to consider the bigger picture when they vote. A party that sticks together as a team is said to be ready to govern; a party that cannot stick together lacks the maturity to govern.

The fact that Canadian politics is a team, meaning party, sport also gives us clear lines of accountability at the highest and most visible level. Not many citizens devote much time to evaluating the performance of individual politicians or Cabinet ministers, and in any case attributing fault or merit to any one individual player on a team is perilous. Americans can never really tell who should be held responsible if they sense something is badly wrong with the political direction of their country. In times of divided government, when different parties control the two chambers of Congress and the executive branch, accountability is diffused through the normal incentives of partisan competition. But even in times of unified government, when one party controls the House, the Senate, and the White House, it can be hard to figure out whom to hold accountable for large-scale failure. In Canada, the line of accountability is clear. The prime minister, for better or for worse, heads the team and ultimately bears the responsibility for the good and for the bad.

The Senate and the Institutional Uses of Partisanship

Justin Trudeau's government recently introduced an experiment in unaccountable and nonpartisan government with its reforms to the appointment of senators. From 1867 until 2015, the appointed Senate was acceptable in a democratic nation because senators were appointed as partisans and were therefore limited in their powers. On paper, the Senate was as powerful as the elected House of Commons. In fact, senators understood that as unelected partisans they ought to defer to the judgement of elected, partisan MPs when exercising their legislative roles. They could make technical changes to legislation adopted by the House. Their committees could study and issue reports on a broad range of public issues. But if senators disagreed with the House on legislative matters they knew the elected branch should succeed. Partisanship checked their powers.

Harper tried to reform the Senate in two ways: by shortening the tenure of senators and by allowing the prime minister to consult the voters of a province before making appointments to the Upper House. Taken together Harper's proposed reforms would have made the Senate, like the House, both partisan and accountable to the voters. Like the House, the Senate would have become elected and powerful. Harper would have reinvigorated the Senate as a legislative chamber but submitted it to the discipline of regular elections. The Supreme Court of Canada ruled Harper's reforms could not proceed by simple legislation, effectively killing off the effort (Brodie 2014;

Morton 2015). It found that a substantial change to the nature of the Senate required a formal constitutional amendment.

The Trudeau reforms are pressing at the edges of the Supreme Court's decision. Shifting the Senate from a partisan to a non-partisan body by making most senators "independents" without attachment to any party marks a fundamental change in the nature of the Upper House. A Senate that is not limited by partisanship or elections is dangerous. The Senate's effort to block one of the Trudeau government's budget bills in spring 2017 put it on a path to a constitutional overreach. Crisis was only averted when the independent senators backed down (Bryden 2017). Policy, especially budget policy, should be the preserve of democratically accountable chambers. The Senate can be either unelected and partisan – unaccountable and weak – or elected and partisan – accountable and strong. Democratic principles cannot tolerate a legislature that is unaccountable and strong.

To say that parties are essential to the democratic operation of responsible government is not to say that the parties we have today are essential, or that those parties must operate the way our parties operate today for responsible government to work properly. But the fact that all of our political parties today feature strong leaders and disciplined caucuses is not a coincidence. Parties are the vital crucibles for forming politicians, political leaders, and, in the end, popular consent in our form of government.

Parties and the Electoral System

Understanding the balance of forces inside our political parties is only one aspect of how parties matter to the health of our form of government. There is another measure that matters, and that is the balance of forces between the parties. Voters should be able to alternate the party in government when they think it is appropriate, and to make that possible at least two of the parties must be competitive in the race for government. Étienne Parent grew worried Papineau did not see a need for any party other than the Patriotes; while we do not need to worry about one-party politics, we should be concerned about the balance between the parties. Ideally, the voters change governments regularly and see clearly how their votes produce a change of government. A new government brings a refresh of priorities, new approaches to existing challenges, and cleans the carbuncles that build up on every governing party. It is sometimes said that governments and diapers both need changing regularly, and for the same reason. The electoral system's role is to provide that competitiveness and to demonstrate to voters how their votes can force a change in government, and Canada's Westminster-style, first-past-the-post electoral system certainly fills that requirement. Political science has long understood that first-past-the-post discourages the creation of new parties. The discipline also knows that under our system, a small swing in votes from election to election often produces big swings in the number of seats won by the competitive parties. In the 2011 federal election, the Conservatives won 40 percent of the votes cast and 54 percent of the seats up for grabs. In 2015, they won 32 percent of the votes and only 29 percent of the seats. First-past-the-post magnified the relatively small share of votes lost into a much larger loss of seats.

First-past-the-post is often criticized for electing a group of MPs that fails to reflect the diversity of the Canadian electorate. But the House of Commons will never reflect the full diversity of the Canadian electorate. The very purpose of representation, as opposed to direct democracy, is to simplify and reduce the diversity of views and beliefs of the whole electorate to something that can be managed in a deliberative chamber. Responsible government and the procedural rules of the House then further reduce that diversity into a series of binary choices. Are you for or against the government? That determines where you sit in the House. Are you for or against this piece of legislation? MPs can vote yea or nay, or they can abstain. Votes do not reflect the diversity of views in the House let alone the broader electorate. Certain groups of identities within the electorate – women, indigenous persons, some ethnic or religious groups – are underrepresented in the House. We should always be alert to institutional factors that block someone from entering politics, but as long as a broad range of popular views and beliefs is represented in the House that is probably the most we can hope for.

In their 2015 election platform, the Trudeau Liberals promised to replace the first-past-the-post electoral system, but once in office, and following a long public consultation, they abandoned the effort in 2017. Trudeau later explained that the Liberals "had a preference to give people a ranked ballot so they could reduce the aspect of strategic voting" by allowing voters to specify their second and third choices on the ballot rather than having to guess which parties would be competitive in their riding before marking their vote.[16] The problem of vote splitting disappeared when the Liberals were elected; Trudeau and his election team successfully appealed to progressive voters in addition to traditional Liberals in that campaign, reducing the arguments for voters to cast their ballots for the NDP. The Liberals had done exactly what the existing electoral system encourages them to do, and they had done it well. Normal party politics rather than institutional reform turned out to be enough to fix the problem. Proportional representation, the electoral system favoured by the NDP, would, Trudeau said, "weaken one of the great things about Canada," namely that "we come together in our diversity to work together on big things." The fragmentation of political parties that would like occur under a proportional representation system would weaken Canada by introducing too much diversity into the House. And, he continued, the Conservatives did not want to change the electoral system. So his government abandoned the effort altogether.

Political scientists sometimes criticize the fact that first-past-the-post can produce a majority government out of an election where none of the parties gets 50 percent of the votes (Cairns 1968; Russell 2008). First-past-the-post exaggerates the size of election victories, and for political scientists that focus primarily on the House of Commons as a representative institution that is a shortcoming. But the House is more than simply a representative institution, and by exaggerating the size of election victories our electoral system serves the important function of forcing a decisive change of government every so often. The first-past-the-post system made it easier for the Liberals, with a modest 40 percent of the votes cast, to replace the Conservatives. The ranked ballot system that Trudeau preferred would likely have made it easier for the Liberals, as long as they remain the second choice of most Conservative and NDP voters, to continue to form government. However, preserving first-past-the-post makes it more likely that another party will eventually replace the Liberals. Canadians, regardless of their party allegiance, can be grateful for that.

8

Democratizing or Bureaucratizing the Constitution?

Is It *Still* a Constitutional Form of Government Today?

Donald Savoie is not the only one to raise questions about whether Canada's form of government still counts as a constitutional one. Many writers on responsible government reject the idea that our form of government establishes a separation of powers, and without a separation of powers no durable system of checks and balances is possible. As Dennis Baker notes, the "conventional wisdom" in Canada is that our form of government "has no functioning separation of powers between the legislative and executive branches, and thus no effective checks and balances" (2010, 8), citing comments from distinguished legal scholars such as Peter Hogg, Patrick Monahan, Barry Strayer, and the political scientist James Kelly. "That Canada's system of responsible government precludes a separation of powers between the executive and the legislature has clearly become the orthodoxy among scholars" (ibid.).

The most comprehensive argument about the end of constitutional government in Canada since Savoie is *Democratizing the Constitution* (Aucoin et al. 2011). Aucoin's criticisms of political parties featured in the last chapter, but the book makes a far broader point, namely that Canada has "A constitution without effective constraints" (56). The central failing, he argues, is that "The House of Commons is unable to constrain the prime minister from abusing power, beyond attempting to mobilize public opinion, because the powers to summon, prorogue and dissolve Parliament are assigned to the governor general and not the House" (57). This is especially a problem when a prime minister heads a majority government "if the prime minister has excessive control over Cabinet and caucus as has been the case in Canada for some time" (ibid., citing Samara 2011). The House, he argues, could not constrain decisions of Prime Minister Stephen Harper's that Aucoin claims were made in bad faith. Aucoin paints a desperate picture of Canada's constitution.

The crux of Aucoin's case against Harper, and the rallying cry of many of Harper's partisan opponents, was his decision to ask the governor general to prorogue Parliament in December 2008. Events of that autumn are now well behind us, and there has been a change of government. Perhaps it is time for a sober re-evaluation, one that takes into account a full consideration of the political context of that prorogation. Remember that, shortly after the 2008 election, Liberal Leader Stéphane Dion announced his resignation as party leader. His hold on his party's caucus was tenuous and although he had stopped Harper short of a majority the Liberals had lost seats and lost share of the popular vote. Dion took responsibility for his party's poor showing. But, instead of following the normal practice, which would have seen him step down and allow the Liberal caucus to select an interim leader, he insisted on staying on until his successor could be selected. This peculiar decision was an early hint of trouble to come. When the House reconvened, the Harper government presented an autumn economic update that stood pat on the macroeconomic situation. This was a wise decision even in the face of the global financial crisis then in full swing. His government had passed a large fiscal stimulus a year earlier and taken ambitious steps to respond to the collapse of Lehman Brothers in the middle of the election campaign. The US was in the midst of a presidential transition. Design a further crisis response for a small open economy without knowing the future direction of US policy would have been foolhardy. Harper decided to wait and see.

The economic update did, however, contain one surprise: it proposed to phase out the quarterly public subsidy that was then paid to political parties. Despite the government's protests, this was widely seen as an effort to hurt the opposition parties, in particular the Liberals. They had not yet figured out how to raise enough small-money donations from individuals to make up for the large-money corporate fundraising that Chrétien's political finance reforms had made illegal. Errol Mendes (2008) was particularly strident in his criticisms, accusing the Harper government of trying to "bankrupt most of the political opposition" in an effort that "could well result in a 'Putin'-style authoritarian democracy in Canada." He even hinted that ending the party subsidy could be unconstitutional since it was a "constitutional trade-off" for ending corporate and large-money individual donations. Harper was destroying a "constitutional balancing act."

Dion and NDP leader Jack Layton used the controversy over the public subsidy to announce they had agreed, with the support of the Bloc, to vote non-confidence in the Harper government and form a new government. The Liberal-NDP pact was stunning news. The election had cost the Liberals eighteen seats, and Dion had resigned as leader. Layton had fought his third election as NDP leader, and his success seemed stalled. He could not seem to be able to lead his party past 20 percent support in an election and faced internal grumblings about his leadership. When it then emerged that Dion and Layton had discussed ways to displace Harper before the economic update was presented, the Dion-Layton pact started to look like a way for two weakened leaders to protect their own positions against their own party activists. After the initial shock of the pact wore off, Harper went to the governor general and asked that the House be prorogued. This would head off the Liberal-NDP scheme; the Standing Orders of House of Commons allocate no special priority to non-confidence motions. The Liberals and NDP could have pressed for reforms when the Standing Orders were renegotiated after the 2006 or 2008 election, especially since it had taken time to get the motion of non-confidence in the Martin government onto the floor in November 2005. This was a known issue, and if the Liberals, Bloc, and NDP had wanted to fix it, they had the votes to amend the Standing Orders between spring 2006 and December 2008. Instead, just as the Conservatives, the NDP, and the Bloc did after the 2004 election, the opposition negotiated for other rule changes after the 2006 election. When Dion and Layton finally decided they had to secure their positions from dissension within their parties by joining forces, they had to wait for the procedural opportunities to do so. Harper, Layton, and Duceppe had had to do the same in autumn 2005. The governor general decided to grant Harper's request, a decision that was unimpeachable. A governor general must always find a prime minister to take responsibility for her decisions. She had only one alternative to accepting Harper's request: to fire him, call for Dion to form a government, and hope Dion could gain the confidence of the House. The prospect of Dion becoming prime minister while holding his party together by threads would have been daunting. He had already said he would serve as prime minister only through April 2009, when the next Liberal leader was to be selected. Presumably the candidates for the Liberal leadership could not have served in his Cabinet, and the Dion-Layton pact would have become an issue during that leadership campaign. Michael Ignatieff had made a show of being the last Liberal caucus member to sign a letter of support for Dion's gambit and let it be known he had doubts about the arrangement. The new Liberal leader would not have been bound to abide by any agreement Dion had made. The Dion-Layton pact was a farce. There was no parallel to the 1985 Peterson-Rae pact that toppled the PC dynasty in Ontario.

The "prorogation crisis" provoked immediate controversy in the academic world. Legal scholars and political scientists at the University of Toronto convened to produce a quick book on the events around the prorogation (Russell and Sossin 2009) that might have been better if the editors could have found anyone at the university with anything good to say for Harper.

Tom Flanagan (2009) weighed in to note that Harper's comments about prorogation and the Dion-Layton-Duceppe effort were modest and limited, comments that failed to satisfy Harper's political opponents.[1] For evidence that both Her Excellency Michaëlle Jean and Harper acted properly, recall that the "crisis" itself ended pretty quickly. Parliament was prorogued 4 December and returned on 26 January. The government presented a budget on 27 January and was sustained in the House. But by then the Liberals had pushed Dion out and made Ignatieff their leader. Ignatieff, in turn, immediately killed the Dion-Layton pact, and the Harper government continued in office for another two years. Setting aside the rallies, protests, and op-eds, with hindsight and a different party in government, we can now see that the December 2008 prorogation gave everyone time for sober second thought about the Dion-Layton pact. Aucoin argues that this episode shows the House cannot constrain a prime minister intent on abusing his powers: "The several weeks' delay saw the unity among the three opposition parties crumble and support for the non-confidence motion erode" (2011, 54), but Aucoin misses the historical point. There was never any clear evidence that the three parties were really behind the non-confidence motion. Ignatieff's wily decision to show only lukewarm support for the plan indicates the depth of the problem on the Liberal benches. It is quite possible that if Her Excellency had not agreed to prorogue the Liberal and NDP caucuses would have split apart when the roll was called in the House of Commons. It was not the six weeks' delay that led to the crumbling support for the Dion-Layton gambit. If Harper had really overstepped his bounds, the Liberals, NDP, and Bloc would have passed the non-confidence motion even with the delay. Instead, the Dion-Layton pact was a desperate move by a lame-duck leader to give his leadership career a second life by means of a coalition that his own caucus colleagues quickly figured out was not in their political interests. As soon as the House was prorogued, they overthrew Dion, coalesced behind Ignatieff, and put all talk of a coalition behind them. The only "crisis" was inside the Liberal Party, and prorogation gave the Liberals time to restore their internal checks and balances.

The Role of the Public Service

Is it simply a coincidence that the two major academic books about the centralization of power in Canadian government are by Donald Savoie and Peter Aucoin, both scholars of public administration? After all, the discipline of public administration started as an effort to separate the business public servants and public administration from politicians and politics. Possibly the criticisms of "court government" reflect public administration's lingering discomfort with politics itself.

Public administration was first described in North America by future US president Woodrow Wilson in an academic article (1887). At the time, the "eminently practical science of administration" was starting to be taught and the civil service reform movement had already started replacing political patronage in government with professional staffing by career officials. Wilson's article looked beyond these developments toward a time when the expansion of government would bring more rational organization and method to government. The "science of administration," he wrote, should be *applied* to government but sit *outside* of politics. Administration and democratic government, he noted, were hard to reconcile. The new "unpartisan" and permanent public service, because of its superior training and expertise, should share in governing. Like most progressives of the era, Wilson viewed "politics" as inherently corrupt, unprincipled, unsophisticated, and prone to electing poorly educated leaders. "Public administration" would create a new, cleaner form of government run by a new elite – a new aristocracy – modernized for a modern world and embedded in government.

Public administration has evolved since Wilson's article, but the antipathy to politics and politicians remains. And it runs through Savoie and Aucoin's arguments about the centralization of political power within the executive. Savoie, as we saw in chapter 4, bemoans parliamentary debates that do nothing but create scandals and assign blame. This, in turn, forces the executive to focus its attention on avoiding blame for what it does. The news media and the opposition parties, working together, distort policy-making. Savoie hopes the parliamentary scrutiny of government spending can be marked by reasoned debates and not partisan arguments. Aucoin and his co-authors fret about prime ministers using their powers to advantage their partisan interests. They argue the number of political staff on Parliament Hill should be cut in half, both to reduce the power of the prime minister (although how across the board reductions would reduce the prime minister's power is unclear) and also for "good governance," to "reduce the politicization over processes that are meant to remain non-partisan and impartial" (Aucoin et al. 2011, 235). They have special worries about the Prime Minister's Office. "Political staffs from the PMO also do not shy away from giving politically motivated advice to ministers and public servants, decreasing the likelihood that ministers will ever receive impartial, independent, objective advice that is free from partisan considerations" (ibid). Aucoin and his co-authors want political staff to stay out of the business of setting public service policy or staffing practices. They suggest taking away the prime minister's power to appoint deputy ministers, the senior officials in each department, lest political considerations be seen as muddying the highest levels of the public service and give it to the Public Service Commission, an independent body that oversees the appointment of all other public servants.

As I have argued elsewhere, this kind of hand-wringing about political staff needs to be reconsidered (Brodie 2012). After all, the federal public service is already protected by clear, powerful legislation. It has been a permanent, professional body with carefully selected protections against political interference for about a century. By law, the public service is staffed on the merit principle rather than by political patronage, and the Public Service Commission has powers to protect that principle. By law, public servants are protected from corrupt political influences when spending public money, and both the Treasury Board and the auditor general have powers to protect those principles. The Public Service Act and the Financial Administration Act set out rules and insulate public servants from all sorts of political pressures – not just from political staff but also from ministers and others. They strike a difficult balance between giving public service protections while still allowing accountable political leaders to run the government. To speak of "bureaucratic independence" just as we speak of "judicial independence" is nonsense, and dangerous nonsense at that (Russell and Sossin, 201). The public service is not a separate branch of the government; its protections are intended to guard against government corruption not guard against democracy. Do Aucoin and his co-authors mean to suggest that ministers as well as political staff stay out of decisions about public service policy? If so, who would be accountable to the public for public service rules, public service pay, and public service pensions? If these are not meant to be the domain of politics, who will secure the consent of the governed to pay the taxes required to finance them? Just as the independence of judges has to be carefully justified and the judicial role carefully limited as a result, the protections afforded to public servants have to be carefully justified and the bureaucratic role limited. The greater the job protection of public servants, the more important it is that they be non-partisan and seen as non-partisan.

The original premise of the Civil Service Act – permanent employment in exchange for severe restrictions on the political activities of public servants – has been eroded by judicial decisions granting broad political rights to most government employees. This has put both public servants and elected officials in an increasingly difficult position. The risk of politicizing the public service is a two-way street. Ministers and their aides occasionally overreach, and in those circumstances public servants rely on their legislative protections. Ministers are not similarly protected from overreach by public servants. Public service protections are undercut when even a handful of public servants engage in egregious partisanship. The leaking by low-level employees of draft documents makes it more difficult for ministers to trust other public servants who take their professional roles more seriously. At a higher level, rumours that at one point former Finance Department official and Bank of Canada Governor Mark Carney considered running for the leadership of the federal Liberal Party makes it difficult for other senior officials to gain the trust of their ministers. Carney was highly trusted by Jim Flaherty. Did he harbour political ambitions to run for the opposition party at that time? A lower-level official, Kevin Chan, left the public services as a senior policy advisor in the inner office of the clerk of the Privy Council, to join the office of Liberal Party leader Michael Ignatieff in the midst of the prorogation crisis. Ignatieff assured the public that Chan did not breach any confidences of the government, which was reassuring but hardly sufficient (Bailey 2009). Chan's move, like the reports about Carney's leadership ambitions, raised questions about the private partisan views of other public servants. The Public Service Commission, from time to time, approves leaves of absence from the public service to allow individual public servants to run for political office. When public servants run for non-partisan municipal office, federal rules should provide some leniency. Running for provincial political office should be permitted under some circumstances. But I applaud the Public Service Commission for frowning on public servants who want to take a leave of absence to run for the House of Commons and then return to being trusted non-partisan advisors if they lose the election. The Federal Court of Canada may see a distinction between running for elected office being seen as a problem for a public servant and running for elected office actually being a problem (*Taman v. Canada* (Attorney General) 2017). However, ministers are not fools. Public servants who run and then return to the public service will never be seen as non-partisan again.

The Harper government's decision to curtail the right of long-serving political staff to "parachute" into equivalently paid positions in the public service was a mark of its respect for the status and role of the public service. That change was not meant to stop political staff from joining the public service. Rather, it forced political staff to join the public service through the same merit-based as every other public servant and with no preferential treatment as to pay. When I was PMO chief of staff, I worked with hundreds of officials who had parachuted into the public service from political offices. I never saw a partisan pattern in which ones turned out to be excellent public servants and which ones turned out to be great disappointments. Very few of the public servants I worked with gave a hint of having a party view of any matter even though the best were, rightly, aware of the partisan context of the government. But the underlying idea that the public service should be resolutely non-partisan and neutral is increasingly hard to sustain, and not just because of the role of political staffers or ministers.

Even so, recent years have brought new pressures to find new bureaucratic and non-partisan ways to limit Cabinet's power. In 2014, Canada 2020, an Ottawa think tank, issued a paper on public service renewal by Ralph Heintzman. His report worried that "over the last twenty-five years or so, the federal public service appears to have gradually lost sight of the necessary boundary between political and public service values – and thus between elected and non-elected officials – in a parliamentary democracy" (6). While acknowledging that "public service values" are no better or important than "political values" – in fact, he recognizes that political values have a democratic legitimacy – Heintzman argues that lines have been crossed between the two realms and a "Charter of the Public Service" is needed to restore those lines. The problem of "court government" and the centralization of influence in the hands of prime ministers and their courtiers is not new. In Heintzman's view it dates back to Pierre Trudeau's appointment of Michael Pitfield as clerk of the Privy Council, the Mulroney government's al-Mashat affair, and the sponsorship scandal. Yet, he argues, it reached a new height in Harper's government when the clerk of the Privy Council defended the accuracy of the government's budget projections to the parliamentary budget officer.[2] The Charter would help put things right by stating the importance of the non-partisan nature of the public service, clarifying the power of deputy ministers over their own departments, giving the Public Service Commission the power to recommend the appointment of deputy ministers to the prime minister, and freeing public servants to communicate freely with the public without first checking with the government of day or their ministers. Heintzman's report draws heavily on Aucoin's analysis but stops short of stripping the prime minister of the final say on the appointment of deputy ministers.

In 2015, the Public Policy Forum, an Ottawa-based think tank, issued a wide-ranging report on restoring trust in Canada's public institutions. The report was written by one of Peter Aucoin's co-authors, Lori Turnbull, and overseen by a panel that included former Alberta treasurer Jim Dinning as chair as well as former Quebec premier Jean Charest and former Clerk of the Privy Council Kevin Lynch.[3] It worried that the proper role of the public service was being taken over by a "political service," a corps of increasingly professional political staff (Public Policy Forum 2015). The paper acknowledges that "Political staff are an essential part of our system of government" but asks if they should be "doing the work of the public service" (7), which is to offer "evidence-based policy advice and experience" while also administering the activities of the federal government "on a non-partisan basis" (6). The paper recommends the restoration of Cabinet government by, among other things, protecting ministers from interference by the PMO in staffing their political offices, codifying the role of the public service in proving policy advice and administration, and third-party training and regulation of political staff. It also recommended changes to the House of Commons committee system, which we will turn to later.

In 2016, the Mowat Centre, a think tank at the University of Toronto where Prime Minister Justin Trudeau's advisors put together their policy and implementation agenda before taking office, issued a research paper on the need to overhaul the federal public service. The paper, written by another of Peter Aucoin's co-authors, takes direct aim at the mechanisms that allow a prime minister and Cabinet to influence the vast administrative machinery of the public sector. It recommends creating a "new system of independent appointments" for the deputy ministers to create "more independence for civil service leaders" (Jarvis 2016, 10). The report argues that "Deputy ministers may be more comfortable taking risks if they do not feel as directly beholden to the prime minister that appointed them" (13). Following Aucoin's analysis, the report recommends that deputy ministers be appointed by the Public Service Commission.

Worries about the balance between the public service and the political realm are not new. Nearly forty years ago, similar concerns were in the air in 1979 when the Joe Clark government took power from Pierre Trudeau and then promptly handed it back in 1980. Just as in the late 1950s, when "twenty-two years of Liberal domination of Canadian politics ... came to a temporary end in 1957 [and] revealed how close had become the nexus, carefully nurtured by Mackenzie King, between the Liberal Party and the overwhelming majority of the intellectual establishment in the universities and the civil service" (Mallory 1980, 249), Clark came to office and fired both Clerk of the Privy Council Pitfield and the deputy minister of finance. Other senior officials soon resigned from the public service or were reassigned. J.R. Mallory asked if these moves "in any way damaged the integrity and hard-won neutrality of the public service?" His answer: "Pretty certainly not" (262). Mallory, no enemy of the public service, is sensitive to the democratic mandate of the prime minister and Cabinet. Looking ahead, he concludes that ministers will have to take the risk of undermining the professionalization of the public service "if ministers are to regain control of their capacity to innovate" (262). Larger political staffs for ministers and in PMO might work but political aides "are not around long enough to offer a serious challenge to the bureaucratic control over policy" (ibid.) The problem of "authority and accountability,"

Mallory concluded, "is as far from a solution as ever" (263). Mallory's is a more vibrant view of the political and the public service roles.

As Aucoin recognized earlier in his career, "A professional, non-partisan public service is not required by responsible government, but it has become an important feature of the Canadian government" (Aucoin 2004). PCO itself does not accept Aucoin's formulation. In describing the "Mission of the Privy Council" [*sic*], PCO declares that one of its values is "a non-partisan public sector is essential to our democratic system" (Privy Council Office 2014). PCO's statement goes too far. Canada's professional public service is only a century old, but the country has been democratic longer than that. In the US, a new president is empowered and expected to replace everyone in the top three or four layers of the executive branch with the consent of the Senate. To make this possible, the United States has developed two executive branches, one in office and the other biding its time in law firms, think tanks, international organizations, and universities. When the White House changes hands, the two groups swap places. Even with this limited degree of public service professionalization the US remains a democratic country. And even so, American scholars worry about how much power of the administrative state lies outside of political accountability (Hayward 2017; Hamburger 2015).

The special expertise of a permanent public service like Canada's is said to rely on their use of evidence rather than on political considerations as a basis for their public policy recommendations. I came to respect the expertise, experience, and judgement of many public servants. Public service advice is no doubt valuable to ministers and prime ministers. Developing the capacity for that advice needs space, resources, and political respect. But there is a constant risk of overreach on this count. Some public servants claim that their role is to "speak truth to power." That is the first step on the path toward the argument for the public service as a separate branch of government. Public servants who want to speak truth to power should first be certain that they are speaking the truth and not simply advocating a particular view about the role of government or a contestable vision of public policy. Ministers who suspect public service advice is tilted or less than complete may see the "truth to power" claim as arrogant. "Truth to power" is a role to be taken up with humility and self-awareness. The best advice is given in confidence. For in the end, democratically accountable ministers have the final say over public policy. It cannot be any other way.

The risk of overreach in claims about the "truth to power" mission can be found in Kevin Page's memoirs of his time as the first parliamentary budget officer (2015). I first met Page shortly after the 2006 election. He was in charge of the macro-economic analysis shop in PCO. I found him to be a decent person, a competent analyst, and knowledgeable about fiscal policy. When the Harper government started looking for Canada's first parliamentary budget officer, one of his PCO colleagues pointed out Page had recently suffered a family tragedy and he was looking for a new challenge in his professional life. Setting up the PBO would be a challenge but a rewarding one for a good budget analyst, and Page was soon on his way to this new role. The idea of the parliamentary budget office was part of our 2006 platform, and I remain convinced it was a good idea. Our platform argued that parliamentarians needed an independent source of big-picture fiscal analysis. The prime minister and Cabinet can draw on the expertise of the Department of Finance. Parliamentarians do not have a similar source of advice. So, just as the work of the Public Accounts Committee is impossible without the support of the Auditor General, and just as a successful auditor general must have a close relationship with that committee, we thought parliamentarians on many committees could depend on analysis from the PBO and a parliamentary budget officer would form close relationships with several House and Senate committees.

Making budget projections is an imprecise exercise. The Department of Finance, PBO, and private organizations all try to predict federal revenues and expenses one or two years into the future and sometimes longer. They all used sophisticated models and rely on proven indicators. However, economics is not a precise discipline. When making budget projections a year into the future, showing a surplus or deficit to the nearest few million dollars gives a false sense of accuracy to the exercise. The economy may grow faster or slower than projected, and that makes revenue projections tricky. On the spending side, some expenses can be reliably predicted. Others are estimated. Some projections are little more than guesses. The farther into the future the projections reach, the more likely they are to be wrong. Trying to estimate fiscal numbers far into the future is a nearly pointless exercise. Everyone involved in federal budgeting understands that. Experts make their best estimates, and governments use those estimates because there is no better way to work. Budget projections are not "facts," and if two sets of projections are different, that difference does not indicate someone is lying or trying to deceive. All these considerations mean that the task of the PBO is inevitably more difficult than the role of the auditor general. The auditor general audits past spending of the government. Reports on past spending are facts. Deciding whether a certain expenditure showed "value for money" is a political judgement, but it is a political judgement about facts. Projections about future spending are not facts and are eventually likely to be proven wrong. Given the shifting sands of fiscal projections, I expected Page to proceed carefully and with a healthy dose of prudence in setting up the PBO. On Parliament Hill, we would have to build new relationships and gradually establish the credibility of his work. Instead, Page not only immediately crossed swords with Conservatives on the Hill. He also crossed swords with others (Page 2015, 97). Instead of taking heed of the early setbacks to his office, he took an even more sharply political path. That blunted the impact of the PBO.

Page writes that he had "strained' relations with the Harper government but satisfies himself by claiming the Harper government "rarely had anything negative to say about the *work* we produced ... [A]s time passed they learned to keep quiet about the content of the reports themselves – because the content was always solid and based on reliable data" (103, emphasis in the original). But consider one of the highest profile reports prepared under Page's direction – the PBO analysis of the F-35 purchase – and it becomes easier to see the risks of his "truth to power" mantra.

After I left the PMO, the Harper government decided to purchase the F-35 Lightning II to replace the ageing CF-18 Hornet flown by the Royal Canadian Air Force. Canadian governments had been contributing to the development of the Joint Strike Fighter project for several years. Those contributions meant that if Canada decided to buy the F-35, Canadian firms would be part of the production consortium for all the F-35s built. Every complex military system encounters problems during its development, and the F-35 encountered a lot of them. The US government compounded the risk in the way it decided to develop and produce the aircraft. When I was in government, I knew that Canada would have very few types of aircraft to choose from when the CF-18 fleet reached the end of its life. In the future, the US and its allies should never put all their military jet eggs in one basket again. But that decision had been taken long before Harper was elected and long before I moved to the PMO.

Before the Harper government settled on the F-35, the auditor general reported on two earlier decisions to buy new military helicopters. That report (Auditor General of Canada 2010) should have received more public attention than it got. It showed that the Department of National Defence had not shared the true scope of two helicopter projects with the Treasury Board (i.e., Cabinet), saying the helicopters it wanted to buy were "off the shelf" models when it knew would both need significant customization before they could go into service. This was a serious finding. No government should tolerate a department hiding the scope of a major expense from the political authorities who are ultimately accountable for it.

The auditor general also found that the DND had failed to identify the full lifecycle costs of the aircraft. This was a more contentious finding. If projecting government revenues and expenses more than one or two years into the future is fraught with imprecision and uncertainty, estimating the full lifecycle costs of a major purchase is even more difficult. After the Harper government announced it would buy the F-35, parliamentarians asked the PBO to provide a "cost" of the aircraft purchase. Page and his staff should have proceeded with caution. Since no contract had even been negotiated, it was impossible to estimate the basic "fly away cost" of the purchase. The price of an F-35, everyone knew, would drop over time as the Americans worked out problems with the design and production of the airplane. The US Air Force would absorb those costs since it would buy the first few dozen airplanes. Canada would buy later at a lower per-plane cost, and the "fly away" cost of the Canadian purchase would not be clear until then. The cost of renovating RCAF facilities to accommodate the new airplane and the transitional training costs for pilots, crew, and maintenance technicians could not be estimated with any confidence until that point. Even so, in response to the auditor general's report on the two helicopter project the Department of National Defence came up with a twenty-year cost estimate for the F-35 program.

The twenty-year price tag of $16 billion was sketchy for all the reasons that any budget project is sketchy. What will it cost to train an F-35 pilot in 2030? No one can possibly know the answer to that question today. Pilot training evolves over time as training techniques change, simulator technology progresses, and safety issues for particular aircraft emerge. What will it cost to buy military aviation fuel cost in 2030 and how much of it will the F-35 fleet need that year? Again, no one can know the answer to that question today. Will our RCAF jets fly a little that year or a lot? Will there be a war that year, or will it be a peaceful year? Will Canada be asked to provide military jets to a UN or NATO mission that year? If so, will the government of the day agree? How many jets will it send? Estimating these costs means estimating the decisions of future Canadian governments, and another word for that is "guessing."

The PBO went well beyond the sketchy DND estimate in its report on the F-35. Page and his team tried to estimate the total lifecycle cost of acquiring, maintaining, upgrading, and operating the fleet. In his memoirs, Page acknowledged that these costs were unknowable at the time: his office was "trying to cost a *moving target* in that the technology [of the F-35] was continuing to change, making it extremely difficult to arrive at a fixed cost" (128; emphasis in original). And instead of projecting these unknowable costs twenty years into the future, the PBO decided to project them thirty years into the future. Why? Because, in Page's words, "realistically, no one gets rid of planes after twenty years" (128). That might or might not be an accurate estimate. The lifecycle of a fleet of military jets depends entirely on decisions taken by a future government. But one thing is certain. Adding an extra decade of estimates (guesses) to the projected "price tag" meant feeding even sketchier numbers to the political debate. Since the current CF-18 fleet has been operating for thirty-five years and will likely fly for more than forty, why did the PBO add ten years of estimates (guesses) to the DND estimates (guesses) instead of fifteen or twenty years of estimates (guesses)? Page writes that he believes PBO's number was "realistic" because "we were factoring in costs such as equipment upgrades over an extended period of time, which translates into big money. There might even be two upgrades over ... that additional ten-year time span" (128). But if that figured into the PBO projections that meant their figures were even sketchier! Decisions about future upgrades will be made by future governments based on future technologies at future costs PBO had no way of knowing. Extending the lifecycle estimate to include possible future upgrades did not add more "facts" to the analysis. It added more unknowables.

PBO's report on the costs of the F-35 was not an exercise in truth-telling. It was an exercise in technocratic arrogance. That arrogance is reflected in Page's account of his exchange with the Harper government over the PBO report: "The notion that forecasts should include not only the cost of acquisition but also maintenance costs of the life cycle of the planes had apparently never crossed their minds" (129). That is nonsense. Everyone involved in the F-35 project understood that the aircraft will incur maintenance costs over its life. The DND had produced a twenty-year estimate of the cost of the plane. PBO's thirty-year estimate (or a subsequent KPMG report commissioned by the government that produced a forty-year estimate) was no more accurate than the twenty-year estimate. Adding additional decades to the projections probably made them less accurate. No one has ever bothered to calculate the total lifecycle cost of the existing CF-18 fleet, since that number would be meaningless. But it could be calculated since it is based on actual spending based on past decisions. Page compares the analysis needed to buy a jet aircraft to the analysis needed to buy a car. But even the best economist does not try to estimate the cost of maintaining a car and fueling it over three decades. The limits of the DND, PBO, and KPMG analyses become even clearer when you look for the corresponding *benefits* analyses in their reports. What are the benefits of purchasing the F-35 over the next two, three, or four decades? Theories of deterrence suggest that adding to the military capabilities of the Western alliance discourages would-be aggressors from starting wars. By that reasoning, adding sixty-odd F-35s to the RCAF presumably adds to that deterrence. How many wars will be headed off over the next twenty, thirty, or forty years because of the F-35 purchase? What is the value of the death and destruction that is prevented by that purchase? Of course, such an estimate would be nonsense. The deterrence value of the F-35 program, if it even exists, cannot be estimated accurately. Neither can the thirty-year or forty-year lifecycle costs of the program. PBO's effort to do so did not add to the public debate. It subtracted from it. Page later agreed with a reporter that the Harper government "wanted Canadians to think that these planes would cost a lot less money" (132). That might be true. Officers of Parliament, however, should be careful in attributing bad faith to political leaders. Page claims that the PBO report was "just telling the truth" (133). He provided Canadians with, in his words, the "best numbers." But his numbers were just a guess, and the PBO report made Canadians less informed, not better informed, about the cost of the F-35 purchase.

A better view of the contrast between public servants and ministers and their political staffs comes from the practical memoirs of Andrew Griffith. Griffith was the director general of multiculturalism when Jason Kenney was given ministerial responsibility for that program (Griffith 2013). The test of any parliamentary democracy, he writes, is the "professionalism, responsiveness and loyalty of the public service in adjusting to the different priorities of a new government." But, in his field of multiculturalism, this norm was "severely tested" when the Harper government was elected and in particular when Jason Kenney took the government's lead. Multiculturalism policy had been marked by a high degree of consensus of governments since the early Trudeau years (see Pal 1993), but Kenney wanted to make big changes. Griffith could have relied on traditional theories of public administration to condemn Kenney for trying to make changes, but, rather than rely on the "truth to power" argument, Griffith instead explores the "dilemma for public servants when a government that has a radically different world view and evidence-base of issues and approaches" takes office. The struggle to produce a new citizenship guide ended up with a better product because of the interplay between the minister, his genuinely expert political staff, and the public service. Once decisions are made, of course, public servants have a duty to implement them loyally. Along the way, Griffith argues, the political side of government has to create space for fearless advice to be provided. He worries that, if public servants keep offering advice that is rejected, they may be seen as "neither professional nor non-partisan." However, as long as public service appointments are secure individual public servants can always quietly wait out a government they find objectionable.

Griffith's account of the Harper government and its policy initiatives around multiculturalism is an optimistic one. It recognizes the limits of both public service expertise and political considerations in the formulation of policy and the conduct of public affairs. When public servants or any other body of specialists claim to have special expertise and want to speak "truth to power" citizens and political leaders have a duty to be skeptical.

Étienne Parent, Joseph Howe, and Lord Durham all rejected the idea that anyone had a permanent right to rule by virtue of either aristocratic birth or democratic election. Power was meant to chance hands regularly and to change hands at the demand of the voters. If Parent, Howe, and Durham were unimpressed by arguments for aristocracy or democratic absolutism, they would likely not be impressed with arguments for the natural rights of public servants to rule either. Proposals to increase the independence of the public service, especially ones that envisage it nearly becoming a separate branch of government, never consider why citizens or elected officials would be uncomfortable trusting so much power to a permanent set of officials. Further entrenching the independence of the public service means its policy advice will be increasingly isolated and therefore less influential. Building up the Public Service Commission in an effort to hem in the decision-making powers of ministers will not eliminate the pressure of politics. Governments will still face the ballot box every so many years, and elections will produce both governments and oppositions. Ministers will decide accordingly. A government that is willing to accept the advice of the public service will be followed by a government that chafes at that advice and eventually ignore it. There is danger in the effort to hem in ministers and force them to accept public service advice. That is a fool's mission in any case. Public administration may be skeptical about political parties and politics itself. But public administration has not killed off politics.

Reviving Parliamentary Scrutiny of Public Spending

Any strengthening of the checks and balances in our form of government will have to rely on modern elected institutions, not would-be non-partisan aristocrats. We need republican remedies for the diseases of republican government. To do that, we have to recognize the checks and balances we already have and work on the proper mix in our separation of powers. As Dennis Baker argues, the "vast bulk of separation of powers theory and practice" only allows the mixing of the legislative and executive powers across branches, they see mixing the powers as essential to "the desirable checks and balances that healthy liberal-democratic government requires" (2010, 55). The great constitutional theorists Montesquieu and Blackstone both commend the partial independence of the branches of government, and Madison argues that a separation of powers was wholly compatible with the branches of government having "partial agency" in the acts of others. The president has a veto over legislation and the Senate must advise and consent to executive branch appointments. That mixing of powers is essential to the operation of the checks and balances. In Canada, as Baker writes, the "finely tuned interaction" between Cabinet and Parliament is most apparent in the money bill rule of the BNA Act, ss. 53 and 54. The executive proposes a fiscal policy, including spending measures, taxation measures, and borrowing authorities. The House of Commons reviews the plan and consents to it or defeats the government. The operation of the money bill rule has become routine in Ottawa, with ministers moving budget implementation acts, tabling spending estimates, and advancing appropriations bills many times per year. Almost no one pays attention off of The Hill. As we saw in chapter 4, while the business of private members' legislative has expanded over the last thirty years, the House has not succeeded in improving its oversight of spending. In the spirit of the McGrath Report, and recognizing that the House and its committees are partisan political institutions, can the power of the purse be invigorated? After all, private members' legislation plays an important role but the far larger part of government and the far larger need for stronger checks and balances is in the government's spending plans, the estimates.

Why is there so little parliamentary scrutiny of the estimates? There are two central problems. First, there is an enormous gulf – a nearly unbridgeable chasm – between the budget information reported by the executive branch and the ability of parliamentarians to absorb that information. Savoie (2013), Samara (2010), and others have recommended better training for MPs and the Library of Parliament puts on regular training sessions for MPs. Training, however, cannot close the information gap between government departments and parliamentarians. Members of Parliament, as individuals, in committee, or in plenary session, will never absorb all the budget information needed to fully understand the spending estimates tabled in the House. Since the 1960s, most of the scrutiny of the estimates has gone on in committee, where individual MPs can focus on a slice of the overall spending plan. As it is, MPs complain that departmental financial reports are too long and too detailed to be useful, and departmental officials complain that standing committees do not digest the information that is provided. This information problem has its roots in a second central problem. MPs do not have much political incentive to spend time and energy on the estimates. Government MPs fear that looking into the estimates too closely will hurt their relationships with ministers and colleagues. Opposition MPs only look into the estimates if they can find something that hurts the government in public. Unless a committee uncovers a scandal, committee hearings do not get much attention from anyone, so the incentive is to let most spending estimates be "deemed reported" back to the House. Then, when the estimates get to the floor of the House, they are confidence measures. Defeating the resulting appropriations bills runs the risk of defeating the government, and the opposition parties cannot even delay the votes to make the government sweat a bit to get them passed. As one veteran Library of Parliament researcher notes, "Although there is always the possibility that scandal or pointless activity can be identified and remedied, most work on estimates will remain unglamorous. Administrative issues and incremental progress do not attract the media spotlight reserved for more dramatic issues of ethics or principle, are of limited comprehensibility or interest to voters, and therefore offer limited incentives for investments of time by parliamentarians" (Stilborn 2006–07, 27).

To invigorate Parliament's power of the purse requires changing the incentives against scrutinizing the estimates. More specifically, it means changing the incentives for backbench government MPs. Opposition MPs are already free to dig into the government's spending estimates. How can a government backbencher do that the estimates without becoming a trained seal for the chief government whip? A backbench government MP would need an assurance from the prime minister that genuinely scrutinizing the estimates is valued, and the prime minister would need to stick by that assurance. Why would a prime minister give such an assurance? First, as it stands, a prime minister can never be sure that Cabinet ministers really control or supervise their departments' spending. When the executive forms its spending plans, as Savoie puts it, Cabinet has many spenders but few guardians. During all the Cabinet meetings of the Chrétien government, "No one ever suggested cuts to existing programs, or tradeoffs that might make some of their ideas more affordable" (Goldenberg 2006, 107). Every few years, prime ministers set up a "program review" exercise to find ways to reduce spending. They give a Cabinet committee, a central agency, or their own political staff the power to decide which government programs to cut. But, without a program review, government spending plans are worked out by public service officials over many months and sometimes longer. If important government priorities are at stake, the PMO and PCO might be involved (Good 2007). The prime minister and the finance minister decide the broad outlines of the budget but do not have time to look into the details of the spending involved. Deputy ministers present their ministers with finished versions of the spending estimates just days or sometimes hours before they have to be tabled in the House. And all hell breaks loose if a minister refuses to sign a department's spending estimates or is late in signing them. Even capable ministers with capable political staff can sometimes do very little to challenge the budgeting power of the public service. The bargain between officials and ministers is clear. Sign the estimates and, if you get questioned about them in committee, read the talking points prepared by the department. Retired Treasury Board secretary J.L. Manion argues that "The annual Estimates cycle is the engine of a frantic annual process which has been so impossibly burdensome that Ministers and Parliament alike have effectively given up" (quoted in Savoie 2013, 48). Robert Giroux, another former secretary to the board, prepared ministers for testimony about the estimates by saying, "Don't worry about all that information, you will not get a question on that. We know what to expect and that is what will enable the opposition to score political points" (ibid, 46).

Even the Cabinet committees given responsibility for program reviews have trouble coping with the volume of decisions that must be made. If a prime minister let government backbenchers to take a closer look at the estimates, this imbalance of ministerial and bureaucratic budget power could be evened up. Getting more political eyes to pay more attention to more line items would force ministers to pay more attention to the estimates. Officials would have to involve ministers in preparing the estimates earlier in the budget cycle and be more careful getting ministers ready to answer questions about them. Over time, that would improve the oversight of spending at all levels. Better oversight would come with a cost – less capable ministers would be embarrassed in public. But a capable minister could frame the vigorous parliamentary scrutiny of the estimates as a useful exercise, especially if the prime minister assured everyone involved that this opening up of the process was valuable.

If backbench government MPs can get a private member's bill through the House, presumably they can scrutinize the estimates. The job requires careful research and coordination with colleagues. The MP might ask for information in advance of committee hearings and follow up afterward. The MP could put in a standing request to have all of a department's program evaluations sent to the committee. If the MP is not given enough time or information to perform their duties, a loud complaint in front of the prime minister at caucus should get the attention of the minister concerned. MPs should ensure that ministers who try to ram spending estimates through committee pay a political price for doing so. When the estimates contain truly questionable items, it might be appropriate to draw attention to them in the weekly caucus meeting before doing so in public. A government MP who wants to play a more vigorous role in scrutinizing the estimates should always frame their actions in a way that gives a minister a lever over departmental officials. Nothing the government MP does or says can be seen as undermining confidence in government as a whole. But within those restrictions, there is lots of room for an MP to do good work. Think tanks and government watchdog groups could play a role. The Canadian Taxpayers Federation, the Fraser Institute, the Manning Centre, the Canadian Centre for Policy Alternatives, and other institutes have long raised concern about government spending over the years. They should devote some of their time and resources to equipping sympathetic MPs to raise these issues at committee when the estimates are up for discussion, and they should embarrass MPs who do not take this part of their job seriously. Just as MPs need the professional help of the Parliamentary Counsel to draft private members' bills, the Parliamentary Budget Office should focus its resources on helping MPs with their scrutiny of the estimates. The financial information presented to Parliament, including the estimates, needs to be streamlined, simplified, and decentralized if the scrutiny of the estimates is going to improve. The Trudeau government has indicated it will start to do that (Treasury Board Secretariat 2016). A drill-down, roll-up system that puts together the annual budget, the spending estimates, and the public accounts on a cash basis is an essential part of invigorating Parliament's role. Ideally, the drill-down, roll-up system would let users aggregate spending at the riding, municipal, and provincial level. MPs, local or provincial politicians, and outside watchdogs could track proposed and past spending in a way that is politically useful. Departmental reports on program objectives and performance can set the context for government spending, but that reporting needs to be connected to the riding or local level to attract the interest of parliamentarians and others.

Since the 1960s, the standing committees of the House of Commons have taken the lead in scrutinizing the estimates. The opposition parties can call one minister before the Committee of the Whole House to defend one set of spending estimates in each cycle, but at night when no one is paying attention. Otherwise, the House has roughly one standing committee to correspond to each portfolio in the executive. The spending estimates of the Department of National Defence and its agencies are referred to the Standing Committee on National Defence, the spending estimates of Health Canada and its agencies are referred to the Standing Committee on Health, and so forth. The Public Policy Forum report (2015) on restoring trust in institutions referred to above recommends reducing the number of standing committees in the House again, although it is silent on whether committees would then be larger as they once were. Disrupting the one-to-one relationship between portfolios and committees might not be the best place to start reinvigorating the scrutiny of the estimates. The report also recommends making the members of standing committees more independent, having committee chairs elected in secret ballots by vote of the entire House, and ensuring committees and their chairs remain in place for the term of an entire Parliament. These ideas are worth considering, provided everyone understands the limits imposed by responsible government and party discipline. These reforms might help, but it will be far more important for a prime minister to make it known that the closer scrutiny of estimates pays off for government MPs. The Public Policy Forum group hopes that committees might dig into longer term issues facing Canada, and maybe some will. Parliamentarians are busy, though, and if the House has a smaller number of standing committees each committee will have a heavier load of government and private members' bills. The report recommends greater efforts to get the public involved in committee hearings, although how and why members of the public would follow committee work that is less partisan is not clear. Officials and ministers must guess what aspects of their responsibilities will engage the interest of parliamentarians. They will therefore tend to over report to committees. Many and possibly most departmental reporting to committees will remain unread. This is not a sign of failure. If committees have access to drill-down, roll-up reporting on every dollar in the estimates and the public accounts, perhaps committees will be able to formulate more precise demands on departmental reporting for the future.

Even if we could solve the problem of incentives, provide MPs with better expert support in scrutinizing the estimates, and make government financial information more accessible, parliamentarians still need to find time to do the work involved in scrutinizing the estimates. When would this take place? As things stand, when the estimates are tabled on 1 March, there is not much time for parliamentary committees to do proper investigations of the estimates before the House rises for summer, usually in early or mid-June. The House might need to sit beyond mid-June to do this work. Interim supply might need to fund government operations through the end of July to allow this to happen. Alternatively, the Government of Canada could move its year end to 30 June. The government could then announce its budget plans in January or February, table its Main Estimates in March, prepare for committee study of the estimates in April and May, and attend hearings in June. Parliament could then approve the Main Estimates and adopt an appropriations bill before the new fiscal year begins on 1 July. The Trudeau government has indicated it is open to changing the budget calendar (Treasury Board Secretariat 2016).

Invigorating Parliament's review of the estimates would mean repealing the "deemed reported" rule, at least for the Main Estimates. If every committee had to hold a vote on the estimates, committee members might feel obliged to hold at least one hearing before the vote. Repealing the "deemed reported" rule would open the door to filibusters, delays, and procedural games. These are the tools that give the opposition a measure of influence over government legislation, and letting government MPs use them too would be helpful. Invigorating parliament's role in approving spending plans is risky. The revolt against King John was risky, too. It could have gone badly for the barons. In the end, John had to sign Magna Carta. Magna Carta was so successful that all of John's successors have accepted to its conditions upon ascending to the throne. Giving MPs a say in public spending is essential to restoring the power of the purse and making the separation of powers on fiscal policy as strong as the separation of powers on other kinds of legislation.

Pretending there was once a golden age when Parliament did better work is not helpful and undermines public confidence in parliamentary institutions. Expecting politicians to be non-partisan or apolitical is expecting too much. If we want to strengthen the checks and balances in our form of government, reform has to take place within our form of government. Canadians should not expect MPs to have decisive and visible impacts on every dollar of public spending. Nor should they expect Parliament will routinely refuse to approve the estimates or change departmental requests. They should expect committees to scrutinize the estimates by questioning ministers and officials. They should expect MPs to report on the estimates, usually in a partisan, adversarial way. Ministers will make their own decisions about how react. A minister who opts to take a different course in the future might not credit the committee with having influenced policy or administration, but observers who want to be fair to the institutions and the players, instead of holding them to unattainable standards, will give credit where credit is due.

Executive Leadership

The Canadian consensus that our prime minister is too strong looks a bit quaint when we turn to the situation in the United States. The US has seen a very real accrual of power in the hands of the executive branch at the expense of Congress over the years. The Bush Administration expanded executive authority on matters of national security in the wake of the terrorist attacks of 11 September 2001. The Obama Administration expanded the executive authorities over national security, reading the original 2001 congressional authorization for the use of military force broadly. It also made aggressive claims of executive authority in other policy areas, such as immigration and healthcare.[4] The framers of the US Constitution created the potential for a strong presidency in 1789. Worried about the about the threat of overreach by the legislative branch, the one closest to the people, they adopted bicameralism to ensure no one legislative chamber could claim to speak for the people (Federalist no 51 in Hamilton 2001). They also opted to abandon the failed form of government in the Articles of Confederation by instituting a unitary executive with a legislative veto and direct authority for officials of the executive branch. That unitary executive would be both energetic and safe, exercising "decision, activity, secrecy, and dispatch" while remaining overtly accountable for its actions (Federalist no. 70 in Hamilton 2001). The argument for a strong executive picked up influence through the Progressive movement, with its emphasis on the public will and its discomfort with checks and balances. The American argument about the proper role of the executive continues. William Howell and Terry M. Moe argue that the US Constitution is a relic and undermines effective government. The solution they prefer, as evident in the title of their recent book (*Relic: How Our Constitution Undermines Effective Government, and Why We Need a More Powerful Presidency*), is a more powerful presidency. Congress is composed of parochial members and tied down in a web of entrenched interests devoted to protecting the status quo. Congress and its legislative pathologies must be pushed aside in favour of presidents, whose overriding concern for their legacies means they alone will govern with an eye to the future and the histories that will be written of their terms in office (Howell and Moe 2016). Howell and Moe stop short of proposing the wholly novel constitution that their analysis might suggest is needed. Instead, they recommend giving the president more power to set the legislative agenda of Congress, a suggestion that a Canadian observer will see bears some resemblance to our form of government. A more searing analysis that is at once more balanced in its historical and constitutional analysis and more bracing in its view of the future of the United States form of government is F.H. Buckley's *The Once and Future King: The Rise of Crown Government in America* (2014). Buckley, a Canadian-born law professor, agrees that executive power has grown in Canada, the US, and the UK. But his twin arguments should be reassuring to Canadians. First, he argues that despite the power of the executive, parliamentary government makes Canada a freer country than the US. Secondly, he argues that the separation of powers regarding fiscal policy means Canada is better governed. The US and the US Constitution have been unable, in Buckley's view, to thrive with the growth of political progressivism, public administration, and the resulting imperial presidency. Canada's institutions of responsible, Cabinet, party, and parliamentary government get the Madisonian balance better: both free and effective government.

Opening Our Eyes: A Postscript for Citizens and Scholars Alike

Designing a constitutional regime is a tricky business. In the Federalist Papers, Hamilton, Madison, and Jay catalogued all the failures to establish free self-government up to that point in human history. The ratification of the US Constitution should not make us any more optimistic about our ability to structure a constitution properly. The populist dream of parliamentary government with 300 free agents sitting in the House of Commons has been proven impractical here and around the world. We know such a regime would be constantly threatened by demagoguery. The alternative of technocratic government by meritorious public servants and experts is no more solid an option. It would fail to govern with the consent of the governed. Aristocracy by any other name is still aristocracy.

Academic works should help us discover the truth about the world around us. The works of political scientists should be particularly valuable in helping citizens and scholars see our government and politics as they truly are. Rigorous political science is an indispensable aide to self-government. Citizens need informed observers like Donald Savoie, Jeffrey Simpson, Peter Aucoin, and others to raise the alarm when our form of government risks running off track. Someone must watch the watchers. The reader may not be persuaded by the argument of this book that, despite the alarms being raised, all is fundamentally well in our form of government. The reader may not even find the argument, despite the author's best efforts, plausible.

To citizens and scholars who are not persuaded by the argument, and who find the "prime minister as dictator" argument more compelling, there is one final message: do not succumb to confirmation bias. Do not let arguments about the centralization of power in the prime minister's hands divert you from paying attention to Cabinet, Parliament, and our political system more broadly. The shortage of serious study of Canada's Parliament is appalling. The glib assumption that Cabinet ministers are mere ciphers is a disservice to citizens and scholars alike. If you are not persuaded by the argument, at least open your eyes to a fresh look at our form of government. You might be as surprised to discover its vibrancy and resiliency anew.

Afterword

Leaving Government: Another Autobiographical Note

In mid-January 2008, I got back to the office after three weeks of nearly unbroken vacation. It was the longest break I had had from politics since moving to Ottawa spring 2003, but I was not as refreshed as I had expected to be. Vacation has brought clarity on two issues, however. It was time for the Brodies to add to our family and the Brodies could not manage a larger family and PMO at the same time. I sent a memo to Prime Minister Harper to say I would either see him through a spring election and then step aside or, if we avoided a spring election, step aside 30 June. We had had a short discussion about my continuing role a year earlier, but this time I was setting a firm departure date. He was surprised that I was so insistent about leaving but understood the priority of family life. I did not announce my plans to anyone else but did start some policy and human resources initiatives designed to give my successor options for autumn 2008.

The spring was busy. I wanted to see the Manley Panel and the renewal of the Afghanistan mission to a satisfactory conclusion and to ensure the spring budget set a strong path through what seemed to be the beginning of stormy waters. Credit markets were starting to seize up. As he travelled that spring Harper met the premiers one-on-one to gauge their readiness for difficult fiscal and economic conditions. The Manley Panel reported in January, and that led to international meetings with our allies and domestic consultations with the opposition parties. Manley's major recommendation was that we only renew our commitment in Kandahar if our NATO allies sent at least an additional thousand troops to reinforce the southern sector of the country. Harper called the leaders of the largest NATO countries to give them his view of the mission and the Manley Panel's report. This forced the allies to read the report carefully and brief up ahead of the calls. Most of the calls were quite predictable, but the call with French President Nicolas Sarkozy delivered a surprise.

Conversations with President Sarkozy were always casual and unstructured affairs. This time Harper reached his French counterpart en route to a ribbon cutting of some sort. President Sarkozy seemed distracted but told Harper that he was rethinking France's troop commitment in Afghanistan. He might move the French army out of Kabul to join the US in the country's eastern sector of operations. Kabul was relatively safe while the eastern sector was just as challenging as the south. But perhaps, Sarkozy mentioned, his troops should join the Canadians in the south. Could Harper send a team to brief his military and diplomatic advisors? Of course, Harper responded, he would send a team right away. We were not prepared for this turn of events. Would the French really dispatch 1,000 troops to Kandahar? The chance was worth a concerted push. The prime minister asked me to travel to Paris as head of a delegation that would include Foreign and Defence Advisor Susan Cartwright, PMO communications officer and former navy officer Jacques Fauteux, and Chief of Defence Staff Rick Hillier, who would join us in Paris on the way home from a NATO meeting in Vilnius.

Canada's ambassador in Paris was Marc Lortie, an experienced diplomat who was once seconded to Prime Minister Mulroney's PMO. Lortie arranged an early meeting with President Sarkozy's diplomatic advisor, Jean-David Levitte, and senior military advisor, Admiral Édouard Guillaud, as well as a separate meeting with Sarkozy's top aide, Claude Guéant. Lortie met the civilian side of the delegation when we arrived in Paris and briefed us on Sarkozy's political challenges. Levitte, the former French ambassador to the United States, probably leaned toward deeper French military cooperation with US forces in Afghanistan, and the French military leadership probably preferred working with American partners. But Sarkozy was unpredictable, and he alone would decide how to redeploy French forces. The next day, once Hillier and the rest of the delegation arrived, we proceeded to the annex across from the Elysée Palace. Hillier presented an overview of the situation in Kandahar area and what could be done with an additional 1,000 troops. He outlined the kind of equipment and capabilities that those troops would need in an environment filled with IEDs, the roadside bombs that posed such a threat to Canadian troops. The French, I could tell, were skeptical. One of officers attending the meeting had served with the French special forces in the area a few years earlier. He knew the terrain and the challenges of operating there. The political meetings in the Elysée did not offer much cause for optimism about the prospects for French reinforcements either.

The next step in finding the 1,000 troops was a trip to Washington, DC. Michael Wilson arranged a long day of meetings with senior Bush Administration officials for 25 February. Once again, I led the delegation. We had three meetings – at the Pentagon, with Eric Edelman, the undersecretary of policy for the Defense Department, at the State Department, with Tom Shannon, the head of the western hemisphere bureau and his counterpart for Europe and Eurasia, including Afghanistan, Dan Fried, and finally at the White House, with President Bush's national security advisor, Stephen Hadley, Deputy National Security Advisor Doug Lute, and, briefly, with my counterpart, White House Chief of Staff Josh Bolten. We agreed to meet Wilson at the Canadian embassy before heading to the Pentagon.

Wilson was tied up when we arrived at the embassy, giving me a chance to chat informally with some of the senior career diplomats. The US presidential elections were running hot at the time and then-senator Hillary Clinton faced a surprisingly strong challenge for the Democrats' nomination from Barack Obama. The Ohio primary was a week away and both the Democrats were piling on about the damage supposedly done to the US economy by the North American Free Trade Agreement. I asked Wilson's senior team about the risk of NAFTA being an issue after the election. They told me Canadian diplomats had been in touch with advisors for both campaigns and been assured there was nothing for Canada to worry about. Once Wilson arrived, we were off to see Edelman and his team, who were extremely well briefed on the *Manley Report*. After a detailed discussion, Edelman assured us that the Pentagon wanted Canada to stay and would not leave us short the extra 1,000 troops Manley had recommended. The State Department delegation was less focused on troop levels and more focused on the regional political situation. The last meeting at the White House was encouraging. Bolten, Hadley, and Lute all echoed Edelman's earlier comments that the US wanted Canada to stay and would find 1,000 troops if that is what was needed. Every American we met acknowledged the price Canadian troops were paying in the Kandahar area. Even though the Americans were taking heavy losses in both Iraq and Afghanistan they appreciated that our troops were holding the line in a difficult mission.

The next day was budget day in Ottawa. The finance minister delivers the budget speech to the House of Commons late in the day after the eastern financial markets have closed. The Finance Department runs "lockups" earlier in the day to give reporters, financial analysts, and other interested commentators access to the budget documents and technical briefings so they can be ready to respond when the budget is made public. In 2008 the main media lockup was at the Government Conference Centre, the old Ottawa train station. Jim Flaherty held an embargoed press conference in the morning, and Finance Department officials were available the rest of the day to answer reporters' questions. Flaherty and his team sent word to PMO that the budget was well received by the reporters. We did not know if we would survive the budget vote a few days later, but it was good to know the earlier reviews were positive. After lunch I went over to the lockup to take my own temperature of the room. I also had a mission – to ensure the senior political reporters knew we had included at least one of the pre-budget requests from each of the opposition parties. I touched base with the main bureau chiefs. The room was so cramped that the CTV bureau was located in a cubby hole off the main room. I talked to Craig Oliver and Bob Fife, the two senior CTV journalists in the lockup. Oliver thought the opposition would be hard-pressed to defeat the budget and send us to an election. I was glad to hear his take. He and Fife had already figured out there was something for each of the opposition parties in the document. As I left CTV's cubby hole, David Akin approached me. I did not know Akin well. To the best of my recollection, he asked me about public transit funding. I do not remember him asking about NAFTA or anything else.

The budget was well-received, and it soon became clear we would not be defeated in the House. I started to focus more attention on leaving PMO on 30 June. I forgot about the budget lockup until a few days later when Wilson called me. CTV Washington correspondent Tom Clark was calling him about a conversation I had had during the lockup. Had I talked about Canada getting assurances from the Democrats on NAFTA? I did not recall saying anything about it. My usual practice, whenever anyone asked me about conflicts in the Canada-US relationship, was to downplay the issue. Two years earlier, Wilson and I had been in touch regularly during the softwood lumber negotiations. Whenever someone asked me about those negotiations or any other flash point, I always expressed my optimism that everything would work out well. I told Wilson that if anyone had asked about the Democrats criticizing NAFTA I was sure I had downplayed that as well. Over the next few days, the story that would eventually be called "NAFTAgate" leaked out. Clark had got a lead about my comments from Akin, Akin apparently burned me as his source in front of a class of journalism students, and my name became public. The story became a scandal in the US when someone leaked the original diplomatic report of a meeting between Canadian consul general in Chicago Georges Rioux and Obama economic advisor Austan Goolsbee to the Associated Press. The AP story landed right in the middle of the Ohio primary, a primary that Senator Clinton ended up winning. Some Canadian reporters and opposition parliamentarians accused me of burning Canadian diplomats in an effort to shore up Republican chances in that autumn's election.

A scandal that reaches into PMO creates a particularly difficult issue for political staff to manage, and the difficulty multiplies when the PMO chief of staff is ensnared in it. Harper was, rightly, furious at me, all the more so because I could not remember what I had said to Akin in the lockup. I did not remember him asking about NAFTA. All I could say was that if I had been asked about NAFTA I was sure I had downplayed the potential impact of election-time comments on the relationship. But I could not remember exactly what had happened. Other PMO staffers were not sure whether I would survive the day as chief of staff and I could tell some of them were starting to worry about that rather than figuring out how to respond to the story. For six years I had worried about Stephen Harper's interests first, last, and always. For six years I had expected my staff to do the same. Now I was the story. Harper took matters into his own hands, and for a while I took a back seat in running the office. The search for my replacement kicked into higher gear without my participation. The office's collective ability to make timely decisions, even on quite simple matters, was hurt. I was not involved in the PMO's handling of the Senate expense scandal that ensnared Nigel Wright, but from a distance I could see the same internal dynamic at work. Any scandal that reaches into PMO leaves a prime minister unable to depend on his aides for help. Fortunately, someone came up with the idea of a PCO-led investigation to uncover the facts. PCO contracted an experienced team of former RCMP and CSIS investigators to assist them. I was questioned twice about the matter. After the initial NAFTAgate story broke but before the leak to AP, a PMO staffer had handed me the original diplomatic report from Chicago about Rioux's meeting with Goolsbee. After reading it I assumed it was classified material and disposed of it in my secure waste box. I did not know any political reporters in DC and did not know anyone from AP. I would never have done anything to enflame Canada-US relations on NAFTA or anything else. The investigators seemed to believe my assurances and their report satisfied the prime minister of my intentions. The final report on the matter (Lynch 2008) could not say who had leaked the diplomatic report to AP, and since no one at CTV cooperated with the investigation it also could not shed light on what I had said to Akin at the lockup. But it did clear me of leaking the report. I gather that all the documents and findings of the investigation were prepared for quick release under the Access to Information Act, but if anyone ever has requested those records they did not generate any more news reports.

To this day I do not know who leaked the diplomatic report on the Goolsbee meeting to the Associated Press. It was not me.

Nearly a decade later, we can see the cumulative damage done by three decades of political attacks on NAFTA. In 1992, then-governor Bill Clinton had sharply criticized the agreement, although after negotiating side deals on labour and the environment he managed to get it ratified. Over the next few years candidates for lesser offices followed Clinton's lead and criticized the agreement. Then-secretary Hillary Clinton and then-senator Obama both took shots at it in the 2008 presidential campaign. Over all these years, both Mexico and Canada refrained from responding to correct the record or stand up for the benefits that a generation of trade liberalization brought to all three countries. No one called out these campaigns for their irresponsible rhetoric. Or, rather, no one called them out until President Trump took aim at NAFTA, and at that point it was too late. Canada and Mexico may be able to wrestle an improved NAFTA from the Trump Administration, but as of the date of writing this is not certain. I regret whatever damage I might have done to Canada-US relations, if any was caused. I also wish some of the people who attacked me had directed some criticisms to American politicians taking unwarranted shots at NAFTA's impact. That might have helped head off the far more serious problems created by President Trump's presidential campaign.

Mr and Mrs Harper hosted a going-away party at 24 Sussex Drive for me in mid-June 2008 and I had a touching send off from caucus at the last caucus meeting before the summer break. The PMO staff threw a moving surprise party for me in the Langevin Block on my last day. I hope no one will think it was a breach of public service values that the senior staff of PCO invited me to one of their weekly lunches for a low-key celebration. I was touched by all the kind gestures around my retirement from politics. I had arranged to stay on the PMO payroll for an extra month to serve as an advisor to new Chief of Staff Guy Giorno and was grateful to hand off my PMO BlackBerry and the responsibility for serving Prime Minister Harper to him. Lachlan, a brother for our daughter, Chloe, arrived in early 2009.

Notes

Preface
1 Tom has a different version of events in his book, *Harper's Team* (Flanagan 2007, 142), but I believe my account is correct.

Chapter Two
1 The tendency to focus on 1 July 1867 as the start date of Confederation is similarly diverting. Focusing attention on the original four provinces of Confederation usually means overlooking the plain ambition, written into the BNA Act, to bring British Columbia, Prince Edward Island, and the Northwest Territory (from which Manitoba was created in 1870, and Alberta and Saskatchewan in 1905) into Confederation. Section 146 of the BNA Act also provided for Newfoundland to join, an ambition that would take eight decades to fulfill.

Chapter Three
1 By way of full disclosure, I serve as an independent director of the Canada Health Infoway, one such organization.
2 By way of full disclosure, I serve in the Advisory Committee of the Canadian Global Affairs Institute. Manley chairs the committee.
3 Tom MacGregor, "Defence Conference hears of Canada's role in Afghanistan," 4 June 2008, *Legion Magazine*. By way of full disclosure, I joined the board of directors of the Conference of Defence Associations Institute after I left the Prime Minister's Office.

Chapter Four
1 By way of full disclosure, I am a member of the Program Committee for the Halifax International Security Forum.
2 Harper did not elect an MP from PEI until 2011. At that time, Gail Shea joined the Conservative caucus and was immediately appointed to Cabinet. Likewise, when Leona Aglukkaq was elected from Nunavut, she went to Cabinet immediately.

3 In the interest of full disclosure, Fortier hired my brother, Neil, as a political aide when he was minister of public works. Neil was then Fortier's chief of staff during Fortier's brief tenure as minister of international trade. My brother had worked on the 2004 and 2006 national election teams, but once we were in government it turned out that only a strong and self-assured minister like Fortier wanted to take the brother of the PM's chief of staff into his ministerial office.

4 The article is written in a light tone that Harper rarely uses, and it jokes about the author drinking beer. Harper does not joke about drinking.

5 The analysis that follows does not count secretaries or ministers of state.

6 The definitive academic study of the structure and operation of cabinets is Aucoin 1986. A fuller account of Burney's contribution can be found in Zussman 2013.

Chapter Five

1 Proceedings of the Special Senate Committee on Senate Reform, Issue 2 – Evidence Thursday, 7 September 2006.

2 Bill Curry, "MPs to Act as Watchdogs of Government Spending," *The Globe and Mail*, 28 January 2016.

3 BNA Act, s. 20.

4 Charter of Rights and Freedoms, s. 5.

5 Emergency debates take place by adding additional hours to the normal sitting week of the House, usually in the evening. Take-note debates typically take place in the same manner.

6 Over time, the Harper PMO started asking backbench members of the government caucus to use their statements to reiterate government communications lines. If done effectively, this use of statement time can contribute to the public debate. If it prevents MPs from using a bit of House time to speak to their constituents about an important local issue, that eventually harms caucus relations.

7 The Standing Orders also envision time allocation being used with the support of all the opposition parties or just one of the opposition parties. In those cases, time allocation can be used with a shorter supplementary debate.

8 8 February 2005, on Bill C-280.

9 Criminal Code (RSC, 1985, c. C-46), s. 223.

10 M. Rabson, "Parliament Mired in Crime-Bill Mess." *Winnipeg Free Press*, 5 September 2014.

Chapter Six

1 Letter of Robert Déry dated 25 May 1999, cited in *Smith v. Canada*, 2009 FC 228 at page 4.

Chapter Seven

1 See Parliament of Canada Act, s. 46(2): "The number of Parliamentary Secretaries … is not to exceed the number of ministers for whom salaries are provided in section 4.1 of the Salaries Act." Section 4.1 of the Salaries Act provides salaries for thirty-four ministers plus the prime minister. Therefore, there can be no more than thirty-five parliamentary secretaries at a time. They serve for one year.

2 "Québécois nation motion," Wikipedia.org, retrieved on 7 March 2016.

3 For the New Build Canada Fund, see Leslie Young, "Map: New Infrastructure Funding Spent Mostly in Conservative Ridings," globalnews.ca, 8 July 2015, accessed on 8 March 2016. For an earlier program, see Steven Chase, Erin Anderssen, and Bill Curry, "Stimulus Program Favours Tory Ridings," *The Globe and Mail*, 21 October 2009.

4 Steven Chase and Bill Curry, "Tories Stung by e-Privacy Backlash," *The Globe and Mail*, 16 February 2012.

5 Tobi Cohen, "Backbenchers Join Backlash against Bill C-30," *Ottawa Citizen*, February 13, 2013.

6 Canada Post Corp. v. Key Mail Canada Inc. (2005), 259 DLR (4th) 309 (Ont. C.A.) and Canada Post Corp. v. G3 Worldwide (Canada) Inc. (2007), 85 O.R. (3d) 241 (Ont. C.A.) appeal to the Supreme Court of Canada dismissed 1 November 2007 (Docket 32093).

7 See House of Commons, Debates, 26 October 2006 at p. 4306 and Bill C-14, An Act to Amend the Canada Post Corporation Act, 39th Parl., 2nd sess.

8 See House of Commons Debates, 20 November 2007 at 1620-40, per Joseph Volpe.

9 The author was Executive Director of the Conservative Party at the time and present at the meetings where the Party Constitution was drafted.

10 David Staples, "Wildrose Candidate Allan Hunsperger on Gays," *Edmonton Journal*, 15 April 2012.

11 Randy Burton, "Free Thinker or Real Stinker?" *Saskatoon Star-Phoenix*, 21 October 2006, A2.

12 See the excellent speech by Senator Denise Batters in the Senate's debate on the Reform Act. Senate Debates, 22 June 2015.

13 "Off with Their Heads: Why MPs Should Sometimes Run Prime Ministers out of Town," *National Post*, 18 September 2015, A8; Andrew Coyne, "Unelectable Leaders. Democracy in Action," *Calgary Herald*, 15 September 2015, B5.

14 Colby Cosh, "The System Down Under," *National Post*, 15 September 2015, A11.

15 *Sydney Morning Herald*, 22 July 2013.

16 See his comments at a news conference on 27 June 2017, reported at Payton 2017.

Chapter Eight

1 An excellent overview of the academic debate can be found in Knopff and Snow 2013 and Schneiderman 2015.

2 Heintzman sees the Clerk's intervention as unduly partisan. I saw the Clerk standing up for the professionalism of the public servants who prepared the budget projections in question.

3 In the interest of full disclosure, I was on the Public Policy Forum's advisory council for the project.

4 Analyses of the expansion of executive power since 2001 range across the political spectrum in the US (see Healy 2008 and Savage 2015).

Works Cited

Ajzenstat, Janet. 1995. "The Constitutionalism of Étienne Parent and Joseph Howe." In *Canada's Origins : Liberal, Tory, or Republican?*, edited by Janet Ajzenstat and Peter J. Smith. Montreal/Kingston: McGill-Queen's University Press.

– 1988. *The Political Thought of Lord Durham.* Montreal/Kingston: McGill-Queen's University Press.

– 1987. "The Separation of Powers in 1867." *Canadian Journal of Political Science* 20 (1): 117–20.

– et al. 1999. *Canada's Founding Debates.* Toronto: Stoddart.

Aucoin, Peter. 1986. "Organizational Change in the Machinery of Canadian Government: From Rational Management to Brokerage Politics." *Canadian Journal of Political Science* 19 (1): 3–28.

Aucoin, Peter, Mark D. Jarvis, and Lori Turnbull. 2011. *Democratizing the Constitution: Reforming Responsible Government.* Toronto: Edmond Montgomery.

Bagehot, Walter. 1961 [1867]. *The English Constitution.* London: Oxford University Press.

Bailey, Ian. 2009. "PCO Aide Made Move Himself, Ignatieff Says." *The Globe and Mail*, 15 January 2009.

Baker, Dennis. 2010. *Not Quite Supreme.* Montreal/Kingston: McGill-Queen's University Press.

Beaudoin, Gerald-A. 1982. "The Democratic Rights." In *The Canadian Charter of Rights and Freedoms: Commentary*, edited by Walter S. Tarnopolsky and Gerald-A. Beaudoin. Toronto: Carswell.

Bercovici, Vivian. 2016. "Why Diplomats Are Agog at Trump's Ambassador to Israel." *The Wall Street Journal.* 19 December. Accessed 2 January 2017. www.wsj.com/articles/why-diplomats-are-agog-at-trumps-ambassador-to-israel-1482192085.

Bowden, James W.J. 2016. "1841: The Year of Responsible Government?" *Dorchester Review* 6 (2): 69–71.

Brodie, Ian. 2014. "Harper's Gitmo: The Sisyphean Task of Senate Reform." *C2C Journal* 8 (2): 18–21.

– 2012. "The Tansley Lecture: In Defence of Political Staff." *Johnson-Shoyama Graduate School of Public Policy.* 19 April. Accessed 2 January 2017. www.schoolofpublicpolicy.sk.ca/documents/research/archived-publications/tansley-publications/2012_Tansley%20Publication.pdf.

Bryden, Joan. 2017. "Senate, MPs Locked in Test of Wills over Budget Bill." *Global-News.ca.* 21 June. Accessed 21 June 2017. globalnews.ca/news/3545612/senate-approves-most-of-federal-budget-but-removes-booze-tax/.

Buckley, F.H. 2014. *The Once and Future King: The Rise of Crown Government in America.* New York: Encounter.

Cairns, Alan C. 1968. "The Electoral System and the Party System in Canada, 1921–1965." *Canadian Journal of Political Science* 1 (1): 55.

Campbell, Kim. 1996. *Time and Chance: The Political Memoirs of Canada's First Woman Prime Minister.* Toronto: Doubleday Canada.

Carson, Bruce. 2014. *14 Days: Making the Conservative Movement in Canada.* Montreal/Kingston: McGill-Queen's University Press.

Ceasar, James W. 1978. "Political Parties and Presidential Ambition." *Journal of Politics* 40 (3): 708–39.

Chagger, Bardish. 2017. *Letter to Candice Bergen and Murray Rankin.* Ottawa: Office of the Government House Leader, 30 April.

Champion, C.P. 2011. "Pushing at an Open Door." *Dorchester Review* 1 (1): 46–50.

Chong, Michael. 2014. "Restore Canada's Parliament by Returning Power to MPs." *Inside Policy,* April 2014, 16–18.

Commissioner, Office of the Conflict of Interest and Ethics. 2010. *The Raitt Report.* Ottawa: Parliament of Canada.

Conservative Party of Canada. 2016. *Constitution of the Conservative Party of Canada.* Ottawa: Conservative Party of Canada.

– 2006. *Stand up for Canada.* Ottawa: Conservative Party of Canada.

– 2005/06. *Stand Up for Canada.* Ottawa: Conservative Party of Canada.

– 2004. *Demanding Better.* Ottawa: Conservative Party of Canada.

Cooper, Barry. 2009. *It's the Regime, Stupid: A Report from the Cowboy West on Why Stephen Harper Matters.* Toronto: Key Porter.

– and David Bercuson. 1991. *Deconfederation: Canada without Quebec.* Toronto: Key Porter.

Cooper, Michael. 2017. "How to Fix Question Period: Ideas for Reform." In *Turning Parliament Inside Out: Practical Ideas for Reforming Canada's Democracy,* edited by Michael Chong, Scott Simms, and Kennedy Stewart. Vancouver: Douglas & McIntyre.

Craft, Jonathan. 2016. *Backrooms and Beyond: Partisan Advisers and the Politics of Policy Work in Canada.* Toronto: University of Toronto Press.

Dawson, R. MacGregor. 1957. *The Government of Canada*. Toronto: University of Toronto Press.

– 1948. "The Cabinet: Position and Personnel." *Canadian Journal of Economics and Political Science* 12 (3): 261–81.

Delacourt, Susan. 2013. *Shopping for Votes: How Politicians Choose Us and We Choose Them*. Toronto: Douglas & McIntyre.

– 2003. *Juggernaut : Paul Martin's Campaign for Chrétien's Crown*. Toronto: McClelland & Stewart.

Department of Justice. 2017. *Table of Public Statutes and Responsible Ministers*. Ottawa: Department of Justice.

Diamond, Martin. 1992. "The Separation of Powers and the Mixed Regime." In *As Far as Republican Principles Will Admit: In Honor of Martin Diamond*, edited by William A. Shambra. Washington: American Enterprise Institute.

Docherty, David C. 2005. *Legislatures*. Vancouver: UBC Press.

Docherty, David. 1997. *Mr Smith Goes to Ottawa*. Vancouver: UBC Press.

Elections Canada. 2017. *Political Financing Handbook for Electoral District Associations and Financial Agents*. Ottawa: Queen's Printer for Canada.

Finance Canada. 2007b. 2007a. *Economic Update. Strong Leadership. A Better Canada*. Ottawa: Government of Canada.

– *Aspire to a Stronger, Safer, Better Canada*. Ottawa: Government of Canada.

– 2006. *Canada's New Government Announces Tax Fairness Plan*. Ottawa: Government of Canada.

Fitzpatrick, Meagan. 2012. "MPs Denounce Motion to Study When Life Begins." *CBC News*. 27 April. Accessed 25 July 2017. www.cbc.ca/news/politics/mps-denounce-motion-to-study-when-life-begins-1.1232053.

Flanagan, Tom. 2014a. *Winning Power: Canadian Campaigning in the Twenty-First Century*. Montreal/Kingston: McGill-Queen's University Press.

– 2014b. "Don't Let Party Caucuses Unseat Leaders." *Inside Policy*, April 2014, 19.

– 2009. "Only Voters Have the Right to Decide on the Coalition." *The Globe and Mail*, January 9: A13.

– 2000. *First Nations, Second Thoughts*. Montreal/Kingston: McGill-Queen's University Press.

– 1997. "The Staying Power of the Legislative Status Quo: Collective Choice in Canada's Parliament after Morgentaler." *Canadian Journal of Political Science* 30, no. 1 (1997): 31–53.

– 1995. *Waiting for the Wave*. Toronto: Stoddart.

Franks, C.E.S. 1987. *The Parlament of Canada*. Toronto: University of Toronto Press.

Goldenberg, Eddie. 2006. *The Way It Works: Inside Ottawa*. Toronto: McClelland & Stewart.

Good, David A. 2007. *The Politics of Public Money: Spenders, Guardians, Priority Setters, and Financial Watchdogs inside the Canadian Government.* Toronto: University of Toronto Press.

Griffith, Andrew. 2013. *Policy Arrogance or Innocent Bias: Resetting Citizenship and Multiculturalism.* Ottawa: Anar Press.

Hamburger, Philip. 2015. *Is Administrative Law Unlawful?* Chicago: University Of Chicago Press.

Hamilton, Alexander, John Jay, and James Madison. 2001. *The Federalist.* Indianapolis: Liberty Fund.

Harper, Stephen H. 2016. *Jim Prentice Remembered at State Memorial: "He gave Canada and Alberta his very best ."* 28 October. Accessed 2 January 2017. globalnews.ca/news/3026508/jim-prentice-memorial-live-coverage-friday/.

– 2014. "Stephen Harper's Full Eulogy for Jim Flaherty Funeral." cbc *News.* 16 April. Accessed 2 January 2017. www.cbc.ca/news/canada/stephen-harper-s-full-eulogy-for-jim-flaherty-funeral-1.2612835.

Hayward, Steven F. 2017. "The Threat to Liberty." *Claremont Review of Books,* Winter 2016/17, 53–8.

Healy, Glenn. 2008. *The Cult of the Presidency: America's Dangerous Devotion to Executive Power.* Washington, DC: Cato Institute.

Heintzman, Ralph. 2014. *Renewal of the Federal Public Service: Toward a Charter of the Public Service.* Ottawa: Canada 2020.

Hockin, Thomas A. 1979. "Flexible and Structured Parliamentarianism: From 1848 to Contemporary Party Government." *Journal of Canadian Studies* 14 (2): 8–17.

House of Commons. 2016. "House of Commons Notice Paper." *Parliament of Canada.* 18 May. Accessed 25 July 2017. www.ourcommons.ca/Document Viewer/en/42-1/house/sitting-58/order-notice/page-12.

Howell, William G., and Terry M. Moe. 2016. *Relic: How Our Constitution Undermines Effective Government, and Why We Need a More Powerful Presidency.* New York: Basic.

Høyland, Bjørn, and Jean-François Godbout. 2015. "Unity in Diversity? The Development of Political Parties in the Parliament of Canada, 1867–2011." *British Journal of Political Science* 47 (3): 545–69.

Jackson, R.J., and D. Jackson. 2001. *Politics in Canada.* Toronto: Prentice Hall.

Jarvis, Mark. 2016. *Creating a High-Performing Canadian Civil Service Against a Backdrop of Disruptive Change.* Toronto: Mowat Centre.

Jeffrey, Mike. 2013. *The Future of Foreign Military Training.* Canadian Defence & Foreign Affairs Institute and Canadian International Council. March. d3n8a8pro7vhmx.cloudfront.net/cdfai/pages/95/attachments/original/1413683815 /The_Future_of_Foreign_Military_Training.pdf?1413683815.

Knopff, Rainer, and F.L. Morton. 1992. *Charter Politics.* Toronto: Nelson.

Knopff, Rainer, and Dave Snow. 2013. "'Harper's New Rules' for Government Formation: Fact or Fiction?" *Canadian Parliamentary Review*36 (1): 18–27.

Kornberg, A., and W. Mishler. 1976. *Influence in Parliament, Canada*. Durham, NC: Duke University Press.

Lagassé, Philippe. 2015. "Military Deployments and a 'Political Convention' of Commons Support." *Policy Options*. 24 March. Accessed 25 July 2017. policy options.irpp.org/2015/03/24/military-deployments-and-a-political-convention-of-commons-support/.

Landes, R.G. 1983. *The Canadian Polity*. Scarborough: Prentice-Hall Canada.

Lewis, J.P. 2015. "A Consideration of Cabinet Size." *Canadian Parliamentary Review* 38 (3): 14–24.

Loat, Alison, and Michael MacMillan. 2014. *Tragedy in the Commons: Former Members of Parliament Speak Out about Canada's Failing Democracy*. Toronto: Random House Canada.

Lynch, Kevin G. 2008. "Report on the Investigation into Unauthorized Disclosure of Sensitive Diplomatic Information." *Privy Council Office – Bureau du Conseil Privé*. 22 May. Accessed 18 July 2017. www.pco-bcp.gc.ca/index.asp?lang=eng& page=information&sub=publications&doc=iudsdi-rednards/report-rapport-eng.htm.

Malcolmson, Patrick, et al. 2016. *The Canadian Regime: An Introduction to Parlai-mentary Government in Canada*. Toronto: University of Toronto Press.

Mallory, J.R. 1984. *The Structure of Canadian Government*. Toronto: Gage.

Malloy, Jonathan. 2004. "The Executive and Parliament in Canada." *Journal of Legislative Studies* 10 (2): 206–17.

– 1996. "Reconciling Expectations and Reality in House of Commons Committees: The Case of the 1989 GST Inquiry." *Canadian Public Administration* 39 (3): 314–35.

Marland, Alexander J. 2016. *Brand Command: Canadian Politics and Democracy in the Age of Message Control*. Vancouver: UBC Press.

Martin, Don. 2007. *Belinda: The Political and Private Life Of Belinda Stronach*. Toronto, Ontario: Key Porter Books Ltd.

Martin, Paul. 2008. *Hell or High Water*. Toronto: McClelland & Stewart.

May, Elizabeth. 2017. "Westminster Parliamentary Democracy: Where Some MPs Are More Equal than Others." In *Turning Parliament Inside Out: Practical Ideas for Reforming Canada's Democracy*, edited by Michael Chong, Scott Simms, and Kennedy Stewart. Vancouver: Douglas & McIntyre.

McGrath, James A. 1985. *Report of the Special Committee on Reform of the House of Commons*. Ottawa: House of Commons.

Morton, F.L., and Rainer Knopff. 2000. *The Charter Revolution and the Court Party*. Peterborough, ON: Broadview Press.

Morton, Ted. 2015. "No Statecraft, Questionable Jurisprudence: How the Supreme Court Tried to Kill Senate Reform." *SPP Research Papers*, April.

Mulroney, Brian. 2007. *Memoirs*. Toronto: McClelland & Stewart.

O'Brien, Audrey, and Marc Bosc. 2009. *House of Commons Procedure and Practice*. Ottawa: House of Commons.

Office of the Government House Leader. 2017. "Reforming the Standing Orders of the House of Commons." *Government of Canada*. March. Accessed 25 July 2017. www.canada.ca/en/leader-government-house-commons/services/reform-standing-orders-house-commons/2017/march.html.

Organisation for Economic Cooperation and Development. 2012. *Canada: Development Assistance Committee Peer Review 2012*. Parison: OECD.

Page, Kevin. 2015. *Unaccountable: Truth and Lies on Parliament Hill*. Toronto: Viking.

Pal, Leslie A. 1993. *Interests of State: The Politics of Language, Multiculturalism, and Feminism in Canada*. Montreal/Kingston: McGill-Queen's University Press.

Paris, Roland. 2014. "Are Canadians Still Liberal Internationalists? Foreign Policy and Public Opinion in the Harper Era." *International Journal* 69 (3): 274–307.

Payton, Laura. 2014. *CBC News*. "Justin Trudeau Clarifies Abortion Stance for Liberal MPs." 18 June. Accessed 25 July 2017. www.cbc.ca/news/politics/justin-trudeau-clarifies-abortion-stance-for-liberal-mps-1.2679783.

Privy Council Office. 2014. "Mission of the Privy Council – about PCO." *Government of Canada, Privy Council Office*. 7 February. www.pco-bcp.gc.ca/index.asp?lang=eng&page=about-apropos&doc=mission-eng.htm.

Public Policy Forum. 2015. *Time for a Reboot: 9 Ways to Restore Trust in Canada's Public Institutions*. Ottawa: Public Policy Forum.

Rathgeber, Brent. 2014. *Irresponsible Government: The Decline of Parliamentary Democracy in Canada*. Toronto: Dundurb.

Redlich, J. 1969 [1908]. *The Procedure of the House of Commons: A Study of its History and Present Form*. New York: AMS Press.

Robertson, J. 2005. *The Evolution of Private Members' Business in the Canadian House of Commons*. Ottawa: Library of Parliament.

Russell, Peter H. 2008. *Two Cheers for Minority Government: The Evolution of Canadian Parliamentary Democracy*. Toronto: Emond Montgomery.

Samara Canada. 2010. *The Accidental Citizen?* Toronto: Samara Canada.

Savage, Charlie. 2015. *Power Wars: Inside Obama's Post-9/11 Presidency*. New York: Little, Brown.

Savoie, Donald J. 2013. *Whatever Happened to the Music Teacher?* Montreal/Kingston: McGill-Queen's University Press.

– 2008. *I'm from Bouctouche, Me: Roots Matter*. Montreal/Kingston: McGill-Queen's University Press.

– 2000. *Governing from the Centre: The Concentration of Power in Canadian Politics*. Toronto: University of Toronto Press.

– 1990. *The Politics of Public Spending in Canada*. Toronto: University of Toronto Press.

Schneiderman, David. 2017. "Harper's New Rules Revisited: A Reply to Knopff and Snow." *Canadian Parliamentary Review* 38 (1): 17–22.

Segal, Hugh, and Michael Kirby. 2016. *A House Undivided: Making Senate Independence Work*. Ottawa: Public Policy Forum.

Simpson, Jeffrey. 2001. *The Friendly Dictatorship*. Toronto: McClelland & Stewart.

Smith, David E. 2013. *Across the Aisle*. Toronto: University of Toronto Press.

– 2007. *The People's House of Commons*. Toronto: University of Toronto Press.

– 2003. *The Canadian Senate in Bicameral Perspective*. Toronto: University of Toronto Press.

– 1995. *The Invisible Crown*. Toronto: University of Toronto Press.

Snow, Dave, and Rainer Knopff. 2013. "'Harper's New Rules' for Government Formation: Fact or Fiction?" *Canadian Parliamentary Review* 36 (1): 18–27.

Sossin, Lorne, and Peter Russell. 2009. *Parliamentary Democracy in Crisis*. Toronto: University of Toronto Press.

Stilborn, Jack. 2006–07. "Parliamentary Review of Estimates: Initiatives and Prospects." *Canadian Parliamentary Review* 29 (4): 22–7.

Sutherland, Sharon. 2010. "The State of Research on Canada's Parliament." *Canadian Parliamentary Review* 33 (3): 49–55.

Taman v. Canada (Attorney General). 2017. Federal Court of Appeal. Neutral citation 2017 FCA 1.

Treasury Board Secretariat. 2016. *Empowering Parliamentarians through Better Information*. Ottawa: Treasury Board Secretariat.

Turner, Garth. 2009. *Sheeple: Caucus confidential in Stephen Harper's Ottawa*. Toronto: Key Porter.

Ulrich, Martin, and Peter Dobell. 2002. *Parliament's Performance in the Budget Process: A Case Study*. Montreal: Institute for Research on Public Policy.

UNAMA. 2011. *Treatment of Conflict-Related Detainees in Afghan Custody*. Kabul: United Nations Assistance Mission to Afghanistan and UN Office of the High Commissioner for Human Rights.

von Heyking, John. 2016. *The Form of Politics Aristotle and Plato on Friendship*. Montreal/Kingston: McGill-Queen's University Press.

Ward, Norman. 1962. *The Public Purse*. Toronto: University of Toronto Press.

White, Graham. 2015. "The 'Centre' of the Democratic Deficit: Power and Influence in Canadian Political Executives." In *Imperfect Democracies: The Democratic Deficit in Canada and the United States*, edited by Patti Tamara Lenard and Richard Simeon. Vancouver: UBC Press.

Wilson, Woodrow. 1887. "The Study of Administration." *Political Science Quarterly* 2 (2): 197–222.

Zussman, David. 2013. *Off and Running: The Prospects and Pitfalls of Government Transitions in Canada*. Toronto: University of Toronto Press.

Index

Abbott, Tony, 114
Act of Union, 1840, 14
adjournment proceedings, 84–5
Afghanistan mission: American view of,
    35; Bev Oda and, 70; Cabinet Commit-
    tee on Afghanistan, 67, 72, 73; detainee
    issue, 123–5; John Manley and (see Man-
    ley Panel); parliamentary votes approv-
    ing, 48–51, 119, 180
Ajzenstat, Janet, x, 14–21, 23, 25, 130
Akin, David, 183–4
Alberta Report, xi
Allen, Mike, 56
Ambrose, Rona, 41, 59
Anders, Rob, vii, xi
APEC, 6, 36, 37
appropriations: see estimates
Archer, Keith, ix
Arone, Shidane, 125
Articles of Confederation, 16, 24, 178
Ashfield, Keith, 68
Atlantic Accord, 4
Aucoin, Peter, 12, 156, 160, 179; and politi-
    cal staff, 160–1; on the power of party
    leaders, 132–3, 141; and prorogation, 157,
    159; on the public service, 163–5; and
    Reform Bill, 143–4
Auditor General of Canada, 71, 161, 166–8

backbenchers, 21, 132, 137; and estimates,
    173–4; likely influence of, 139–40; and
    party discipline, 77; and private mem-
    bers' business, 96–7; and role in legisla-
    tive process, 84–6, 89;
Bagehot, Walter, 20, 74, 95, 130

Baird, John, 57, 68, 113, 117
Baker, Denis 155, 171
Bakvis, Herman, 7–8
Bank of Canada, 31, 162
Beardsley, Keith 117, 121
Bercuson, David, ix
Bernier, Maxime, 57, 59, 62, 66–7, 68, 70,
    127, 148
bicameralism, 80, 178
Bill 101, x
Bill 178, x
Bill C-14, 140
Bill C-30, 139–40
Bill C-43, 141
Bill C-51, 92–4
Bill C-53, 94
Bill C-288, 98
Bill C-292, 100
Bill C-293, 100
Bill C-304, 100
Blackburn, Jean-Pierre, 57, 62, 68
Blainey, Steven, 57
Bloomfield, Garnet, xiii
Boessenkool, Ken, xvi
Bolten, Josh, 182
Brodie, Neil, 11
Brodie, Vida, vii, xiii–xvi
Buckler, Sandra, 136
Buckley, F.H., 178
Build Canada Fund, 45
Burney, Derek, xvii, 27, 73
Burns, George, xi
Bush, George W., 34–5, 177; administra-
    tion of, 181–2
business of supply, 89, 104–7

Cabinet: appointing ministers (*see* Harper, Stephen, appointment of ministers); and estimates, 76, 104–5; centrifugal forces within, 113, 114, 116, 129; Committee on Afghanistan, 67, 72 compared to US Cabinet, 61; diversity of, 61–2; and federal-provincial relations, 41; and fiscal policy, 31–2, 103; as "focus group," 5–6, 53, 70–2, 74; and foreign relations, 37–8; loyalty to PM, 61–2; managing the agenda of, 51–2, 70–4, 109–14, 118–20; Operations Committee of, 73; origins (*see* responsible government); and Parliament, 78, 81, 83–6, 88, 89–93; PCO and, 51, 118; Priorities and Planning Committee of, 73; size of, 54–5; Treasury Board, 73

Calvert, Lorne, 44–5

Cameron, Mark, xvii

Campbell, Gordon, 45

Campbell, Kim, 54, 57

Canada Elections Act, 131

Canadian Alliance, xi, xiv, 6, 47, 61, 134; caucus (*see* caucuses); internal life of, 133; Stephen Harper as Canadian Alliance MP, 59; Stockwell Day as leader (*see* Day, Stockwell)

Canadian Bill of Rights, 1960, 24

Canadian general elections: of 2004, xvi, 145, 158; of 2006, 26; of 2011, 30, 68, 100, 154

Cannon, Lawrence, 40, 41, 45, 57, 68

Cardow, Lanny, viii, 66

Carney, Mark, 162

Carson, Bruce, 63–4, 120

Cartwright, Susan, 137

Casey, Bill, 47, 55, 137, 147

caucuses: Canadian Alliance caucus, 131, 146–7; caucus meetings, 107, 134–41, 185; caucus officers, 46, 77; Chrétien caucus, 10, 47; Conservative caucus unity, 47, 99–100; government caucus, 7, 11, 31, 74, 77–8, 84, 86, 134–42, 156, 175; Harper caucus, 30, 41, 128; and leadership "spills," 147–8; Liberal caucus in opposition, 49, 50, 157; opposition caucus, 86, 92; Reform Party caucus, 47, 56; role in

selecting and firing party leaders, 77, 98, 132–3, 147–8

C.D. Howe Institute, 31

centralization of power, 5, 7–11

Chan, Kevin, 162

Charest, Jean, 45, 163

Charlottetown Accord, 135

Charter of Rights and Freedoms, x, 3, 24, 132; death penalty and, 128–9; democratic rights, 82

checks and balances, 4, 6–7, 171–2, 177; direct democracy lacking, 21; missing in Canada, 3, 156; in responsible government, 23, 96, 103; in US, 7, 23, 132

Cheney, Richard, 35

Chief Elections Officer. *See* Elections Canada

Chong, Michael, 57, 59, 62, 67, 96, 132, 136; as minister of federal-provincial relations, 40–1; Reform Bill, 11, 80, 101, 143–9

Chrétien, Jean, 5–10, 28, 32, 39, 41, 47, 71, 113, 173; Cabinet appointments, 54, 61, 64, 67; and caucus, 134, 147–8; Election finance reforms, 143, 157; private member's bill, 98; retirement from politics, 98

Clark, Joe, 61, 147, 164

Clark, Tom, 183

Clement, Tony, 11, 57, 62, 65, 113

Clerk of the Privy Council, 8, 27, 32, 162–3. *See also* Himelfarb, Alex; Lynch, Kevin; and Pifield, Michael

Clinton, Bill, 184

Clinton, Hillary, 39, 182, 183

Commonwealth Summits, 36, 119–20

Confederation, 14, 20, 24, 48, 13, 137

Conference of Defence Associations Institute, 50

confidence matters, 14–15, 18–19; backbenchers and, 148, 175; budget as, 7–8, 33, 104, 147; during minority government, 76, 79, 119; estimates as, 14, 73; foreign relations and, 35; Harper and, 119–20; House of Commons as confidence chamber, 77, 79; income trusts decision as, 29–30; military deployment

and, 50; prorogation as a (*see* proroga-
tion crisis of 2008); Standing Orders of
the House of Commons and, 148
Conservative Party of Canada, xv, xvi, 42,
60, 130; 2004 election platform, xvi, 80;
2006 election platform, 29, 80; candi-
date screening, 145; caucus of (*see* cau-
cuses); creation of, xiv, 55, 133, 143, 146;
unity of, 61–2
Constitution Act, 1867, 82, 130–1
Constitution Act, 1982, 41
Constitutional Act, 1791, 15
Consular services, 125–9
Cooper, Barry, vii, ix
Cooper, Michael, 150
Copps, Sheila, 61
Corbett, Lynette, xii
Crean, Simon, 148
Crown Share Adjustment, 44
Courtois-Eaton, Nicole, xv
Cummins, John, 140

Dawson, McGregor, 61, 78
Day, Stockwell, xii; Cabinet unity and, 61;
and Canadian Alliance caucus, 147, 148;
as minister, 56, 113, 127; retirement from
politics, 68
death penalty, 127–9
Democratic Reform Caucus, xii–xiii
departments: ACOA, 66; and Afghanistan
mission, 72; central agencies, 5, 7, 8, 89,
173; creation of, 74; and estimates (*see*
estimates); Finance, 5, 31–3, 37–8, 111,
166, 182; Fisheries and Oceans, 113–14;
Foreign Affairs and International Trade,
127; Foreign Affairs, Trade and Development, 37; and governing by lightning
bolts, 3, 6; and government planning
cycle, 118–20; Health, 175; Indigenous
and Northern Affairs, 112; Justice, 111,
112, 128; National Defence, 167–8, 175;
and Prime Minister's Office, 9; Privy
Council Office, 5, 8, 13, 27, 32, 38, 42, 46,
49, 51–2, 66, 72, 74, 75, 81, 111, 115–16, 118,
162, 163, 164, 165, 173, 184, 185; Transport,
54–5; Treasury Board Secretariat, 5
deputy ministers, 111; appointment of,

160–1, 163–4; central agency experience
of, 8; clerk of the Privy Council as, 8;
of federal-provincial relations, 52; of
finance, 164; powers of, 163, 174
Diamond, Martin, 23–5
Diefenbaker, John, 30
Dion, Stéphane, 113; and Afghanistan mis-
sion, 49, 119–20; and detainees, 123; and
Liberal caucus, 50, 148, 157; and Stephen
Harper (*see* Harper, Stephen: and
Stéphane Dion). See *also* prorogation
crisis of 2008
Doyle, Norman, 42, 56, 113
Duceppe, Gilles, 41, 48–9, 135, 158, 159
Duffy, Mike, 68
Duncan, John, 57, 68,
Dunderdale, Kathy, 147
Durham, Lord: checks and balances of,
23–4, 103, 171; equality and, 25; report
of, 15, 17, 19–21; and strong executive,
21–2

earmarks, 33
East Asia Summit, 36
Edelman, Eric, 181–2
Elections Canada, 142–3
Emerson, David, 62, 63, 113, 117; appointment to Cabinet, 59–60, 136, 146; and
Cabinet Committee on Afghanistan,
67, 72–3; as foreign affairs minister, 59,
67; retirement from politics, 67; and
softwood lumber, 52
equalization. See Harper, Stephen:
federal-provincial relations of
Essex, Chris, xi
estimates: appropriations in Lower
Canada, 17, 22; and the battle for parliamentary time, 46, 83, 85, 89; Brison
reforms, 80; ministerial role, 81, 172;
reinvigorating parliamentary role, 76,
104–7, 172–7

F-35 Joint Strike Fighter, 167–70
Fife, Robert, 183
Financial Administration Act, 161
Finley, Diane, xiv, 57, 62
Finley, Doug, viii, xiv

Flaherty, Jim, 28, 31–2, 119, 182; and income trusts decision, 29–30; influence of, 33, 41, 113, 117; selection as minister, 57, 63, 64–5, 68, 70, 120
Flanagan, Tom, vii–viii, xi, xiii; on Bill C-43, 141; as campaign manager, xii, xiv–xv; departure from Harper's team, xvi; on Preston Manning, 79; on prorogation, 159; on Reform Bill, 147; work for Reform Party, 146
Fortier, Michael, 52, 63, 67; appointment to Cabinet, 59–60
Francophonie summits, 36–7
Franks, C.E.S., 78

G7/G8 summits, 31, 36, 37, 39, 119, 120
G20 summits, 31, 36, 37, 64
Gander Airport, 42
Gerstein, Irving, xv
Ghiz, Robert, 45
Gibbins, Roger, ix–x
Gillard, Julia, 148
Goldenberg, Eddie, 8; on budget decisions, 28, 32, 33, 71, 173; on cabinet, 9–10, 32, 39, 61–2, 113; on caucus, 47, 54, 98; on role of PMO, 9, 115; on opposition, 87
Goodale, Ralph, 50, 86, 113
Goods and Services Tax, 30, 32, 120; and 2006 election, xvii
Goolsbee, Austan, 183–4
Governing from the Centre, 3–10
government whip. See whips
Governor General, 87, 119, 156, 158
Graham, Bill, 39, 48–9
Griffith, Andrew, 170

Hacker, Jim, 111, 114
Hadley, Stephen, 35 182
Halifax International Security Forum, 56
Hamilton, Alexander, 13, 179
Harper, Stephen, ix, xi; 2006 election campaign, xvi–xvii, 26, 27; and Afghan detainees (see Afghanistan mission: detainee issue); appointment of ministers, 27, 53, 55–61, 63–6; and Barack Obama, 114; and Canadian Alliance, xii–xiv; and caucus, 134–7, 140–1; and centralization

of government, 10–11; and Conservative Party of Canada, 143, 152–3; and death penalty, 127–9; did not participate in party fundraising, 142; federal-provincial relations of, 39–46, 120, 180; firing ministers, 66–70, 113; and fiscal policy, 29–33, 52; and foreign relations, 34–6, 38–9; Garth Turner and, 136–7, 146–7; and George W. Bush, 34–5; and government communications, 118; ministers influencing, 52, 127; and multilateralism, 38–9; and NAFTA-gate (see NAFTA-gate); National Citizens Coalition, xi; and Nicolas Sarkozy, 180–1; in opposition, 86–7; parliamentary management of, 46, 48, 75, 80, 83, 92–4, 99–101; prorogation crisis of 2008, 12, 156–9; and les Québécois motion, 136; and Senate reform, 80; and Stéphane Dion, 50–1, 120; views on appointing ministers from outside Parliament, 60–1
Harper transition team, xvii, 27
Hearn, Loyola, 42, 56, 67, 113
Heintzman, Ralph, 163
Hiebert, Russ, 100
Hill, Grant, xiv
Hill, Jay, 47–8, 68
Hillier, Rick, 124, 181
Himelfarb, Alex, 47
Hockin, Tom, 20, 107
Hogg, Peter, 156
Hosek, Chaviva, 9–10, 113
House of Commons of Canada, 26, 46, 48, 61, 119; diversity of, 154; Finance Committee, 32; Government Operations Committee, 106; influence of, 78–9, 156; Justice Committee, 101, 119; Public Accounts Committee, 105, 166; responsible government and, 14, 21, 33, 71, 76–7; sitting days, 83, 94; Standing Orders of, 103, 104, 158. See also estimates: the battle for parliamentary time
House of Commons of United Kingdom, 7, 18, 20, 75
House leader. See ministers: government House leader

Johnston, Pierre-Marc, x

Kalopsis, Ken, xi
Kenney, Jason, x, xi, 59, 62, 170

Laforest, Guy, x
Lebel, Denis, 59
LeBreton, Marjory, 59, 68
Levant, Ezra, xi
Long, Tom, xii
Lortie, Marc, 181
Lougheed, Peter, x
Lunn Gary, 57, 65, 67–8
Lynch, Kevin, 116, 163, 184

MacDonald, Rodney, 44–5
MacKay, Peter, xiv, 43, 55–6, 62, 65, 66, 113
Manfredi, Chris, x
Manley Panel: aftermath, 50–1, 70, 120, 180, 182; origins of, 49, 120; recommendations, 72; report of, 50
Manning, Fabian, 42, 56, 113
Martin, Paul: and caucus, 10, 147, 148; and democratic deficit, 79–80; as finance minister, 10, 28, 61, 64; as prime minister, 34, 40, 54, 60, 73, 87; private member's bill, 100
Mazankowski, Don, 64
McCallum, John, 39
Meech Lake Accord, x
Meinen, Marian, xiii
Merrifield, Rob, 59
message event proposal, 118
ministers: Aboriginal affairs minister, 68, 112; agriculture minister, 28; appointing, 26–7, 54–61, 77, 137; and the budget, 5, 9, 28–34; and centralization, 6–8, 10, 27, 52, 132, 160–3, 179; Chrétien and, 9, 39, 41, 71, 113; defence minister, 49; discretion of, 27–8, 74, 83–4, 112, 129, 173; double role of, 109–17; environment minister, 40, 114; federal-provincial relations minister, 40–1; finance minister, 9, 28–34, 63–5, 71, 80, 86, 173, 182; firing of, 66–70; fisheries minister, 42; foreign minister, 35, 37–9, 49, 67, 127, 129; government House leader, 46, 81, 94, 101, 111; government leader in the Senate, 46, 59, 68; Harper empowering ministers, 45, 71, 73, 99–100, 119–20, 128; health minister, 38; heritage minister, 71; industry minister, 54, 71; international cooperation minister, 68; justice ministers, 56, 65–6, 127; legislative role of, 81, 89, 91, 104, 115, 134–5, 139, 177; national revenue minister, 67; natural resources minister, 67; number of (see Cabinet: size of); PMO and, 9; president of the Treasury Board, 28; public safety, 127; public servants and, 161–2, 164, 165, 170–1, 173–4; regional ministers, 9, 42, 54–5; and responsible government, 17, 20–1, 71; "Roman Guard," 61; setting government priorities, 9–10, 11, 74, 110–15; trade minister, 35, 37, 59, 67, 72, 111; transport minister, 40, 45, 54, 112
money bill rule, 18, 21, 22, 103, 172; and private members' bills, 97–8
Moore, James, 59
Moore, Rob, 56
Morton, Ted, ix; and Senate reform, 80, 153; working for Stockwell Day, xii
Motion #6, 94–5
Mulroney, Brian, 10, 54, 57, 64, 67, 73, 86–7, 92, 141, 181
Mulroney, David, 72
Muttart, Patrick, viii, xvi, 117–18

NAFTA-gate, 182–5
Nevitte, Neil, ix
Nicholson, 57, 62, 65, 66, 127, 128
Novak, Ray, xii, 43

Obama, Barack, 30, 36–7, 182; executive leadership of, 177; NAFTA and, 184–5
O'Connor, Gordon, 57, 67–8, 99, 124
Oda, Bev, 57, 64, 68
Oliver, Craig, 183
Oliver, Joe, 63, 65
opposition parties, 84; government negotiations with, 46, 48, 81, 92, 94, 158; position guaranteed by responsible government, 20, 22–3, 25, 130–2, 140, 151; during time of majority government,

61, 76, 87, 104; during time of minority
government, 77, 87, 104, 119. *See also* estimates: the battle for parliamentary
time
O'Toole, Erin, 148

Pal, Leslie, ix
Pallister, Brian, 56
Paradis, Christian, 57, 59
party discipline, 46–7, 75, 77, 98, 176;
promises to reduce, 80; and size of Cabinet, 55
Penner, Dave, xii
Perth–Middlesex by-election, xiii
Plett, Don, 42, 143
political parties: balance of power within,
101, 132–4, 141–3; criticisms of, 18; need
for alteration in power, 16; and partisanship, 149–55; power of leaders, 141–3;
public subsidy, 47; and responsible government, 21; selection of party leaders,
77
Prentice, Jim, 52, 59, 63, 65, 68, 114, 117, 120
prime minister: power to appoint ministers, 53–4; as *primus inter pares*, 6, 26.
See also Chrétien, Jean; Harper,
Stephen; Martin, Paul; Mulroney, Brian;
Trudeau Justin; Trudeau, Pierre
prorogation crisis of 2008, 157–9, 162

responsible government: compared to US
Constitution, 22–4; emergence of, 14–
21; strengths and weaknesses, 21–2, 24–5
Richardson, John, xiii
Ritz, Gerry, 59

Savoie, Donald: centralization thesis (*see*
centralization of power); and the estimates, 104–7, 174; and *Governing from
the Centre*, 5–6, 7–10; and role of public
service, 159–60; view of Cabinet, 53;
view of Parliament, 75, 172
Scheer, Andrew, 59, 148
Schellenberger, Gary, xiii
Senate, 11, 40, 46, 77, 81–2, 84, 87, 133; and
battle for time, 89; government leader

in the Senate, 135 (*see also* LeBreton,
Marjory); reform of (*see* Harper,
Stephen: Senate Reform); Trudeau re-
forms, 152–3. *See also* Bill C-51; Fortier,
Michael
separation of powers: American practice,
23; contemporary debate, 156, 171–2, 177;
debate in Lower Canada, 16; and mod-
ern mixed regime, 20, 23; and private
members' legislation, 96; purpose of,
23–4. *See also* money bill rule
Simpson, Jeffrey, 179; *The Friendly Dicta-
torship*, 6–7, 8, 10, 11, 55
Skelton, Carol, 59, 67
Smith, Danielle, xi
Solberg, Monte, 59, 62, 67
Soudas, Dimitri, 43
Spencer, Larry, 146
Stelmach, Ed, 113
Storseth, Brian. *See* Bill C-304
Strahl, Chuck, 56, 68
Stronach, Belinda, 47, 60, 61–2, 137
supply days, 89, 91, 105
Supreme Court of Canada, 80, 109, 130,
152–3

Taras, David, ix
Thatcher, Margaret, 7
Thompson, Greg, 56, 68
throne speeches, 52, 75, 77, 84, 85, 119–20
time allocation, 91–5
Toews, Vic, 56, 65–6, 68, 113
Treasury Board Secretariat, 5, 105, 167,
175–6
Trudeau, Justin, 38, 39, 45, 54, 65, 66, 80,
93, 94–5, 100, 101, 142; electoral reform
and, 153–5; Senate reform efforts of,
152–3
Trudeau, Pierre, 5, 6, 7–8, 10, 12, 63, 64, 67,
74, 86, 92, 163, 164, 170
Trump, Donald, 39, 185
Tucker, Malcolm, 116
Turnbull, Lori, 163
Turnbull, Malcolm, 148
Turner, Garth, 10–11, 47, 126, 136–7, 146–7
Tweed, Merv, 56

UN General Assembly, 36–8

Van Loan, Peter, 50, 57
Verner, Josée, 57, 68

Wall, Brad, 44
Wells, Paul, 76
whips, 46–8, 68, 74, 81, 99, 135, 173
White, Graham, 8, 116

Williams, Danny, 40, 42–3, 45
Williamson, John, 139–40
Wilson, Michael, 64, 181–3
Wilson, Paul, xvi
Wilson, Woodrow, 160

Yelich, Lynn, 59
Yes, Prime Minister, 116. *See also* Hacker, Jim